Current Perspectives in Psychology

Intelligence of Apes and Other Rational Beings

Duane M. Rumbaugh and David A. Washburn

YALE UNIVERSITY PRESS   NEW HAVEN AND LONDON

Frontispiece: A young adult gorilla *(Gorilla gorilla gorilla)* at the San Diego Zoo, ca. 1965. Photo by Duane M. Rumbaugh.

Set in Adobe Garamond type by The Composing Room of Michigan, Inc.
Printed in the United States of America by Vail-Ballou Press.

Library of Congress Cataloging-in-Publication Data

Rumbaugh, Duane M., 1929–
    Intelligence of apes and other rational beings / Duane M. Rumbaugh and David A. Washburn.
        p.   cm. — (Current perspectives in psychology)
Includes bibliographical references (p.   ).
        ISBN 0-300-09983-5 (cloth : alk. paper)
        1. Apes—Psychology.   2. Animal intelligence.   3. Psychology, Comparative. I. Washburn, David A., 1961–.   II. Title.   III. Series.
        QL737.P96R855 2003
        156—dc21

                                                                                2002156629

A catalogue record for this book is available from the British Library.

The paper in this book meets the guidelines for permanence and durability of the Committee on Production Guidelines for Book Longevity of the Council on Library Resources.

10 9 8 7 6 5 4 3 2 1

To the contributions and memories of Austin H. Riesen, Henry Nissen, Harry F. Harlow, Maurice P. Smith, and Allan M. Schrier

Contents

Series Foreword

Current Perspectives in Psychology presents the latest discoveries and developments across the spectrum of the psychological and behavioral sciences. The series explores such important topics as learning, intelligence, trauma, stress, brain development and behavior, anxiety, interpersonal relationships, education, child-rearing, divorce and marital discord, and child, adolescent, and adult development. Each book focuses on critical advances in research, theory, methods, and applications and is designed to be accessible and informative to nonspecialists and specialists alike.

In *The Intelligence of Apes and Other Rational Beings,* Duane M. Rumbaugh and David A. Washburn show that learning by apes—and even by animals usually considered to have little or no intelligence—can illuminate our own processes of cognition. That humans and other animals have much in common is only the point of departure for the authors' portrayal of the richness of learning, perception, and communication skills across the animal kingdom. Relying on their own research as well as that of colleagues and others in the field, they provide a comprehensive overview of both theoretical and empirical advances with regard to cognition, perception, emotion, and behavior in both humans and animals.

Multiple species have been studied and have revealed fascinating evidence of elaborate intelligence and rational processes. Rational and creative processes among animals have been elaborated in clever ways both in nature and in experimental settings. The authors provide examples of animals managing competition, understanding numbers, and even learning computer tasks. They describe the processes by which animals come to understand and negotiate their everyday lives. Surprisingly, these processes include language, communication, problem solving, and creativity beyond the limitations long assumed for animal learning and behavior. The engaging stories and studies of animals that illustrate these processes convey how astute observation and one-to-one interactions with animals complement experimental research.

The Intelligence of Apes and Other Rational Beings contributes in important ways to learning theory and research, central foci of psychology. Specifically, the book elaborates a type of learning that explains how new behaviors and competencies are created. The authors—each a peerless contributor on his own to our understanding of learning—have here combined their skills to cast new light on the intelligence of animals, and the underpinnings of human learning and performance as well.

Alan E. Kazdin
Series Editor

Foreword

I remember well the thrill of my first close encounter with an adult chimpanzee. I was visiting the Yerkes Laboratories of Primate Biology, then located in Orange Park, Florida. That was more than forty years ago, a time when it was possible for visitors to roam alone around the spacious grounds surrounding caged chimpanzees. One animal in particular caught my attention, and it was obvious that she meant to do so. She was at the front of the cage holding between her lips a pine straw that she had pushed through the wire. It seemed obvious from the way she looked at me and from her behavior with the straw that she wanted me to take it. When I did, she quickly moved to another location nearby and extended her lips against the wire, clearly looking to me to return the straw, and when I gave it to her she chose a different location and once more offered the straw. We continued with this little game into which I had been recruited, playing by the rules she imposed, until I finally tired of it and quit. Late in the day when I described the incident to Henry Nissen of the Yerkes Laboratories, he immediately identified the animal and told me the game was one of her favorite pastimes.

In light of the many accounts of exceptional intellectual achievements of the great apes, my experience does not seem extraordinary. But for me it was a powerful reminder of how little I knew about the psychology of animals and how much there was to learn.

That theme is central to this book. The richness of behavior and the challenges it presents are major features of the authors' experience. The book illustrates, with unusual force by a host of well-chosen examples, the idea that the phenomena we observe that intrigue and amuse us lay beyond the obvious, and touch on the perennial mysteries of the animal mind. The essential nature of the motives, perceptions, understandings, and desires of the individuals we observe does not sit on the surface, like colorful pebbles at the seashore waiting to be picked up by any passerby, but can be discovered only by careful probes and explorations that go beyond the surface, that point toward events that we still can only speculate about. The investigation of the animal mind is a hugely demanding enterprise, requiring philosophical vision, intellectual discipline, compassion for the animals, a flair for innovation, and courage, too. Rumbaugh and Washburn (and their colleagues) have surely demonstrated to the satisfaction of even the most relentless critic that they are completely prepared for the task.

William A. Mason

Preface

It will be contended by us (if not by Watson) that "behavior-acts," though no doubt in complete one-to-one correspondence with the underlying molecular facts of physics and physiology, have, as "molar" wholes, certain emergent properties of their own. And it is these, the molar properties of behavior-acts, which are of prime interest to us as psychologists.

Tolman 1932, 7

The writing of this book has been driven by the career-long research of the first author, Duane M. Rumbaugh, and by a solid fifteen years' research by the second author, David A. Washburn, on issues of complex learning and intelligence in primates, notably rhesus monkeys, chimpanzees, and bonobos. This book presents our view of behavior, learning, and intelligence from the perspective of comparative psychology. It has been our goal to define trends and principles that undergird complex learning and behavior.

Many of the principles offered are the same as those for our own genus and species, *Homo sapiens*. This is not surprising, given that our taxonomic designator is in the grand order, Primates. There are remarkable continuities in the psychologies that embrace the learning and intellectual operations of monkeys, apes, and us. There are also differences, as there should be, given that diversity and differences are the hallmark of genetic relatedness.

To us, learning is a marvelous accomplishment of life, affording both short- and long-term unity and scaffolding to the structuring of intelligence, symbolic operations, and creativity. Although the history of learning in the twentieth century was dominated pervasively by behaviorists—who were so radical in their commitment to models afforded by the natural scientists that they shunned any sense that a living, sentient, rational organism might exist—there has been a concerted effort in recent years to retrieve the life and rational processes of at least some species into the study of behavior and the writing of psychology. Descartes's proclamation that animals were none but beast machines, devoid of feelings, thought, and the capacity for pain, was not based in anything like scientific data. Yet his proclamation still holds broad sway. Sadly, only a small part of the human population of the world believes otherwise.

Behavioral science of the past fifty years has given us more than enough reason to declare that Descartes was wrong. Animals can become very rational in the psychologies, they can think in terms of abstract symbols, and they can come to understand human speech and the syntactic complexities that organize it into novel sentences for comprehension and request. They learn many of the more complicated skills of life, not by specific repetitive training but by observing the behaviors of others, then translating the principles that they have extracted from their observations into formulations of their own behavior.

Like Professor Tolman and others before us, we have not approached this study with the purpose of assailing either the methodological tenets or the findings of behaviorism. Indeed, we propose to embrace the phenomena demonstrated in so many studies of conditioning. That said, we are compelled by a growing corpus of rational, novel, purposive, and relational behaviors to propose a third class of behavior that psychology must explain. In doing so, we have tried neither to apply the principles of conditioning to cognitive phenomena nor to apply particularly cognitive explanations to operant or respondent conditioning. Rather, we have pointed to an interesting group of behaviors that resist a conditioning explanation but seem to reflect animals' natural and active inclination to seek predictive relations, to recognize patterns, to make sense of the world. We call them *Emergents*.

We readily acknowledge that the questions of "how Emergents emerge" and "why animals occasionally learn associatively when there are rulelike relations that could be learned" await answers from future research in psychology and neuroscience. We are hopeful, however, that emphasizing these behavioral phenomena and our framework for understanding a wide range of behaviors both simple and complex will be more integrative and less circular than is the reinforcement perspective. Above all, we hope that positing this rational view of behaviorism will have the same heuristic effect on the field as the purposive behaviorism to which our view owes such debt.

Here we present for the reader's pleasure a new perspective of learning, intelligence, and Rational Behavior. The perspective is an attempt to unify all behavior—from instinctive, classical and operant conditioning, concept formation, Emergents, and rational thought—into a framework called Rational Behaviorism. That framework happily embraces all of the data accrued via studies by ethologists of unlearned behaviors and by classical and operant conditioning studies and those that define the conditions whence new skills, abilities, and competencies emerge seemingly by magic. They emerge not by magic, of course, but without the researcher's having a clue that they are taking form. These skills, abilities, and competencies have no specific histories of reinforcement or experience, but rather take form in response to generalized classes of experience.

Emergents are natural products of a natural world's system whereby new behaviors and competencies are created. We are coming to understand their antecedents and how to predict their consequences, just as we do with all behaviors. As we do so, however, we note a marked shift from the tenets of radical behavior to those of Rational Behaviorism.

Behavior is the grist of our science. Whether the organism is or is not an agent in the formulation of any of its behaviors, particularly variations on old themes and new ones, is the question. Radical behaviorists declare No! Rational behaviorists proclaim Yes!

In fact, the intelligent behaviors that are presented herein simply cannot be reduced to the operations of stimulus-response-reinforcement frameworks or even to others of that kind. So we shall take you, the reader, into a new vista for understanding animal—and human—behaviors.

We gratefully acknowledge the encouragement and support extended by Yale University Press for this book, especially the kind letter of invitation by Alan Kazdin and the unstinting editorial support of Erin Carter. We are grateful for the loyal and ready support of Judith Sizemore, Kim MacQueen, and Charlene Weiters of the Language Research Center and the colleagueship afforded by William A. Hillix,

Charles R. Menzel, Emil Menzel, James L. Pate, R. Thomas Putney, Herbert Roitblat, William A. Mason, Robert B. Voas, Michael J. Beran, Graham Sterritt, Harold Warner, Charles Bell, Josephine V. Brown, Dan Bockert, James Kavanagh, Nicholas Toth, Cathy Schick, Francine Dolins, Gary Greenberg, James E. King, Len Rosenblum, Steve Suomi, Bill Hopkins, John Gulledge, Bill Fields, Ty Partridge, Samuel F. Carriba, Claudio Cantalupo, Daniel Rice, Melvin Konner, H. Carl Haywood, Russell Tuttle, Terry Maple, E. Sue Savage-Rumbaugh, and Stanley Rapoport. Finally, we gratefully acknowledge support of friends and family—Elizabeth and Heather Pugh; Doris Radloff; Joan, Marc, Aaron, and Micah Gartenberg; Shane and Stacy Savage-Rumbaugh; and Cathy Washburn and her family.

Special thanks are extended to Professor Richard Jessor, one of several professors at the University of Colorado who guided Duane Rumbaugh's graduate studies in the Psychology Department, chaired by the late Maurice P. Smith. And special recognition is extended to E. Sue Savage-Rumbaugh for her highly creative research of the past twenty-five years that helped establish important points and principles for this book.

The affiliations with and support from the following organizations are gratefully credited: the American Psychological Association and Psi Chi (and notably its chapter at Texas Christian University), the American Society of Primatologists, the International Primatological Society, the Southern Society for Philosophy and Psychology, the National Institutes for Child Health and Human Development (HD-06016 and HD-38051) of the National Institutes of Health, the National Aeronautics and Space Administration, the U.S. Navy and the funding branches of the Department of Defense, the Yerkes National Primate Research Center, and the San Diego Zoo.

Special acknowledgment is due Georgia State University, its Foundation, and its College of Arts and Sciences for financial and administrative support. Duane Rumbaugh gratefully acknowledges his standing as a Ted Townsend Fellow with Iowa Primate Learning Sanctuary and the recognition given him by Steve W. Woodruff, who has established a scholarship at Georgia State University to support study and research in psychology as articulated throughout this book.

We extend special recognition to the late Carol Rice McCormack and the late Timothy V. Gill for their sterling contributions to early project work at the San Diego Zoo and at the Yerkes Center, respectively, and also commemorate the valued contributions of Austin *(Pan troglodytes)* of the Language Research Center and of Albert *(Gorilla g. gorilla)* of the San Diego Zoo. As with all of our apes, Austin and Albert taught us far more than we ever taught them.

I
The Need for a
Rational Behaviorism

1

Introduction

Thorndike tried to dispose of the difficulty (of thought) 55 years ago by denying its existence. He buried thought in 1898, but the ghost insists on walking. Often we decline to say that animals think; but comparative psychology has been unable to avoid concluding that animals have expectancies, insights, hypotheses, conceptual activities, a variable attention and so forth. These are but aspects of thought; and if we cannot deal with the comparatively simple behavior of animals without taking account of thought, how adequate can a thought-less human psychology be?

Hebb 1953, 99

The need for a better understanding of animal intelligence has become clear in recent years as, particularly in the laboratory, animals have done truly remarkable things, things that would not have been anticipated even ten years ago. Here we will make the case that to view animals as irrational, unsmart creatures is no longer tenable. In measure, we must now view them as beings with intelligence and rationality appropriate to their species. Otherwise, how can we account for their remarkable achievements in advanced levels of communication (including, in some cases, language), in counting, and in computer-based tasks? The intelligence of animals is just now coming to be understood, and the search for an appropriate understanding of it has been joined only recently. The following example serves to illustrate the point. How is this example to be understood and appreciated as a natural phenomenon in a natural world?

Panzee, a chimpanzee *(Pan troglodytes)*, age eleven, had been coreared with Panbanisha, a bonobo *(P. paniscus)*. From six weeks of age, these two apes were constant companions, and researchers worked with them intensively. The apes were together day and night and were cared for much as one would care for a human child (fig. 1).

The purpose of this study of corearing was to examine the apes'

Figure 1. Panzee (left, a chimpanzee, *Pan troglodytes*) and Panbanisha (right, a bonobo, *Pan paniscus*) were reared together to determine whether environment or species differences underlay the spontaneous learning of lexigrams and the ability to comprehend human speech in Kanzi and Mulika, both bonobos. Panzee came to learn symbols spontaneously and to understand spoken words, though not as well as Panbanisha. Photo by Rumbaugh.

spontaneous, untutored mastery of the word-lexigrams (defined and discussed in Chapter 9) and to see whether Panzee would come to comprehend human speech. We assumed that Panbanisha would, as her half-brother, Kanzi, had come to do so spontaneously during the course of his early rearing at the Language Research Center of Georgia State University. Both apes did in fact learn to comprehend their word-lexigrams and to comprehend novel utterances of human speech (Brakke and Savage-Rumbaugh 1995).

Our question here is, "What did the apes do with their language skills that otherwise they could not have done?" We take an example of Panzee's accomplishment to illustrate generally what is meant when we assert that apes display intelligence by using their acquired skills and knowledge innovatively to unique advantages in solving novel problems.

A researcher, Charles Menzel at our Language Research Center, placed one of Panzee's favorite foods, a kiwifruit, several feet away from the back of Panzee's fenced exercise yard in an area of dense brush and trees. She appeared to be fascinated with his so doing but did nothing about it until later, when she recruited another researcher, Shelly Williams, to help her. Williams was inside the building and knew nothing about the food having been placed among the twigs and leaves on the forest floor. Panzee first had to attract the attention of Williams, who was nearby, and did so by presenting her hindquarters. When Williams acknowledged this greeting verbally, Panzee went promptly to the keyboard mounted on a wall of her cage and pointed to the word-lexigram for kiwifruit. She held her finger on the lexigram until Williams acknowledged what it stood for—kiwifruit. With that assurance, Panzee moved up into her tunnel that led to a large outdoor cage. Then, covering her eyes with a hand—her standard way of uttering "hide"—she gestured with outstretched arm to the tunnel door. Williams surmised that Panzee was telling her that a kiwifruit was hidden somewhere. Williams said, "You want me to go outdoors?"— whereupon Panzee ran through the tunnel outdoors. At first, Williams didn't know what she was to do. Panzee then seemingly set about giving her specific instructions. Panzee vocalized and gestured with an extended arm toward the general area where the kiwifruit had been placed. Williams understood that she was to go the area behind the cage. Panzee then went to the spot closest to the kiwifruit and pointed with her finger to the fruit's specific location. As Williams approached the spot to which Panzee pointed, Panzee began to make low-frequency vocalizations of excitement—all the while focusing her eyes specifically upon the kiwifruit. Williams could not see the fruit at first because it was well nested in among sticks and leaves. Panzee became increasing excited whenever Williams approached the location of the kiwifruit. After a brief search, Williams found the kiwifruit, whereupon Panzee headed back indoors after making a beckoning hand movement to Williams to return indoors. Thus Panzee got her prized kiwifruit through the coordinated use of her several skills. She had solved a novel challenge, one never encountered before.

This procedure has been replicated dozens of times, with a host of foods and variety of personnel to help Panzee. Panzee has no problem remembering what food was hidden and where it is hidden. Although typically she will recruit someone within twenty-four hours to help her, she has on occasion waited several days and even weeks to ask for assistance to get an item specified by name. Panzee is only rarely incorrect in her use of lexigrams in identifying the hidden object and in pointing to the several locations where the food has been hidden (Menzel 1999). Only rarely has she recruited someone to assist her when, in fact, no item had been hidden.

Without mastery of her word-lexigrams, Panzee would not be able to identify the food hidden and the materials that hide it. Her early rearing afforded her experience in pointing and gesturing in communicative settings. All that said, the impressive behavior is that years later she put various skills together, all with speech comprehension—not by conditioning, shaping, or by selective reinforcement. Rather, the skills were put together by her highly complex brain and its covert cognitive processes. No trial and error was involved. Panzee was competent even on her first challenge with hidden food—the episode recounted above in which she recruited Shelly Williams. She was able to structure the solution to a problem that never before had been faced by her or modeled for her by others.

Now how did Panzee do this? What enabled her to do it? Without a reinforcement history that would quite probably lead her to the task solution in some specific manner, what mediated the solution?

Pointing at Intelligent Behavior

As we shall discuss in some detail, language skills and enriched early rearing were critical requisites to Panzee's creativity in this case. We will investigate the ways that silent learning and covert operations afforded by a complex brain and enriched rearing generate emergent behaviors, skills, and invention. Panzee provides us with a fine example with which to start this book that focuses upon questions of animal intelligence.

We cannot account for intelligence in terms of basic reinforcement of responses to stimuli. In a relatively recent book, *Cognitive Aspects of Stimulus Control*, Honig and Fetterman (1992) tacitly reject that the central challenge for psychology was to "define the stimulus."

Rather, they argue that even the analysis of stimulus control, as advocated by traditional behaviorism, can benefit from the use of cognitive constructs. They recognize, as do we, that even relatively simple animals can learn seemingly complex concepts with great facility if the materials are relevant to their environments. When tested in the artificial surroundings of a laboratory with methods of yesteryear, animals can appear to be the plodding trial-and-error learners that historically they have been declared by Descartes and others even to this day. Accordingly, we will argue here that we must look beyond the basic conditioning procedures of traditional behaviorists to understand both animal and human intelligence. At the same time, we recognize that the long and rich history of research into the parameters of both respondent (Pavlovian) and operant (Skinnerian) conditioning have provided us with a vast repository of valuable findings that are not to be rejected. Those findings need only be embraced with a new framework that allows us to look beyond the procedures of traditional behaviorism if the full richness of animal intelligence is to be defined.

Historical Perspective: (Nonhuman) Animals as "Beast Machines"

For much of history, animals have been viewed essentially as wild beasts or as chattel. Indeed, the Cartesian view (Descartes 1637) that animals are senseless beast machines probably is still more commonly believed (at least tacitly) than is Darwin's (1859, 1871) postulate that humans share psychological, as well as biological, dimensions with animals. Thus animals remain important sources of food, sport, work, and pleasure. Though admired for their beauty, strength, and agility, animals generally have been declared dumb—that is, without intelligence and language.

In fact, there has historically been great pressure to discourage writing and the collection of data that might document psychological dimensions shared with animals, even with our nearest primate relatives, the great apes. G. J. Romanes's initial efforts to document animal intelligence through use of anecdotes, in an 1882 book called *Animal Intelligence*, proved to be nothing short of a disaster. His report, which was intended to be followed by empirical research, was so ridiculed that the whole concept of animal intelligence was discredited. The American psychologist Edward L. Thorndike, who also wrote a book called *Animal Intelligence* (1911), meticulously and colorfully documented the mindless trial-and-error behavior of animals in problem boxes. He concluded that animal problem solving and learning basically was highly mechanistic, sans intelligence, and should be conceptualized as the gradual establishment of bonds between stimuli and randomly successful responses.

This perspective became the basis of the school of behaviorism founded by John B. Watson (1913) and supported by the later behaviorists, notably B. F. Skinner (1953), Clark L. Hull (1943), Edwin R. Guthrie (1935), and Kenneth W. Spence (1956, 1960). All of these scientists rejected rationality as a parameter of behavior—either animal or human. Their conclusions, based on studies of rats, pigeons, and chickens, were advanced as valid for understanding all aspects of human behavior! All behavior, except perhaps for language, was to be explicated by studies of rats making choices in mazes or pigeons pecking targets in a box. Language was allowed as a possible human distinction (although Skinner 1957 generated a complex and largely unsuccessful treatment of "language behaviors" based on the same associative-learning mechanisms that are evident in rats and pigeons). Language, it was assumed, allowed for a new psychology based on thought, and because earlier scientists of the twentieth century were convinced that no nonhuman had language, they were convinced that no nonhuman could think.

Strange!

It was held that it was unsafe to posit thinking in nonhuman animals. Why? Because nonhuman animals could not tell us of their thoughts and experiences, as we do with one another. Interestingly, the verbal report of humans was accepted as a valid reflection of consciousness, thought, intelligence, values, and so on. Yet a moment's reflection makes it clear that even as two humans talk with each another, one has no proof whatsoever that the other's speech accurately reflects his thought. One human assumes that because her interlocutor is a human, he shares the private experiences of her own self. Although this assumption is probably generally true, there is no way of proving the inference. Thus in a real sense we trustingly "anthropomorphize" among ourselves all the time. We assume that it is proper to attribute to other humans aspects of our own private lives. But to do so with non-human animals had been declared by behavioral scientists as unscientific, unwarranted, silly, even dangerous. Yet now, in light of comparative behavioral research of the past fifty years, it is no longer tenable *not* to allow for advanced operations of cognition and even language—at least in our nearest living relatives, the great apes (Savage-Rumbaugh and Lewin 1994; Savage-Rumbaugh et al. 1993; Rumbaugh 1990).

During the heyday of behaviorism, opposing views, although rare, were also influential. Robert M. Yerkes unabashedly discussed primate intelligence in his monograph of 1916, *The Mental Life of Monkeys and Apes,* reflecting a comparative perspective that included learning, intelligence, and the mental lives of apes, monkeys, mice, rats, frogs, crabs, turtles, dogs, cats, pigs, and even earthworms. During World War I, Wolfgang Köhler (1925), a cofounder of the school of Gestalt psychology, studied chimpanzees' problem solving and concluded that it could be insightful. That is, apes were able to solve novel problems by reasoning and creativity—not simply by trial and error as held by Thorndike. In the decades that followed, the avowed behaviorist Edward C. Tolman (1948) created a cognitive framework that he called "purposive behaviorism" to account for maze learning by rats. Tolman ascribed learning to the perception of relationships, called "cognitive maps," between such stimuli as those that depict relationships between routes to the goal box of a complex maze.

The key issue that divided Tolman and Köhler from Thorndike and his followers was how to account for the observed performances of animals. Thorndike considered the animal to be like a machine that generated a series of random responses until one of the responses succeeded in bringing about a "satisfying state of affairs." The response was hence "stamped in" or learned, and the probability that the response would recur in that situation in the future was increased. Clearly this view credits animals with little or no intelligence! By contrast, Tolman and Köhler viewed organisms as thinking beings that, given the opportunity, would evaluate situations and choose responses that were likely to satisfy a purpose or achieve a goal. Such organisms could learn passively as well as actively, through observing the performances and successes or failures of others.

Harry F. Harlow (1949; see also Chapter 17) provided a bridge between these contrasting perspectives with his research on learning set, or "learning to learn." Harlow studied changes in learning proficiency by monkeys over a long series of problems. Initially their learning was essentially like that of Thorndike's trial-and-error improvement—slow and arduous. With experience, however, the monkeys became increasingly skilled and learned new problems with apparent insight—quickly and nearly errorlessly. Thus Harlow defined the course whereby certain protracted experiences provide for the emergence of insightful, one-trial learning, even of novel problems of a kind that initially required gradual trial-and-error learning. Moreover, Harlow's learning-set procedure became the basis of numerous subsequent attempts to assess species differences in learning and transfer ability and, by extension, intelligence.

Wild Animals

We are fortunate today that a wide variety of animals still abounds. It won't always be that way. A United Nations report asserts that the primary causes for the loss of biodiversity are the destruction of habitats and introduction of species not native to an area. The report lists more than eleven thousand endangered animal and plant species. Nearly 25 percent of the world's mammals are at risk for extinction. Even now E. O. Wilson (2002), a Pulitzer Prize winner and a sterling scientist, views with alarm an imminent crash in the variety of species, and he states that this crash will be more abrupt and devastating than any previous mass destruction. Recovery from it will not be likely. Wilson presents a plan to forestall the calamity, one that we would be well advised to implement lest the consumptive needs of exploding human populations devastate too much of the environment needed to support animal and plant life. Even the seemingly indestructible mountain gorilla's extinction is threatened by the combined assaults of volcanic eruption and human encroachment into its fragile forests. Current rates of extinction are now between one hundred and one thousand times greater than normal, qualifying our day as an era of mass extinction (Levin and Levin 2002).

Despite their dwindling numbers, animals adhere the best they can to the lifestyles and cycles for which they are adapted; but their abilities to survive as individuals, and hence as species, no longer work as well as they did before our own populations soared from a few hundred thousand to billions. To preserve wildlife in large reaches of their natural habitats might well be in the interests not only of the animals' survival but of our own species' survival in other than a totally artificial environment.

Each animal that we see in our world is making a statement not only of itself, but of its genetic, biological, and behavioral lineages from the beginning of life itself. Critical junctures in their histories include several stories about how they came to be what they are in appearance, but just how they came to be what they are is certain to be more obscure than obvious.

Understanding the behavior of animals is no simple challenge. Why do they do what they do? How are they able to do it? What were the selective pressures that now cause and/or enable them to do as they do? What kind of neural processes support various behaviors? Can they think? Are they sentient? Do they perceive their own and others' feelings and emotions as do we? Apart from meeting their own basic needs, do they care about anything? Can they become depressed because of their plight of the moment, or because they have lost their parent or offspring or favorite companion? In some quarters it is unacceptable even to ask such questions. That the same questions are asked about humans and their behavior does not make them objective, but unless such questions are asked, techniques for even beginning to answer these basic questions will never be devised. Here we will use whatever questions and data we can that promise to assist our efforts to understand animals and their behavior. At times, our individual assessments—yes, as humans—will be offered in balance with scientific data to at least chart the course for the future. Lifetimes of experience in research and study are not without their value in understanding our fellow humans and animals.

By following these and other questions, we here undertake the quest of exploring animal behavior to a number of ends, not the least of which is the answer to the question—When is intelligence a useful concept in understanding why animals do as they do? How is intelligence best described and understood? Is nonhuman animal intelligence in any manner similar to our intelligence? Does it have roots in common with ours? What might an understanding of animal intelligence tell us of the foundations of our extraordinary competence as a species?

Indexes of Intelligence

We shall posit two major classes of intelligent behaviors, one based in the dictates of genes and heredity and the other based in learning processes and the creative processes of complex brains. Facile learning, the ability to transfer even small amounts of knowledge to leverage an advantage in adaptation, the ability to manifest cross-modal skills (Davenport and Rogers 1970), to symbolize, to learn words via comprehension and competent use, to make tools, to draw, to write, to use technology, and in general to harvest patterns of relationships and to generate knowledge through observations of events and of others' behavior—these capacities will serve as some, but not all, of the hallmarks of what here we will say is intelligence.

Our quest to achieve a better understanding of animal intelligence is fueled in part by how we view and value our own intelligence as a species and as individuals. The structure and function of our own intelligence promises to remain highly controversial (Sternberg 1994). The reason for the controversy is that there is no single way to define, let alone measure, intelligence. It is a construct. There is little or nothing absolute about it. Consequently, it is subject to redefinition. Its redefinition and measurement have become important for a variety of reasons, not the least of which is that intelligence tests of yesteryear (the Wechsler 1935, 1944, 1974, and the Stanford-Binet) are now known to be biased by socioeconomic factors. Although perhaps no one would quarrel with Wechsler's definition of intelligence as "the capacity of an individual to understand the world about him and his resourcefulness to cope with its challenges," the challenge remains to obtain relevant measurements and to avoid major error and egregious conclusions. We have come to reject Wechsler's assumption that essentially all children and adults have the same opportunities to learn information that is vital to doing well on those tests.

A close associate serves as a prime example. He had poor instruction in arithmetic in the first few grades and never received remedial education. As a sad consequence, he underrated his own intelligence. Later he failed to graduate from a state university because he was unable to pass required courses in mathematics and science. Eventually, however, he got a bachelor's degree from a fine arts institute, where they cared little about competence in those areas. There the level of his intelligence became clear. When he then took the Graduate Record Examination for graduate school application in fine art, his scores were well above the 90th percentile in everything but—you guessed it—quantitative skills. His score there was below the 8th percentile! He was still deficient in mathematics, but no question whatsoever remained about his intelligence. And yes, he obtained his master's degree from a fine university in the Northeast and now is teaching in a fine liberal arts college.

Because the definition and measurement of intelligence can have profound implications for individuals and the opportunities extended to them in their diverse lives, strong feelings can be generated in discussions of it. Even now, the definition of mental retardation determines whether the death sentences of some prisoners are commuted to life imprisonment. Given the gravity of defining intelligence of humans, it should come as no surprise that major differences are held for the definition and measurement of animal intelligence. For some, the very notion of animal intelligence is anathema (Kennedy 1992). Such an extreme view is clearly at odds with Darwin's principles of continuity of both biological and psychological parameters between animal and human.

Many attempts have been made to develop a culture-free test of human intelligence. Although those efforts have been of great interest and have substantial validity, they have not been widely accepted. Currently, strong efforts are being put forth to assay intelligence in terms of performance of various kinds, achievement, and even emotional appropriateness or effectiveness. As interesting as those efforts are, they are beyond the scope of this book, except as they illustrate a basic point when we focus on animal intelligence. Just what is animal intelligence? Does it have dimensions in common with human intelligence? If so, how do we know? Do factors that are known to influence human intelligence, task performance, memory, perception, and so on have comparable effects upon animals' behaviors and performances?

Apes surely have their own structures and/or patterns of intelligence, but their brain is so much like ours, except in size (it is about one-third the size of our brain) that it would be a surprise if they and we held no intellectual operations in common. Then, too, there are the lesser apes (the gibbon and siamang). They walk erect, and comfortably so, when they descend from the trees to the ground. Does their erect posture and bipedal walking, reminiscent of our own, mean that they are highly intelligent? (That question is discussed in Chapter 7.)

What are the origins of primate intelligence? Surely the enhancement of the brain has been a requisite for intelligence, but what favored large brains—ones that could learn rather universally about things and events, invent, and could devise cultures and technologies? Mason (1958) proposed that it was within the crucible and complexities of primate social life that advanced learning capacities and intelligence became advantageous. Byrne (1995) and Dunbar (1992) advance their perspectives based on food preparation and the size of social groups, respectively. Stanford (1995) associates hunting skills with the selection of social intelligence, and de Waal views advanced cognitive capabilities as basic to the complexities of apes' social politics and culture (see de Waal 2001b for current articles by these authors). The pervasive importance of the ability to deceive others has been also been advanced as a mover for primate intelligence (Parker and Gibson 1990). It seems likely that just as intelligence serves a broad field of purposes, it was selected by a broad array of challenges and adaptive pressures. The facilitation of open means of communication and language, the need to provide for new food and water resources with changes in climate, the need to care for highly dependent offspring, the need to fend off predators, and so on also surely supported selection for intelligence and elaboration of large brains.

The behavior and intelligence of animals is best understood from a comparative perspective that embraces the influences of genetics, rearing, development, social behavioral systems, and ecology. We need to know about ways in which biology affords behaviors in support of survival and reproductive fitness. We need to learn about learning and to examine perspectives, both historic and recent, that affect the ways we go about learning about learning.

The function of behavior is to bring an animal into interaction with the resources of its environment for nourishment and shelter. Animals must learn of their capabilities for movement—flying, leaping, grasping, biting, and so on—in the interest of behaving competently. Why and how do they initiate such actions on their very first occasion? Through their behavior, animals might be able to obtain food, water, shelter, social companions, and safety to support their own survival as individuals and as species.

Behavior entails substantial costs, inasmuch as it always takes energy (and thus fuel) to keep a body alive and behaving. It costs more to do some things than others, and that can become a controlling factor in determining what animals (ourselves included) do. Animals must learn about that, too.

There also are risks of making mistakes, incurring injuries, getting lost, and going without some of the resources being sought. Animals learn of risks relative to the value of the resources that they are trying to obtain and how to minimize them. Nature is a high-risk context. It has many dangers about which animals must learn if they are to survive.

At least some of the primates, if not animals more generally, learn about what they can and cannot control. We will consider how and why animals learn of control and some of the things they try to control. A guiding assumption is that the evolution of the more complex life forms has brought an increasing effort for exercising personal control over outcomes rather than being subject either to random events or being under the control of other individuals or agencies. Thus the more complex behaviors might well have in common an orientation to achieve at least perceived control over cause-effect relations, between action and consequence. (See Rumbaugh and Sterritt 1986 for a review of relevant literature.) Working with four specimens of ten species of primates ranging from prosimians to great apes, Parker (1974a, 1974b) found that the great apes as a group demonstrated far more complexity than any other group in their manipulations of a rope. Within the great apes, orangutans were more creative than were gorillas and chimpanzees, in turn, in their use of both rope and hoe for obtaining food (Parker 1969). Parker also found a positive relation between the amount of responsiveness and its relevance to the task during the initial phases of working in the situation and the subsequent solution of problems.

Thus Parker's studies within the order Primates support the argument that with the evolution of the advanced great apes both the amount and quality of responsivity increased, a combination of behavioral proclivities that would enable them to cope with an increasingly complex challenge from the environment. Studies by Glickman and Sroges (1966), Ehrlich (1970), Butler (1965), Jolly (1964), and Torigoe (1985) of curiosity and responsivity to objects and novel events in zoo and other animals affords additional evidence in support of Parker's conclusions. In Parker's words, "man the manipulator" had his origins in such a trend. It wasn't only that "man made tools," it also was that "tools made man."

These and the other issues listed above have inspired proclamations by authorities of yesteryear, philosophers both ancient and contemporary, folklore, and general observations by citizens across the board. They remain of high interest to researchers who pursue experimentally the understanding of behavior. Observations by scientists who concentrate their studies in the field and in captive social groups also contribute important information to our quest for understanding of animal behavior and intelligence (Whiten et al. 1999; de Waal 1989, 2001; Suddenford and Whiten 2001).

Comparative Psychology

The most useful studies of intelligence in animals take a systematic approach to viewing behavior within a framework. Nissen defined the perspective with precision: "Unless there is a continuity or homology of behavioral mechanisms from the lower to the higher animals (including human), there would be no rationale for the comparative method. This does not mean, necessarily, that the higher (later) is merely an extension or elaboration of the lower (earlier), although that is and has been a most provocative and fruitful working hypothesis. Quantitative complication may become so great that it produces in effect, qualitative differences with new 'emergent' properties" (1951, 351). Nissen agrees with Novikoff that "each level of organization possesses unique properties of structure and behavior which, though dependent on the properties of the constituent elements, appear only when these elements are combined in the new system. Knowledge of the laws of the lower level is necessary for a full understanding of the higher level; yet the unique properties of the phenomena at the higher level cannot be predicted, a priori, from the laws of the lower level" (Novikoff 1945).

An important point of emphasis is that relational forms of learning require that an organism defy the contingencies that have characterized, perhaps strongly, past experience. This is not to suggest that relational learning is independent of experience, or even that animals with the capacity to learn relationally are no longer subject to the laws of classical or instrumental conditioning. Humans and apes, of course, also learn associatively. At least under some circumstances, however, they can break the bonds of associative learning and extract the more general rulelike relations that emerge from experience. Thus it appears that humans, the great apes, and some of the larger macaques can extract reliable and meaningful patterns in the events of experience, and can use the information from these patterns to predict future events or consequences of action, to solve problems by insight, and to manifest cognitive competencies.

Our definition of comparative psychology is the search for patterns of similarities and differences in patterns of adaptation among animals so that we might better understand the processes of adaptation. Behavior is a prime mediator of adaptation and frequently makes the difference between life and death, both of individuals and of species. Comparative psychology affords us a framework within which to guide our search for similarities and differences in patterns of adaption and animal intelligence.

Although the comparative approach can draw findings from research on a single species, it generally is helpful to collect comparable data on two or more species. The general rule is that even closely related species offer many unanticipated points of difference as well as similarity; hence studying at least two species concurrently is highly recommended. When we have two or more subject species to compare and contrast, we are less likely to overlook differences and more likely to learn from them. Methods of inquiry must be sensitive to differences between the species that might skew the data speciously and invalidate the whole effort. Selecting an array of related species, particularly within a taxonomic order, is well advised whenever possible, for that strategy serves to reduce the likelihood that any obtained differ-

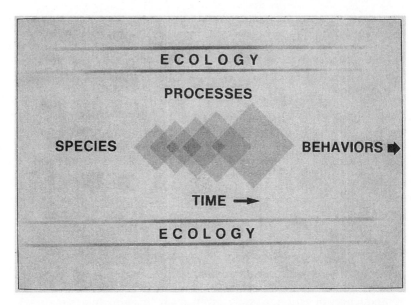

Figure 2. The matrix of comparative psychology. Comparative psychology is more than just research with animals. Rather, it is a framework within which we gain an understanding of similarities and differences in patterns of adaptation across time. Comparative psychology may be viewed as a matrix of five interacting factors: species and their adaptive processes generating behaviors across time within the resources and challenges of ecology (Rumbaugh 1985). Copyright © 1985, American Psychological Association. Reprinted with permission.

ences are attributable to extraneous factors. A survey of species can reveal patterns of change, or trends. It also is generally advisable to use at least two methods of data collection to rule out factors that might be inherent in any given method.

But we need a framework from which to depart strategically in order to weave the fabric of a comparative psychology of behavior. There are several dimensions to the matrix of comparative psychology—species, their behaviors, their basic processes, and the complex interactions of each of these with ecology across time (Rumbaugh 1985; see fig. 2). Let us begin with time.

Time is a relentless agent of change. Species and individuals reveal patterns of growth and the unfolding of abilities and capacities over time. Profound changes in the world itself and attendant changes in the resources and risks of various ecological niches also take place over time. These changes can have an impact upon the selection of life forms and speciation.

Species differ in a variety of dimensions. Each species has some well-defined genotype that sets it apart from others. A species' adaptations to relative specific ecologies can serve to limit its distribution, as might the abundance and competition of other life forms that also depend on some or all of the same resources for nurturing and shelter. The patterns of development and maturation of a species across time can serve to support rich and prolonged socialization, as in the great apes, and manifestations of what scientists view as elements of culture (Bard and Gardner 1996; Boesch and Tomasello 1998; Deacon 1997; de Waal 1982, 1989, 2001; Matsuzawa 1994; Whiten et al. 1999; McGrew 1992).

Behaviors can be relatively predictable within a species. Genetics define many characteristic or signature behaviors, including vocalizations and patterns of movement, as well as appearances. Each species generally has its own proclivities that are not subject to substantive change. For example, orangutans' behavior simply cannot be confused with that of chimpanzees. One can never teach or shape the behaviors of an orangutan to closely approximate those of a chimpanzee, and a gorilla's behavior can never be confused, except in minor detail, with those of the other primates.

Basic processes that serve to generate behavior can be common to several species. For example, simple discrimination learning—choosing one of two or more stimuli to receive a reward, for instance—and many of the general processes of behavior are shared by mammals, birds, fish, and even bees (Bitterman 1975, 1988, 2000; Bitterman and Couvillon 1991; Greenberg and Haraway 2002; Papini 2002). On the other hand, some species may be more able than others to learn relationally, in terms of overarching principles. Their learning processes are not limited to the most basic ones.

Species' sensory and perceptual systems might be quite different in structure and function. Vipers, for example, can see images determined by heat from various sources. Homing pigeons might use different sources of information (magnetic fields, stars, wind currents, odors, and so on) to make their way as weather changes along their course of flight. Bats and some sea mammals have remarkable sonar systems for "seeing" in the darkness of the night and seas, respectively. That a sensory system functions similarly across species does not mean that those species share evolutionary roots and are therefore homologous. The flight of bats is accomplished in a manner quite different from the flight of birds. Accordingly, the relation is only analogous. And common structures do not always function in the same media. Although most birds fly in the air, penguins "fly" in the water. Convergent evolution can lead to similar appearances or kinds of behaviors in unrelated species, though their biological foundations are essentially independent.

Ecology is the crucible within which complex interactions occur across time with the variables of species, behavior, and basic processes. It is within specific ecological niches that all life, animal or plant, must adapt or face extinction. For animals but not plants, behavior affords a ready vector whereby new niches might be found, ones in which adaptation and reproductive success can be achieved if necessary. The temperaments, interests, feeding patterns, and even patterns of social organization can be influenced radically by changes in ecology. During the course of an individual primate's growth and development, it is critical that the animal have a chance to learn broadly how to adapt from every perspective. The profile and demand of a given ecological niche can result in the selection of patterns of behavior that are unique for adaptation in that niche. Thus adaptation in one niche does not necessarily mean that a given individual will be equally adept at adaption in other niches. Only our own species can take its own requisites for life and comfort with it as it has spread around the world and even into the fringes of outer space.

2

Adaptation

Adaptation—survival and reproduction across time—is achieved, in measure, by the physical and behavioral attributes of individuals and species. Adaptation is a continuing challenge and is never perfect. If adaptation begins to fail, dire consequences follow; if it fails completely, the consequence is death or extinction. At any one point in time, successful adaptation generally entails competent behavior, for behavior governs the organism's ability to use environmental resources on the one hand and provides protection from dangers and environmental extremes on the other (Beck 1980; Gottlieb 1984; Kummer 1968). Over the long term, however, adaptation requires selection of species and populations via genetics and the attributes that they control.

The mechanisms for adaptation are shaped by the selective pressures of evolution. Darwin's (1859) contributions to our understanding of evolution include the concepts of natural selection. Since his time, we have come to understand that adaptation via selection can be better imagined in terms of differential reproductive success mediated by genetics. The survival of many of a given species' offspring might threaten the viability of other species. This is particularly likely when a species with a high reproductive success rate competes with other species for a natural resource that is necessary to life but is limited in availability. Extraordinary reproductive success of one species might put another species at risk for survival. Survival and attendant reproductive success of a species might be more than adequate for eons, only to become threatened by sudden changes in any number of conditions and events that are necessary for its sustained success. Global warming, now in progress, promises to have broad and profound effects upon survival of species and their geographic distribution and upon evolution generally. Species' challenges for adaptation surely will become more intense.

Individual variation and differences among members of a given species provide for differential outcomes of natural selection. For example, body weights vary markedly, and selective pressures might favor the heavier individuals at times. To the degree that the weight of individuals is genetically controlled, the species will become heavier in general—until such time as being lean and trim are the more adaptive characteristics.

Mutations and genetic drift afford still other opportunities for change in genotypes. Mutations are transmissible changes in the genotype that are produced by natural forces. Not all mutations favor adaptation, but some can have highly beneficial long-term effects. Recent evidence from the Chicago Field Museum, obtained by testing many mutations, serves to clarify the evolutionary relation between dinosaurs and birds. Other recent reports from the University of California, San Diego, help us understand how major changes in body shapes occurred in early animal evolution.

Examples of changes within the order Primates that also have been discussed as possible mutations rather than results of relatively gradual selection processes include upright posture and bipedal gait, overlapping visual fields and the resultant enhanced depth perception, and the supplanting of claws by fingernails. Indeed, one defining attribute for primates is the presence of nails on at least one digit. Nails afford greater precision in efforts to pick things up manually. Genetic drift is said to occur as the genotype changes gradually, either by chance or in response to relatively minor changes in selective pressures on adaptation. The bones of the fingers of the apes have a natural arch to them, which serves to facilitate hanging for long periods of time from branches in trees. Anatomy serves to simplify doing so and saves work that would otherwise have to be accomplished by stronger tendons and muscle groups.

Separation of breeding groups of a given species can, across time, markedly alter the statistical distribution of genes and eventually lead to speciation. The new species generated by these mechanisms are the bases of taxonomic classification. Closely related species form genera, closely related genera form families. Families form orders, orders form classes, and classes form phyla. Closely related species appear to be similar in many ways. Generally they don't interbreed in nature, but they can and do from time to time. Hybrids thereby produced might or might not be fertile. In captivity, restriction of partners and occasions for breeding can serve to increase the probabilities of breeding between species and genera (Wolkin and Myers 1980). In Atlanta, for example, the happenstance caging of a siamang and a gibbon produced an offspring that lived to adulthood. Interestingly, it had forty-seven chromosomes, the average of the numbers of chromosomes of its parents. Because the chromosomes were mosaics of the parental chromosomes, it is unlikely that the hybrid would have been able to reproduce.

Behavior and Adaptive Processes

Perhaps the most basic characteristic of living cells is that they respond to stimulation from either external or internal sources. With even minimal differentiation of cells so as to form central ganglia and brains, the responsiveness of cells can become selective and specialized.

Cells that have become sensitized to successive encounters with a stimulus source respond more quickly and to lower levels of stimulus intensity than before. By contrast, cells that have become habituated to certain stimuli no longer respond to them. Sensitization operates as if the cells have learned that what will follow the stimulation is not trivial and portends something that is substantially positive or adverse. The same rules apply to organisms. Thus we can become sensitized to minimal cues (for example, a slight weakness or pain) associated with a tendon or muscle that is about to fail, to the crackling of leaves when camping, or to a door that is being opened very quietly. Habituation operates as if we have learned that nothing of consequence will follow; hence it is all right to "stand down" and relax.

Differential responsiveness to events is the basis from which increasingly complex forms and patterns of responding emerge. Increased complexity of response by an organism to a stimulus might be essentially unlearned or automatic, defining reflexive and/or instinctive behavior (Tinbergen 1951). On the other hand, increased complexity of response might be a reflection of learning. Reflexive, instinctive, and learned patterns of behaviors are remarkable in that a system made of tissues (nerves, ganglia, and brains) responds somewhat predictably because of the dictates of genetics or because of the storage of experiences in a form that entails both learning and memory. Just how certain behavior patterns come overwhelmingly under genetic control is not known.

Biological Smartness and Psychological Intelligence

Intelligence is a construct that involves certain special kinds of highly adaptive behaviors. Generally, intelligence is imputed as the underlying basis for facile, efficient, and clever learned or acquired behaviors and skills. Other behaviors, however, are facile, efficient, and clever but clearly are not learned. These are instincts, which are primarily predicated by genetics. How each kind of ingenious behaviors should be defined and measured is subject to continuing debate. Here we will differentiate between biological smartness and psychological intelligence as our point of departure in defining animal intelligence.

We use *biological smartness* to refer to behaviors that are highly adaptive, yet dictated primarily by genetics and maturation within a species' ecological niche. Various species' patterns of migration, reproduction, foraging, communicating, and so forth are familiar markers and serve as examples of biological smartness. They are instinctive behaviors and response patterns, subject to change through experience and learning, that characterize various species. They may require specific age-linked experiences that are generally assured in the species' natural niche. Still other systems of behavioral proclivities, though less specifically guaranteed by biology and genetics, equally distinguish species. Thus gorilla infants find it relatively easy to learn gorilla ways, but not those of leopards. Similarly, the challenge of becoming a competent gorilla is beyond the capacity of a chimpanzee or orangutan or human child, and these species, in turn, have their own genotypes that direct their general styles of behaving and learning. Although biologically predicated behaviors clearly fulfill many species' needs "smartly," their parameters are quite different from those of the next more commonly defined type of intelligence.

While psychologists were debating the relative merits of behaviorist versus cognitive frameworks for comparative psychology, European scientists emphasized biology, genetics, and development in founding the science of ethology—the description of animal behavior in the natural environment, as contrasted with "psychology," in which animal behavior is studied using laboratory or field experiments that involve the manipulation and control of variables that influence behavior. The ingenious studies of Konrad Lorenz (1950, 1965) and Niko Tinbergen (1951) yielded the concept of species-specific or instinctual behaviors that are unlearned and adaptive (for example, courtship routines, imprinting) and that appear at the first opportunity. The right experience at a critical time, however, might be necessary in order for the response to become adaptive; for example, goslings learned to follow their mothers only if they saw them during this critical period. If instead they saw and followed Lorenz first, they "imprinted" on him as though he were their mother. Ethologists generally discounted or ignored the types of learning phenomena that psychologists considered to be important indexes of animal intelligence.

Despite early difficulties in establishing productive communication between stimulus-response behaviorists, cognitivists, and ethologists, it is now almost universally accepted that nature and nurture interact to produce the complex behavioral adaptations of both humans and other animals. The biological preparedness of many forms of wildlife to learn rapidly to avoid certain tastes associated with toxins is a case in point. Memory traces for new tastes can be maintained by special networks that last for many hours to become specifically associated as conditional stimuli "to be avoided" in the future as the result of a single experience. Hence bait shyness—manifested, for example, by predators after ingesting poisoned meat left in fields by farmers to control predation on their herds by wolves—is the product of an interaction between biology and learning mechanisms. This kind of shyness reflects the Garcia effect, whereby some animals associate nausea with specific tastes of foods that were eaten perhaps several hours earlier (Garcia, Ervin, and Koelling 1966; Garcia and Hankins 1977; Garcia,

Kimeldorf, and Koelling 1955; Garcia and Koelling 1966, 1967; Garcia et al. 1968; Revusky and Bedarf 1967). There is a specific neurophysiological system that enables this kind of learning. This learning suggests respondent conditioning but is clearly an exception to the close temporal association otherwise required for an essentially neutral stimulus—the conditional stimulus (CS)—to come to elicit the response produced by the unconditional stimulus (UCS). The adaptive value of this effect is strong for animals that might opportunistically eat carrion and forms of life otherwise foreign to them.

Fixed Action Patterns (FAP) afford a host of instances of biological smartness. An FAP is an innate and predictable pattern of behavior in response to stimuli called releasers. Releasers (Thorpe 1956) or sign stimuli (Tinbergen 1951) serve to trigger certain unlearned behaviors automatically and can serve as distinguishing characteristics for various species. FAPs generate specific behaviors in rather predictable form and pattern, yet ethologists allow for changes in those behaviors with experience and learning across time.

Interesting FAPs are exemplified by the digger wasp's egg laying. As the time of egg laying becomes imminent, the digger wasp digs a nest that can be accessed by a single tunnel. The wasp next paralyzes a caterpillar with its sting, brings the caterpillar to the tunnel's opening, leaves it there, and goes underground as if to check on the chamber's condition. If everything is in order, the caterpillar is pulled down into the chamber. Eggs are laid on and in the caterpillar, thereby providing the young digger wasps, once hatched, a ready source of food. This FAP is mediated by a series of releasers and events brought about by them.

This pattern is efficient in that the digger wasp doesn't need a long history of learning to master the complexity of this behavior, but it has its limitations. One of the limitations is that the behavior pattern's effectiveness is contingent upon things remaining relatively constant in the structure of the environment. For instance, if while the digger wasp is down in the excavated chamber as if to check its condition, the paralyzed caterpillar is moved a bit, the wasp's pattern of egg laying can be so disrupted as to be terminated. If the digger wasp surfaces to find that the caterpillar is not where she left it, she must relocate and position it, then return to the chamber to check it again. If the caterpillar is moved again, the wasp will again relocate it, go down and check the chamber repeatedly. All the while, the caterpillar remains on the tunnel's edge. The behavior and chain of events dictated by genetic influence has been interrupted. Nothing can go forward until the sequence of events is intact. In sum, the digger wasp's behavior, unlearned and efficient, can be easily disrupted. If the wasp is not interrupted, its behavior serves as a good example of an instinct and is endorsed here as a prime example of biological smartness. But it definitely is not an instance of psychological intelligence. Psychological intelligence, as we shall see, offers greater flexibility by way of repair work if something goes awry and novel behaviors are needed to deal with new situations.

The black-headed gull affords another prime example of FAPs. Once the black-headed gull female lays her eggs in a nest, she sets to incubate them and, if necessary, to retrieve them if they have by accident rolled out of the nest when she moves or leaves the nest briefly.

If only one aspect of a stimulus complex is used for the release of an FAP, it might be called a sign stimulus. The beak of the adult seagull, for example, has a red dot on it that encourages pecking by the young gulls in the nest. The pecking of that dot, in turn, stimulates the female gull to regurgitate food for the young to ingest. Another sign stimulus is the bright white interior of broken egg shell. Gould (1982) suggests that the brightness serves to attract predators and that the ejection of the shell from the nest by the adult female serves to reduce predation of its young. The bright interior of the shell appears to serve as a releaser for the gull's FAP of shell ejection. Clearly, the gull's reproductive success would be remarkably curtailed, if not precluded, if she had to learn, by trial and error and across time, that broken egg shells don't serve the interests of the brood's survival (Gould 1982).

Other remarkable FAPs include the weaver bird's building a nest not only distinctive but highly complex, equipped with an opening designed to foil entry by predators. The weaving is accomplished by the use of a variety of knots and materials too complex and intricate to be learned in any arduous trial-and-error manner.

FAPs also can rely upon multiple sensory input. For instance, Meredith and Stein (1983) found that a cat's predation upon songbirds depends upon both sight and sounds of the bird. One type of stimulation is generally not sufficient for predation to be released.

Studies by Chiszar (for example, Chiszar et al. 1982) found marked differences in the predatory strategies and tactics of species of snakes. The garter snake moves quite quickly, and it actively trails potential prey that are relatively defenseless animals, such as small fish and worms. Once the garter snake attacks, it bites, holds, and then consumes its catch. By contrast, the rattlesnake is quite slow in its locomotion, though it is lightning fast when it strikes. By striking quickly, injecting its venom, and withdrawing quickly, it reduces the prospect of injury inflicted by its prey, which is quite commonly equipped with sharp teeth and claws. The rattlesnake does not hold onto its prey as does the garter snake. Neither does it actively trail or pursue its potential prey. Rather, it selects a trail used by potential prey, waits, and then strikes when the prey gets within range. Its strike is controlled both by vision and heat sensors. After the strike, it becomes attracted to chemical stimulation. Only then does it begin to pursue the target of its strike. It might take several hours to locate the prey, now dead from the venomous strike. It can then eat in safety.

Although the hand of genetics can constrain and even define behavior, instinctive behaviors are not necessarily exclusively reliant upon genetic dictation. The development of an organism can afford experiences that are critical to the development and patterns of appropriate behaviors that are provided for and constrained fundamentally by genetics (Thorpe 1972). Consider, for instance, the findings by Marler (1972) and his associates that genetics defines the basic template for the songs that certain songbirds eventually come to sing. Yet the specific songs sung by these birds as adults reflect the songs they hear at very early ages, well before the developing birds begin to sing. The adult songs heard by the very young birds determine the patterns of trills and other nuances of the young birds' singing several months later.

Auditory feedback young birds receive when they first try to sing also has a determining effect upon their singing skill. If they are reared in isolation or if they are deaf and cannot hear their own efforts to sing, the song will be primitive and executed with a relative lack of skill. Notwithstanding, the song is organized with certain major constraints of the basic template of the species. Nottebohm (1981) reported remarkable annual changes in the anatomy of the left hemisphere of songbirds as song learning and singing are perfected.

The execution of behaviors, both unlearned and learned, relies on sensory systems that clearly have been selected for sensitivity to stimulation according to the adaptive efforts for each species. Color vision is associated with diurnal activity and is not common in nocturnal creatures. The reason for this differentiation probably is that the low light levels of the night require an acuity that simply can be accomplished best by achromatic receptors (rods) in the retina. Low light levels render color vision, via cones in the retina, inadequately stimulated for keen vision.

Generally, creatures will use good visual information if available. When it is not, some will shift to other sources for critical information. Homing pigeons use a variety of sensory systems to make their way. If light is good, they use color vision to scan the landscape and discern important cues for flight. If clouds preclude visual cues, they can shift to the use of the stars, magnetic fields, directions of wind currents, and sounds.

Porpoises and whales will use vision whenever possible, but where light is insufficient, they make remarkable use of sonar (Schusterman 1981). Sonar entails the emission of pulses or trains of sounds and interpretation of their reflection. Roitblat (1985) reports that dolphins' use of sonar will permit them to discern not only the shape of an object in the water but also the form of another item that might be within the first object. Griffin's discovery of sonar in bats (Griffin 1958), achieved by the auditory analyses of sounds emitted in pulses, also demonstrated that bats will fly without sonar in familiar environs. This finding was made by placing barriers in the paths of the bats' daily flight patterns, such as from their caves. Procedures indicated that when the bats were not engaging in echolocation, they would fly right into the barriers! Echolocation then was promptly reactivated by the bats.

Although vision seems to be the preferred source of information for most animals, in some cases other sensory systems are preeminent. Taste, smell, and infrared vision are critical to snakes, for example, and electric fields can be critical for effective predation by sharks. Nature has provided for a variety of options of both structure and function to service effective adaption. The pit viper provides one of the more striking examples. Its eyes use infrared waves generated by the heat of creatures about it, and the image thereby obtained is projected on the optic tectum, which in most creatures with eyes is stimulated by mechanisms sensitive only to light (see Fobes and King 1982; Stebbins 1976).

Interestingly, as bats echolocate to find small insects in flight, it appears that the insects have evolved their own defensive flight patterns. Once the insects sense the sound emission chirps of the bat, their flight patterns become erratic as though to make their capture as difficult as possible. Creatures thus appear to conduct their own quasi— arms race: as the predator's mechanisms of preying are refined in the interest of effectiveness and efficiency, the anatomical and behavioral defensive mechanisms of prey seemingly evolve with the effect of confounding the predator's lethal attacks. All of this said, behavior plays primary roles both on the part of the hunter and hunted.

Psychological intelligence contrasts with biological smartness in that it is not "instinctive." Rather, it reflects the individual's ability to benefit flexibly (to learn) from interactions with the environment, physical and social. We regard psychological intelligence as the potential to learn quickly and to solve problems creatively. To do so entails the capacity to transfer learning in ways that give the individual a marked advantage as it encounters new contexts, problems, and challenges. Differences in psychological intelligence exist both within and between species; the quality is not divorced from biology. Psychological intelligence clearly is related to learning, memory, the speed of information processing, problem solving, and language. Although it might be viewed as having a core that is global or "general," it is best viewed as having several more specific dimensions—for example, social, verbal, or performance intelligence.

It is only reasonable that we as humans are curious about whether animals are intelligent in ways that characterize our own intelligence, but it is also important to remember that our intelligence has an evolutionary history. Thus some animals, notably the apes, might have certain dimensions of intelligence that are similar to ours, though limited. Indeed they do! But it is important to acknowledge that the intelligence of animals is organized to service their own adaptations in highly varied ecological niches. They can be highly intelligent in ways that are quite unlike ours. We have yet to identify their kinds of intelligence satisfactorily so as to measure our human abilities against their standards. By doing so eventually, however, we will minimize the risks of anthropocentricity.

3

Sculpting of Tendencies

Even unlearned instinctive behaviors can provide the foundations for learning not only how to do things more efficiently but how to do them differently. That ducklings and chicks instinctively follow the first moving object that they see is generally known. That a duckling can be quite clever in "following" that object is not.

At times, behaviors of relatively complex forms appear as surprises. These behaviors are worthy of attention, for they can point to processes that otherwise go undetected. For example, Dr. Len Rosenblum of the State University of New York, Downstate Medical Center, recounted to one of us how a baby duckling modified its behavior creatively during an imprinting study. Ducklings instinctively will attempt to follow the first moving thing that they see after they hatch. Normally, that object is the mother duck. As the ducklings attempt to follow their mother, they become imprinted to her; that, in turn, helps to ensure that they will receive her protection, that they will find food with her assistance, and so on.

Rosenblum used a mechanical model in lieu of a real mother duck. The model moved about and effectively induced the ducklings to imprint on it. For one innovative duckling, however, following the mechanical model seemed to entail too much effort and wasted energy. Its solution to walking?—To jump up on the model's back and, with its small wings outstretched, to hold on as best it could. The etiology of that clever behavior is not known, but its core was not acquired through trial and error. Although baby geese are known to ride on their mother's back while swimming, this duckling was a Long Island Peking Duck; its "mother duck" was neither swimming nor a goose.

Opening the Door to Intelligence

Cats are generally known for jumping up and grasping door knobs, but they are not well known for the kind of behavior next recounted. Several years ago, a front door to a house I (Rumbaugh) was visiting opened, and in walked a cat. "Who opened the door for the cat?" I asked. The owner of the house said that the cat routinely opened it herself. I found that incredible, for the door was massive and had been securely closed. To demonstrate, he tossed the cat outside and positioned me at a bay window for viewing the front of the door. Shortly, the cat came up to the front door, sat, and gazed up at the sturdy "half heart" wrought-iron piece that formed the handhold used for opening and closing the door. Above the half-heart shaped handle was a thumb latch that had to be depressed for the door to open. The cat leapt up, grabbed the half-heart shaped handhold with its left forepaw, then adroitly hooked its right forepaw onto the thumb latch positioned above the handhold. She pulled down on that latch until it unlatched with a click, then kicked backward and off the door with sufficient vigor to push the door inward! Then, as before, she sauntered into the front room, where a party was being held.

The cat had never been intentionally trained or conditioned by others to open the door. Good fortune combined with tenacious efforts probably had served to sculpt and refine this behavior pattern. Without the benefits of extensive experiences, each of which might be individually explained in terms of operant conditioning, the cat would not have learned how to manipulate the mechanics of the door with such remarkable effect. This is not to say that the cat literally understood anything at all about what it had to do and how it needed to do it in a sequential chain of behavior but rather to assert that the cat's brain somehow organized what it had learned and brought patterns of behavior to its door-opening efforts. That the cat came to open the door does not mean that the extensive and varied efforts that it probably had made assured success. But the brain—even of the cat and of the duckling—has become adept, through the selective pressures of adaptation, both at attending selectively to events and at integrating them toward some specific end. True, some good fortune and luck may have to be involved. The thumb latch had to be sufficiently movable to respond to the force of the cat's weight; the mass of the door could not be so great that it would not move as the cat pushed off and backward from its pawhold; and so on. It had to be a solvable task. Many readers probably know of at least one cat that has opened a door by manipulating some kind of securing mechanism, but of course we also know, as Thorndike did, that for every cat that learns to open a door there are hundreds that don't even try or that try fruitlessly.

A more serious challenge was faced by a squirrel monkey mother. Squirrel monkeys are small, tree-dwelling primates of South America. When they give birth, generally the infant pulls itself from the birth canal by grasping and pulling on the hair on the mother's ventrum. Squirrel monkey mothers do not normally cradle their young or even assist the infant in clinging to her body. The mother's active assistance to the infant is generally limited to the lifting of an arm as the infant tries to gain access from her back to a nipple for nursing. But what if the infant is weak and cannot cling to the mother? In the forest, the infant is probably lost to the forest floor, with the mother doing nothing to rescue it and to care for it. But in captivity she might remain in close proximity. In the 1960s a squirrel monkey, caged with three others, delivered a stillborn infant. Only when the carcass was touched by a probe did the monkey mother attend to it. She did so by dropping to the floor, grimacing and vocalizing all the while. She hovered over the infant, pressing her ventrum against it. Such behavior would have facilitated a live infant's grasp. When the gesture proved futile, the mother surprised observers by sitting on her haunches, picking up the carcass with both hands, and then holding it to her breast as she proceeded to walk bipedally for about three feet. In responding to a dead infant, the squirrel monkey, normally a relatively uncaring mother, became active in caregiving. Furthermore, the dedicated quadruped became a biped—not an easy transition. An experiment with two viable infants whose hands were temporarily gloved so as to preclude their ability to cling elicited the same behaviors from their mothers. The dependency of the infant probably elicited both the cradling and the bipedal walking (Rumbaugh 1965). We submit that even the squirrel monkey mother's modest intelligence and motivation to maintain close proximity to her infant induced in her these two novel courses of action. One might speculate further that maternal instincts themselves evolved across generations in response to neonates' increasing size and decreasing ability to cling to their mothers. These impressive mother-infant care patterns, including assisted nursing and manual support of offspring while the mother is walking upright, probably reflect significant aspects of the mothers' intellects. The proclivity for these behaviors was perhaps spawned in the early stages of the primate brain's evolution, given that even the squirrel monkey did its best to manifest good (albeit novel) maternal skills.

Protracted play with and manipulation of objects clearly developed unusual tool-use skills by a gibbon. In the field, gibbons occasionally will drop branches on people who persist in following them, but otherwise they are not tool users. Yet in a captive setting, a gibbon came to use both a washcloth and a section of rope quite innovatively. The washcloth was initially used to control the initial spurt of water from the gibbon's drinking spigot. It was then draped on a rod so that the water dripping from it would pool on a small ledge, from which the gibbon then drank. The section of rope was used for weaving, as a vine, in and out of the chainlink that formed her cage. But more significant, the gibbon would drape the rope over a rod in her cage, then grasp both ends simultaneously and swing in wide arcs back and forth (Rumbaugh 1970). With no training or reinforcement to develop these skills, the gibbon did so. Why? We believe that her skills reflected her learning about the objects in her cage gained across time. By playing with each object, she learned of its attributes and how it could be used creatively to solve certain challenges. In this instance, a captive environment brought forth behaviors not used in the field.

The Brain as an Integrating Organ

In pursuit of an enhanced perspective regarding the origins of such creative behaviors as those recounted above, let us posit that the brain integrates experiences even of the distant past to enhance not only survival but comfort—as when the cat joined the party and got to enjoy some hors d'oeuvres.

Matata, a bonobo *(Pan paniscus)* liked fresh air in her cage. She would sit for a half-hour at a time in the outer doorway, patiently holding aloft a heavy steel guillotine-style door, first with one hand and then with the other. Finally Matata supplanted this tiring effort by wedging a tire into the doorway as a prop. A simple action it was, but not a simple-minded one. Matata had to know something of the physics of tires and moving doors and likely weights of doors to come up with the solution (assuming, safely we believe, that she did not just get lucky on her first guess of what might have become a long string of trials and errors).

The orangutan Madu used a similarly clever technique to prevent caregivers from locking her outside. Although Madu enjoyed playing in her outdoor enclosure, she hated to lose the option of going in and out, particularly when there was some activity indoors that she might find interesting. Nonetheless, it was occasionally necessary—for example, during cleaning—for her caregivers to lock the guillotine door to prevent her from coming into the building. This task became much more difficult after Madu, without training or modeling, learned that she could jam the lock with a small piece of bark and thereby prevent the door from being securely closed. How did she ascertain this solution? Did she try a variety of solutions—jam the lock with a leaf, jam the lock with a banana, jam the lock with a rock, jam the lock with a branch, and so forth—until she hit upon the successful response? Almost certainly, the solution was not learned from the caregivers, who used different means for pinning the door open or closed. Did she reason this solution based on what could be observed from the operation of the door and the locking mechanism? What was it about the regularity in the operation of the door, the lock, and the affordances of bark that led to this creative (if frustrating for caregivers) innovation?

These single episodes do not constitute conclusive scientific data, but collectively they serve to launch our consideration of a variety of comparative studies that help us understand animals' perceptual and learning abilities and the complexity of their subsequent behavior. For

instance, one might ask from surveying toy houses and children's play
with them whether or not chimpanzees might be able to use scale models of an adjoining area to tell them where an incentive was hidden. If
so, a recent study by Kuhlmeier and Boysen (2002) is relevant. They
used a diminutive model of another room in which the chimpanzees
might search for a prized incentive at a later time. The results indicated
that the chimpanzees were able to learn from the model where the
prized incentive was hidden relative to other furnishings of the adjoining area. Given the opportunity, it seems probable that animals can acquire remarkable understandings of complex situations—in this case
one not understood by children until they are about three years old.

   Do monkeys care what tasks they work on to get food? Can rats
deduce which is the better option of two or more routes when access
to the preferred alley is denied? How does general experience afford
information that subsequently can be used effectively? Does learning
entail specific responses or more general goal-directed and task-com-
pletion behavior? Are rewards requisite to learning? What are the differences between learning and performance? Can monkeys learn to become insightful? Does early experience make a difference in what apes
attend to and what they are able to do as they mature? These and other
questions guide our consideration of research relevant to our overarching question, "Are roots of human intelligence to be found in animals?"—or conversely, "Is there a barrier between us and nonhuman
beings that sets us decisively apart from them?"

   Might animals' creativity be based in large measure upon their attending to the salient aspects of their immediate situation? Might their
readiness to so attend be the result of their genetic proclivities in interaction with contexts of their past experiences which shaped what they
learned and how what they learned might be used creatively in the face
of new challenges? Might the parameters of salience be helpful to our
understanding of animal intelligence? We address these questions in
subsequent chapters.

4

Learning, the Foundation of Intelligence

Learning can do what instincts cannot: it can afford creatures flexibility and problem solving. Its cost is substantial, however. Complex learning generally requires a large and highly complex brain. Large brains, in turn, are very expensive metabolically. Their consumption of energy is massive and continuous, whereas energy consumed even by striate muscle groups of a body tend to be occasional, even intermittent.

But not all learning is complex. Some learning is basic and reflects the neurophysiological design and operations of the body. Such is the case with the most elemental form of conditioning, respondent conditioning. Pet owners and farmers across centuries have long known that their animal charges acquire fears of situations and things because of experience and that the animals also come to anticipate events, such as being fed at certain times of the day. And surely mothers from time immemorial have recognized how they come to make milk ready for their suckling infants even as they began to prepare for nursing to begin. Respondent conditioning was scientifically defined by Ivan Pavlov (1927, 1955), a Russian neurophysiologist.

Respondent Conditioning

The terms *respondent* and *operant* were introduced by B. F. Skinner to differentiate Pavlovian respondent conditioning from the operant conditioning that he advanced. According to Skinner (1938, 1950, 1953), respondents were involuntary responses to an unconditional stimulus (UCS) that could become conditioned to an associated conditional stimulus (CS). By contrast, Skinner's operants were unconnected to any unconditional stimulus but were, rather, strictly the product of conditioning.

The responses elicited by unconditional stimuli are reflexive, not learned. If the level of illumination to the eye is increased, for example, the pupil contracts. If the level of illumination is decreased, the pupil dilates. The net effect is, within limits, to hold the amount of light entering the eye constant. No prior experience or learning is needed for the pupil to react thus; level of light is an unconditional stimulus for the activation of the neuromuscular system that controls the dilation of the pupil—if neurologically the subject's eyes and brain are healthy. Similarly, the eye focuses images upon the retina through activation of the ciliary processes or muscles. If any learning is involved in the eye doing so, then clarity of image must be the goal. Unconsciousness, brain trauma, and toxic states can markedly affect these and other unlearned reflexes. Somewhat paradoxically, the unconditional stimulus both elicits the initial, unconditional, response and, according to traditional conditioning terminology, serves to reinforce the conditioned response.

In a conditioning context, a stimulus that does not naturally elicit the desired unconditional response (for example, pupil dilation or contraction) but is to be associated with it is termed the conditional stimulus (CS). This stimulus should precede the administration of the unconditional stimulus by about one-half second—just enough in advance so as to serve as a signal that the unconditional stimulus is imminent. At that time the unconditional stimulus is administered, thus eliciting the unconditional response. In time, with repeated trials, the desired response occurs even though the conditional stimulus is not followed by the unconditional stimulus. The response observed, termed the conditional response (CR), is similar to the unconditional response (UCR), though sometimes less vigorous or prompt in its appearance.

Thus the association of a conditional stimulus with the unconditional one results in the CS producing a response that approximates the one elicited by the UCS. The conditional stimulus serves, in effect, to announce the imminent appearance of the unconditional stimulus. Nothing entailing awareness, intentionality, or any other such motivation or experience is requisite to Pavlovian respondent conditioning. The term *respondent conditioning* acknowledges that a response has become conditioned through use of a stimulus that otherwise elicits the response involuntarily.

Generally, the unconditional stimulus elicits a response that is under the control of the autonomic nervous system, which is largely responsible for an organism's arousal and relaxation. It also controls and governs or balances opposing tendencies, such as bringing animals to heightened states of alertness, yet also serving to calm them. It controls the release of blood sugars from the liver, as well as digestion, elimination, and so on. Heart rate, blood pressure, and breathing are under the governance of the autonomic nervous system. Responses under the control of the autonomic nervous system have been conditioned to a wide variety of conditional stimuli, including specific thoughts, odors, and so on. Thus blood pressure, for example, can be managed, within limits, through Pavlovian respondent conditioning.

Several phenomena have been defined in association with respondent conditioning. Blocking (Kamin 1969), for example, lends strong support for a central thesis of this book: that learning generally focuses on the predictive relations between stimuli. Stimuli that are reliable in their associations, concurrent or sequential, are more likely to be attended to, learned about, and remembered than those that are not. The salience of stimuli also determines in large measure what we attend to, learn about, and remember. Once a respondent has become associated with and elicited by a conditional stimulus, a second stimulus paired with the onset and termination of the first stimulus fails to become an effective conditional stimulus in its own right. It appears that the new stimulus, paired with the first, is ignored—that is, blocked from attention—as redundant by the subject. On the other hand, if blocking has been established and then the unconditional stimulus is markedly changed, the new component might be included if training continues. Kamin believes that the element of surprise is ba-

sic to the disruption of blocking. A similar phenomenon, overshadowing, also is obtained through use of a compound conditional stimulus
during training. If the elements differ markedly in strength, only the
stronger, more salient stimulus will play the effective role when the elements are tested singly as conditional stimuli.

Operant Conditioning

According to Skinner, operants are emitted, not elicited. The subject
has to generate the desired response or one that might be shaped by selective reinforcement into the desired conditioned operant. In other
words, the initial response might only approximate the response to be
conditioned. For example, if one wants to condition the operant of
marble carrying in a rat, the rat should receive positive reinforcement
for such behaviors as licking or biting the marble, because elaboration
of such behaviors might be shaped into marble carrying.

In operant conditioning there is nothing like the unconditional
stimulus that elicits involuntarily a response to be conditioned. In operant conditioning, the subject must exhibit behavior that then can be
strengthened by subsequent events, termed reinforcers. Reinforcers include anything intended to increase the probability of a given response
occurring or any process by which a response is strengthened; reinforcers are generally assumed to involve more than mere contiguity of
the elements of stimuli and responses (Marx and Hillix 1979, 486).
Contingencies of reinforcement have to do with what happens as a
consequence of behavior. Purdy and colleagues (2001) point out that
reinforcements have relative values rather than absolute ones. Thus
rats initially given a 4 percent sucrose solution licked the vending tube
at a substantially higher rate than others that were given a 4 percent sucrose solution after initially receiving a 32 percent solution (Gordon,
Flaherty, and Riley 1973). For the second group, the initial experience
served to diminish the reinforcement value of the 4 percent solution.

Skinner invented a conditioning device that, against his wishes,
came to be known as the Skinner Box. In its basic design, it gave the
subject something that might encourage a relatively specific kind of response. Thus the box might provide for a bar inserted through one of
the walls. That bar being the only structure within the box, it was in-

evitable that the rat eventually would at least walk toward it and touch it, if not inadvertently push down on it. If that eventuality did not occur, the subject's looking at, walking toward, and touching the bar could, in turn, be selectively shaped via reinforcement. Shaping of the rat's behaviors eventually sculpted the operant to be conditioned.

How were approximations of the desired response reinforced? How was the target response in its full form reinforced? Reinforcement was made possible through use of reinforcer—such as a pellet of food. The reinforcer might be a conditioned reinforcer, one that has been temporally associated with a natural reinforcer, such as food and water. For example, a clicking sound that has always been associated with the delivery of food by the subject in the past can be used for prompt reinforcement of any response that might be shaped into the target or desired operant. Although operant conditioning has neither unconditional or conditional stimulus, there may be a stimulus that can function somewhat analogously to the CS: the discriminative stimulus (S^D). Presentation of the S^D can effectively cue the subject that if it does respond, it will receive reinforcement. Presentation of the S^Δ signals that responding will not be reinforced.

Operants act upon the environment so as to obtain its reinforcing properties for the subject (for example, locomotion can bring the subject to locations of nourishment, shelter, or a mate, contrasted with sources of pain and trauma). As we have seen, reinforcers may be defined as anything that increases the probability that the operant will be exhibited. Whereas in respondent conditioning the unconditional stimulus elicits and serves to reinforce a rather specific response, such as an eyeblink, in operant conditioning a reinforcer might be used to select and strengthen the probabilities of any number of responses.

The Nature and Nurture of Respondents and Operants

The literature available on both respondent and operant conditioning is vast and presents a wide array of procedures and behavioral changes for both types of conditioning. For the purposes of this book, we need only be clear about the difference between Pavlovian (respondent) and Skinnerian (operant) conditioning.

Respondent conditioning determines the occasions for un-learned patterns of responding of the kind generally governed by the autonomic nervous system. If we go to a restaurant, for example, where we have always had good company, music, service, and food, we relax, become comfortable, and have a good time in part because of the positive affective responses conditioned there on previous occasions. By contrast, if we go to a restaurant that we don't like because of its ambience, bad service, menu, or social company on past occasions, the deck is stacked against the probability that we will be able to relax and enjoy a good meal and outing. Moreover, Pavlovian respondents generalize across similar situations. Thus a few experiences with restaurants with a specific ethnic character can prejudice us for or against future selections of places to dine. Food aversions can be established illogically through respondent conditioning. Eating chocolate while already suffering with an upset stomach can lead to an aversion to chocolate (a horrible eventuality!). The chocolate might just push the gastric malaise to a new level of discomfort. Thus the taste of chocolate can serve as conditional stimulus for the unconditional stimulus of biliousness.

Operant or instrumental conditioning, by contrast, encourages responses that bring about procurement of various things and events and states of being. We can learn to ride bicycles, drive cars, ski, play violins, paint pictures, and search for other social and sexual beings. We can learn to manage money, to buy foods and prepare meals, to behave in a socially correct manner at a state dinner, to write poetry, and so on. All of this said, it is still irrevocably true that there is a biology (nature) that enables all that is conditioned by both respondent and operant procedures (nurture). It also is irrevocably true that to write poetry or music surely entails much more than basic conditioning of responses and behaviors.

The argument of nature vs. nurture is fundamentally an impossibly flawed juxtaposition of sources for why things are as they are, either in individuals or in groups. Without biology (life), behavior cannot occur and physical attributes cannot be manifest. Without experiences in diverse environments, the organism cannot achieve development, maturation, conditioning, and other kinds of learning. Interactions between biology and environment are inevitable. These interactions are where the action is and where the answers are to be found—not in the question, "Is this attribute due to nature or to nurture?" Notwithstanding, the variance of behavior can be differentially apportioned, through statistical analyses, to genetics, on the one hand, and to environment on the other.

And the issues entailed are just now becoming understood. Suomi (2002), for example, has conducted long-term studies in order to gain genetic control over the births of "uptight" and "laid-back" rhesus monkeys. Uptight monkeys are noted for their responsiveness, activity, and emotion. By contrast, the laid-back monkeys tend to be tranquil and to take things in the matter of course (Bolig et al. 1998). Yet a recent study reveals that early rearing by a quiescent mother rhesus can essentially inhibit the expression of these genetic proclivities. Maternal and social care can essentially negate the probability that an infant will become uptight or laid back. Suomi asserts a basic principle: deficits in physiological function and abnormalities in the regulation of emotion are the exclusive product of neither nature nor experience but rather the result of an interaction between the two (Suomi 2002). Just as the appearances of plants and their flowers can be profoundly influenced by the altitudes at which they grow, behavior and affect in their manifestations can be sculpted by the environmental parameters of parental and social contexts within which maturation and learning occur.

A host of studies have defined interactions between diets and food preferences. Squirrels as adults prefer the taste of nuts on which their mother fed while nursing. The acquired preference can be so strong as to lead the squirrels to locate primarily in clusters of trees that bear nuts with a particular flavor. If pregnant rats are fed garlic, their pups will prefer milk laced with garlic (Capretta and Rowls 1974). And so, in part, perhaps human culture and preferences for cuisine are similarly determined by interactions between genetics and the uterine and rearing environments.

5

Limitations of
Respondents and Operants

Respondent conditioning can occur at the level of the spinal cord. It does not need a brain (or consciousness) to occur. Nonetheless, the general ineffectiveness of presenting the unconditional stimulus before the conditional one (backward conditioning) supports the thesis that the important function for the conditional stimulus is to signal that some imminent event is at hand.

Thus we have the strong suggestion that the subject learns in a single sequential direction. If the unconditional stimulus is a shock to a dog's paw, serving to elicit an involuntary withdrawal response, the interests of adaptation are well served if the subject learns quickly to lift its paw whenever the conditional stimulus is presented. In a sense, the dog is coming to perceive the conditional stimulus as a forerunner to something that can be avoided—the unconditional stimulus and the attendant pain to the paw. If the lifting of the paw in response to the conditional stimulus serves to keep the dog from receiving the painful unconditional stimulus, the response can be properly viewed as an instance of avoidance conditioning. Even more basic is reconsideration of the conditioned dilation and constriction of the pupil of the eye. If a tone or other neutral stimulus precedes by a fraction of a second the unconditional stimulus of altered level of light, the tone will become effective as a conditional stimulus. In the wake of its presentation, the pupil will dilate or constrict, depending upon whether the light level (unconditional stimulus) is predictably lowered or increased. If the alteration of light level were followed by the tone, there would be no opportunity for the eye to constrict the pupil promptly in order to avoid the discomfort of markedly elevated levels of light to the pupil and the retina.

One rare exception, involving the element of surprise to the subject, is provided by Wagner and Terry (1975). If a stimulus that has served to signal to the subject that there will be no unconditional stimulus is now followed by the unconditional stimulus, which in turn is followed by a novel conditional stimulus, that conditional stimulus might thereby become effective in eliciting a conditional response. In brief, if the subject is surprised by the course of events (by experiencing an unanticipated unconditional stimulus), a novel conditional stimulus presented after that surprise can gain effectiveness in eliciting a response that is similar to the unconditional stimulus that served as the surprise. This finding is, in fact, in keeping with a major theme to be developed in this book—namely, that the subject can learn of complex relations between things—as in a surprising situation.

The alert reader will anticipate that not all conditioning that involves discomfort and pain is necessarily purely respondent in nature. For example, if a mother first punishes her child for bad behavior, then warns that further punishment will follow future misbehavior, the child can learn what not to do only by understanding the words that are heard after the unconditional stimulus is endured. No a priori neutral stimulus can serve as a conditional. Notwithstanding, if the child can understand and remember to refrain from the behavior judged "bad" and punished by the mother, the association should help the child to inhibit that behavior and to avoid punishment. But a child who cannot understand the mother and discern what behaviors will be punished might become generally inhibited in behavior. In the extreme, the child could become a victim of learned helplessness (Seligman 1975; Garber and Seligman 1980).

But what is a conditional stimulus in this circumstance? As we have seen, there is no clear or neutral—let alone simple—stimulus that might come to serve as the conditional stimulus. Perhaps at best the child's thinking of a behavior comes to play the role of the conditional stimulus. The mother's verbal admonitions should precede, not follow, the punishment for them to become effective.

Learning Without Experience

Car accidents are expensive and threatening to life and limb. They present an interesting challenge from the perspective of conditioning and learning. Clearly, it is not practicable for drivers to learn of accidents by having a series of them and suffering the consequences. People must otherwise come to view them as costly and painful unconditional stimuli to be avoided. Some learning might be achieved from verbal and photographic reports of various accidents. Training in defensive driving helps the young driver acquire skills for avoiding accidents. So do a number of specific warning signals, such as taillights on the car ahead turning to red the moment the brake pedal is touched. But if the taillights of the car ahead were to come on only *after* its speed had been reduced, the ability of the driver of the following car to avoid an accident would be significantly diminished. Only the visual looming of the car stopping, possibly accompanied by the sound of skidding tires, might serve to announce the imminence of a potentially painful and dangerous consequence.

But a driver's effort to stop the car because the one in front is rapidly slowing is not an unconditional response to an unconditional stimulus. It is a learned response for avoiding accidents and pain; it is learned primarily through verbal instruction and occasional close calls. One might go a lifetime without ever having suffered the consequences of rear-ending the car ahead. Notwithstanding, verbally, photographically, and conceptually we can learn of the consequences of hitting another car.

A rear-end collision entails greater risk to passengers in the car in front because, among other reasons, there is apt to be no conditional stimulus of the impending event to afford them the opportunity to take protective measures. The car behind may not even be seen in the rearview mirror, the honking of its horn might be lost in the noise of traffic in general, and even the sound of its tires skidding on the pavement might not be heard. And if the screeching tires are heard and that results in the driver of the car about to be hit from behind braking harder, the collision may actually be made worse.

Such effective strategy for avoiding dangerous results (in this case, the unconditional stimulus of the auto accident) is not as readily available in many situations. An intertwining of operant conditioning with respondent conditioning and verbal instruction characterizes this example—something not uncommon to us as we explore and live through the events of each day. We hope that this example will serve to remind the reader that the simplicities of laboratory studies of conditioning rarely match the surroundings of daily life. Because life outside the laboratory is complex, we try to automate measures to ensure safety whenever possible. Airbags serve to attenuate the risks of some (inevitable) car accidents; safety mechanisms are in place to control fusion in atomic power plants and submarines, where the complexity of the context precludes sufficiently quick action and problem solving by even the best of engineers.

Yet the very complexity and intertwining of types of conditioning bring us, from time to time, to encounters in which new behavior must be ventured. Intelligence must play a role and advise us to avoid imminent events that promise nothing pleasant but rather only pain and high cost. We become alert to intelligent assessments of the world about us and learn that old ways of responding do not always bring pleasures and benefits.

Creativity

Hammond (2000) asked how it was that pilots, for example, handled highly complex and rapidly changing crises in flight for which no specific training afforded them a clear course of decision and action. In those situations, intuition was frequently the only source for determining action. One such flight occurred on July 19, 1989, when a DC-10 passenger plane lost all conventional control. Notwithstanding, by intuitive and novel use of the engines' throttles, the pilots guided the plane to an airport and landed it with most passengers surviving. In this and other crises, pilots' collective experiences and knowledge frequently served to generate for them courses of action that were uniquely designed to save the event from disaster. It is fair to say that the pilots generated those courses of action without detailed analysis and without prior training that was directly relevant to the plight of the moment. We do it in our daily lives. Do nonhuman beings do thus as well? Perhaps.

Somehow, organisms must be innovative and venture new behaviors in the interests of efficiency, procurement of benefits and resources, and avoidance of costly consequences. In short, we must be creative. But how can we become creative if, indeed, we are enslaved by specific respondent and operant conditioning of the past? If learning cannot be explained by contiguity alone, repetition alone, reinforcement alone—then what? We now face the question, "What are the sources of creative and inventive behaviors in animals?"

II

A Journey Toward
Rational Behaviorism

6

First Lessons from Primates

With our framework of learning and intelligence now in place, let us recount the kinds of data that have led us to posit rationality in animals' behaviors.

My (Rumbaugh) first academic appointment, to San Diego State University in 1954, is worthy of note here because of the university's proximity to the San Diego Zoo. It was there that I was first overwhelmed by the appearance and behavior of the monkeys and apes that, collectively, form the order Primates. As I watched them, I couldn't help but be impressed with the variation that their numerous species characteristics presented. Some were huge, even by the standard of the largest humans I have known. Others were diminutive, with weight measured in ounces, not pounds. Some appeared to be clever, while others gave every reason to believe that academic affairs were of no interest to them whatsoever! Some were clearly committed to walking on all fours, while others, from time to time, walked erect—as though to emulate those who came to observe them in their exhibits.

In 1958 I set about a variety of research tasks involving the primates so that I might understand them better. I searched for their differences, attributes that might make them truly distinctive and apart from our kind. In the final analysis, however, it was their similarities to our own kind that proved most interesting and served to suggest that neither you nor I are really creatures apart from those other magnificent forms that make up the order in which we share membership, Primates.

Primate species exhibit great differences in appearance and behavior. Within each species, however, there are common features, both physical and behavioral, that are characteristic of all of its members. No one can confuse the appearance or behavior of gorillas with those of orangutans. And chimpanzees always present a similar profile in appearance and behavior. How do gorillas come to behave as gorillas—and how do we *not* come to behave as any of the great apes? With the collaboration of long-term colleagues, a film was released in 1970 that portrayed the taxonomic and behavioral characteristics of the San Diego Zoo's primates (Rumbaugh, Riesen, and Lee 1970) to help teachers and students appreciate the special significance of the order Primates.

Primate species differ markedly in brain complexity. Generally, the larger the primate form, the more complex its brain. Why should that be? What does a large and complex brain do for a primate? Did elaboration of the brain provide for the emergence of skills that we had held to be uniquely human? Might we find that it afforded enhanced learning ability, primitive thought, the rudiments of language and numeric skills?

Despite its vociferous nature, the chimpanzee can, at times, be a paragon of sensitivity and insight. It also can tell us many things about being animal *and* about being human. We share 98.4 percent of our DNA with chimpanzees—an uncommonly high percentage compared with other primate forms. True enough, "percentage of DNA in common" does not tell all of the role played by genetics. The mechanisms that control gene action and expression are critically important as well. Notwithstanding, the percentage of shared DNA is a clue that we should pay heed to our close relative. The relationship makes us sibling species—like the zebra and the horse, for example. And we must remember that evolution produces diversity, not just linear structures and functions. Thus even between such closely related forms as apes and humans, differences in function and role can be expected even though underlying structures and operations might appear essentially identical.

Human Animals, Nonhuman Animals

There is an unfortunate myth in the world today that the behavior of animals is irrelevant to understanding the behavior of humans. This myth is predicated on the mistaken assumption that animals are animals and that humans are *not* animals. Nothing about the body of a human in its basic form or function declares it to be other than animal. Yes, the articulation of the skeleton and, in particular, the articulation of vertebrae of the spine and of the femur to the pelvis are different from those of the chimpanzee, for example. But those are adaptations that serve to enable human posture and erect walking. And they are perhaps no more radical than are differences in the hand that enable knuckle walking in chimpanzees but not in orangutans, who support their weight on fists, not knuckles. Similarly, those arrangements are no more radical than are differences in the dentition of the great apes compared with humans or in the articulation of the bones of the human's hand that enables a superior precision grip. Differences allow us and not chimpanzees to type and to play the violin, and so on; but such skills are only reflections of modifications in the physical anatomy and neuroanatomy of the human hand.

Neither our speech nor upright posture nor social behaviors nor mating patterns nor modes of infant care nor any other attributes of the behavioral domain rest upon distinctively new and different anatomic structures. Every one of our human behaviors is enabled by physical, physiological, and neuroanatomical structures and functions whose origins are clearly recorded in bodies of primates.

The specific elaborations of structures shared with other primates and the profound amplification of some of their functions have enabled us to behave in ways that seem different from the behavior of other animals. Our speech and our advanced potential for discovery, complex learning, and invention give the appearance of human uniqueness; but every one of those attributes has been documented at least at trace levels in the apes. Among the primates there has been an array of quantum leaps from seemingly (though not really) nothing to something—from no language to some language, for example—that has enabled us to develop complex and varied cultures, to write books, to establish institutions we believe to be of lasting value.

What's on Their Minds?

If our bodies do not radically differentiate our species from those of other animals, perhaps it is a psyche or mind that sets us apart. Perhaps. However, such entities as minds are posited, so far as we know, only by human thought. As such, they are constructs which might or might not apply to other life forms. Perhaps psyche or mind exist only through experiencing life as a human. Then again, the mind might be as real to apes as they are (or are not) to individual humans. Constructs or not, psyche and mind are very real to most humans. Are they real to other animals as well?

It can be argued that we have no way of proving that a chimpanzee, for instance, has trace experiences of the same kind that have inspired us to form such concepts as psyche or mind. But in fact, none of us can be sure that we share much, if anything, with one another in our individual private experiences. That we can talk about our private experiences and feelings means, perhaps, only that and nothing more. It is a sheer act of faith as we talk among ourselves that what we say invokes comparable private feelings and experiences. It can be argued, as noted earlier, that we humans anthropomorphize with one another and about our own kind all the time! We make large assumptions about common language and experience as we talk with one another. But are we really sharing common experiences? When someone says, "I understand," do we really know without question that the speaker does understand what the other person is saying? How do we really know that a person who claims to feel a certain way about something is really speaking the truth? We don't. We can only make assumptions, modified by experience of past dealings with others. Of course, failing to make these assumptions would mean never communicating. Essentially the same dilemma holds with animals. Although they don't speak as do we, their behavior does speak in its own ways—and sometimes it does so quite lucidly.

This said, we remain obliged to search for improved methods and techniques of validating what we believe we have in common with other humans. To do so with animals, and notably the great apes, seems like the same kind of challenge. Nor should we be deterred by the admonitions by others in the past. We must press ahead if progress is to be attained in understanding us in relation to the apes and other primates.

Not to listen to apes risks that we will fail to learn about ourselves in comparative perspective. Recall Dr. Charles Menzel's discovery of the cleverness of Panzee through an innovative method, discussed earlier. Dr. Menzel and Dr. Williams, through their innovative methods, "heard Panzee talk." That is always the beginning point. Unfortunately, we cannot always follow up on what we hear, as Dr. Menzel has done so adroitly. At times, we can only recount what is "heard." We shall do that now, again using the young Panzee as the ape subject (Brakke and Savage-Rumbaugh 1996).

How to Listen to a Chimpanzee "Talk"

Ah! But wait, one might say. Just how does one listen to a chimpanzee? The answer is simple. For now assume that not all communication is through speech and hearing. True enough, our species has a marvelous, highly specialized and refined system for speech and for hearing spoken sounds. But we also "hear" (perceive) a great deal with our eyes and other senses. The behaviors of others tell us much about their goals and agendas. Indeed, the best, the most exciting parts of the language of love are exchanged in the sounds of silence. Talk has its place in building the setting for the relation for love; but it is silence and nonspoken signs that carry the most persuasive messages of love and adoration. How many times has a gentle "shhsh-. . . . shhsh" been communicated between lovers? Talk can short-circuit important communications and can undermine the relationship at such times. Silence and "the openness of being" can produce and enable rushes of communication at baud rates that exhaust the body's capacity to process. How informing.

That is not to suggest that to hear a chimpanzee or other ape "talk" we must love it in a sensual way. It is to point out, however, that chimpanzee behavior is always announcing its agenda. That agenda becomes clearer and clearer as we meld our own existence with that of the chimpanzee. If we blend experiences obtained from interactions with chimpanzees and empirical data obtained by scientific methods, we become able to "listen to a chimpanzee" even though it doesn't speak. We will illustrate by recounting an experience with Panzee and then review a substantial body of empirical data that corroborate why Panzee behaved as she did. We admit that the event to be recounted is a favorite; we also recognize that no single account can suffice any more than the credentials of person can be accurately assessed in a single document.

I (Rumbaugh) love jeeps—old jeeps. One of my older jeeps, at the time only recently purchased, had a beautiful black padded cushion across the top of the dash. The flawless cushion was one of the reasons I decided to buy the jeep. With Dr. Sue Savage-Rumbaugh of the Language Research Center and with two young (about two and one-half years old) apes in the jeep, I was employing its four-wheel drive on the rough trails of the forest that surrounds our laboratory. We stopped and walked about for a bit, then returned to the jeep to continue onward. Sue and a bonobo entered from the passenger's door. The chimpanzee Panzee entered through the driver's door—my door.

As I prepared to start the engine, I noted the distinctive pattern of fresh chimpanzee teeth embossed in what had been the flawless, beautiful black padded cushion atop the dash. With dismay, even disgust, I complained, "How did these get here?" The reply from Sue was, "Panzee did it as she came across your seat. You have to watch her!" My penetrating eyes then focused upon Panzee's as I pointed to the teeth marks and asked her in earnest, "Panzee! Did you do this? I'm really disappointed in you." I really didn't expect to be "heard," and I certainly didn't expect a response. Yet very gently but firmly, she then took my right hand, opened and held it, palm up, in her left hand. She then brought her closed right hand across her body, opened it, and gently pressed something—which I did not know that she had—into my hand. She never broke her focused attention to my eyes as she did so. Next, she firmly closed my fingers about the item and pressed my closed hand to my chest. She then looked through the windshield at the trees beyond as though she was ready to go on. Only then did I open my hand and find the item she pressed into my hand, a single flower.

What did she say? I know only what I "heard" nonverbally from her behaviors. The social impact upon me was that I wasn't angry any more. I was impressed, very impressed with what I had heard. What Panzee said was *not* anything that she had been taught, and it certainly

Figure 3. The chimpanzee *(Pan troglodytes)* Panzee at age fifteen years main photo and three years (inset). Photos by Beran and Rumbaugh.

was nothing that she had been rewarded for doing or had seen modeled by others. Her behavior was an invention of the moment—her invention. No words could have been more eloquent, more appropriate to the occasion.

I cannot say with any degree of precision why Panzee did what she did, and I do not offer the experience with her as scientific proof—or even as nonscientific proof—of anything. Anecdotes from interactions with chimpanzees are not scientific evidence, but they may provide insights into the types of questions—and maybe some ways of answering the questions in a scientific way. Rather, I offer it for what it is—a message by a chimpanzee. Although no experiment in the laboratory could be expected to yield such rich behavior, there is a host of studies that have yielded findings in total support of the argument that, yes, a chimpanzee—and perhaps particularly a young chim-

panzee—can "say" such remarkable things. Every parent observes similar communication from prespeech children. The methods of science
are well designed to "set us apart" from receiving many important
communications from animals. We need ways to bridge the chasm.
Technology of the future might help us to do so.

7

Primate Research at the San Diego Zoo

In earlier years, the San Diego Zoo boasted two mountain gorillas *(Gorilla gorilla beringei)* in its collection. After those two magnificent animals died, their popularity probably inspired the zoo to continue to feature gorillas in its collection. With the demise of the two mountain gorillas, the collection was redirected to the lowland species *(Gorilla gorilla gorilla)*. The zoo also had a fine group of orangutans *(Pongo pygmaeus)* and was among the first to have both species of chimpanzee— the so-called common chimpanzee *(Pan troglodytes)* and the so-called pygmy chimpanzee *(Pan paniscus)*. Both common names are somewhat deceptive: the common chimpanzee is no longer common to the forests of Africa, where its populations not long ago were in the untold hundreds of thousands. No longer! Because of the continuing and threatening reduction of its populations in the field, it seems insensitive to continue to call this ape common. The pygmy chimpanzee, for its part, is not, as was thought in the early twentieth century, a pygmoid version of *Pan troglodytes*. It is now recognized as a species of *Pan* in its own right, and its increasingly preferred name is bonobo.

The great and lesser apes (gibbons and siamangs are called lesser apes because of their relatively diminutive sizes) of the San Diego Zoo were the first I (Rumbaugh) studied to try to achieve a better perspective about what large and complex brains contribute to behavior and to learning and problem-solving skills. The gorillas Albert, Bouba, and Bata had been brought in as infants and reared together. Although they were a beautiful trio, the fact that they had been reared together resulted in great reluctance, at least on the part of the male, to copulate. Consequently, the zoo brought in other infant gorillas from Brazzaville, Congo, for the Children's Zoo. Albert did breed with one female gorilla, Vila, thus acquired; the result was the seventh captive-birth of a lowland gorilla.

In 1958 Dr. Charles Shaw, then assistant director of the zoo, asked whether I (Rumbaugh) would be interested in having a test station built, in which I could work with apes who were getting too large to be retained in the Children's Zoo but who were not yet large enough to be introduced to the adult exhibit areas. I had to deliver plans for a modest facility to him by the following morning, so I had my work cut out for the rest of the day. (The facility was to be built adjoining a cage previously occupied by a monkey-eating eagle. Somehow, it seemed appropriate that we took occupancy as it went elsewhere!)

The facility (6 feet × 12 feet) was designed to accommodate apparatus appropriate for discrimination-learning experiments. It was an adaptation of the widely modified Wisconsin General Testing Apparatus, described by Harlow (1949) in reports of his learning-set experiments with monkeys. The apparatus (see figure 4) was quite simple, though it included several new design features necessary for my research. It consisted of a stimulus tray with three pairs of rails within which Plexiglas bins could be placed. The transparent bins were an innovation that would allow the primates to see the various problem objects yet keep them from taking the objects into their cage—which would have been a major distraction to all interests. The bins had small doors that could be raised to allow the placement of stimulus objects— which in pairs and triads constituted discrimination-learning problems. Two vertically mounted doors allowed for preparation of each trial out of the animal's view and placement of a food item beneath the stimulus defined as "correct" for a given problem. These doors, counterbalanced on pulley systems, kept the animal from viewing the experimenter at all times during the preparations of trials for experiments and the presentations of them.

Figure 4. The San Diego Zoo (1959) version of the Wisconsin General Testing Apparatus used for studies of complex-learning skills. Here a gibbon *(Hylobates lar)* has displaced a Plexiglas bin so as to bare a food well, which will hold a reward if the choice is a correct one. Photo by Ron Garrison, Zoological Society of San Diego.

Simple Discrimination Learning and Learning-Set Training

A variety of tasks was presented. With the intention of teaching the animals that they were to attend to the objects within the bins, the first problem required that the subject choose the correct (food-associated or -reinforced) object on 20 of 25 consecutive trials regardless of how long it took. The problem was simply a red circle paired with a red square. It proved not to be a simple problem for the apes to learn. Trials required to reach the criterion ranged from 54 to 704! When the apes did learn, they learned rapidly, generally increasing choice accuracy from slightly better than chance despite dozens of trials to 80 percent or better within the next 25 trials. All of them did eventually learn, and on the assumption that each ape had learned that it was to attend to the stimuli presented within the bins, rather than to the bins themselves, a series of learning-set problems was given to them.

In learning-set training, each problem is presented for a small number of trials—too few for the subject to learn. Each problem consists of a pair of objects which differ from one another in a variety of dimensions—such as size, color, form, and brightness. One of the objects is designated by random as the correct one: if it is selected and displaced, the subject finds a morsel of highly preferred food in an underlying well. Regardless of the animal's level of performance by the end of six trials, the problem is terminated. The objects are never used again except by other animals for each problem in turn.

The trial-2 learning-set data collected at the San Diego Zoo, shown in figure 5, reveal that as a positive function of brain complexity and level of maturation, primates literally learn how to learn such problems (Rumbaugh 1968, 1970; Rumbaugh and McCormack 1967). As a level of intelligence and maturation, young children also learn how to learn problems of this type. Thus the test has an element of validity as a test of "intelligence" with various species of primates. Figure 5 reveals that macaque monkeys do very well. Their accelerated performance with age is in accordance with their relatively rapid growth and maturation. Whereas a macaque monkey is an adult by six years of age, the great apes take twice that long. In general, the improvement of the great apes with age is protracted compared with macaques. An exception to this generalization is with the orangutan subjects, which, with age even to maturity, do more and more poorly. We shall later investigate the hypothesis that the orangutan's intellectual development might be uniquely compromised if it is not in an interesting and challenging environment.

The many species of the Primate order differ in many ways. The

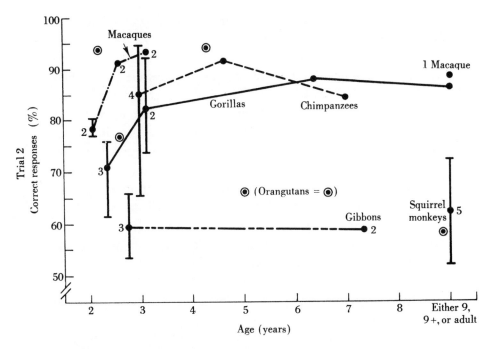

Figure 5. Percentage responses correct by age for chimpanzees, gorillas, orang-utans, gibbons, and macaque monkeys. The data were obtained on fifty test problems where each problem was presented only for two trials: one trial to learn and one trial to test for that learning. This testing occurred after each primate had worked on 500 learning-set problems where each problem was presented for six trials. The macaque monkeys mature more rapidly than do apes and have well-developed learning sets even by the age of three years. (Data on one adult macaque is at the upper right of the figure.) Gorilla and chimpanzee subjects improved with age; however, orangutans did not. The poor performance of gibbons and squirrel monkeys is attributed to the procedure of encasing the objects in Plexiglas bins (Rumbaugh 1968). Copyright © Academic Press.

elaboration of the brain's cortex increases disproportionately as we move from the most primitive primate forms, the prosimians, to monkeys and the great apes. The gibbons and siamangs, taxonomically sandwiched between the monkeys and apes, have elaborations of the cortex appropriate to their taxonomic status. But there is an interesting story to tell about them, one that is not in keeping with the generalization that there is a positive relation between elaboration of the cortex and the ability to learn how to learn—that is, how to benefit in a generalized way as a function of limited experiences in trying to solve each of a series of problems of a given type.

Gibbons and siamangs did uniformly poorly in the learning set (see fig. 5). Although macaque monkeys and the great apes learned how to learn, none of the gibbons and siamangs did. That finding was a real surprise. When on the ground, both gibbons and siamangs walk erect and do so with considerable competence and grace. Back in the late 1950s, when I (Rumbaugh) saw them walk in that manner, I thought that they must be exceedingly intelligent to do so. But they weren't, at least as measured by learning-set training and testing procedures. Why? Probably because of their highly developed talents as ricochetal brachiators in trees. Both gibbons and siamangs are able to swing from branch to branch with such speed and force that they become airborne. To calculate all that is necessary to keep from falling from the trees surely entails priority use of large portions of the brain. (Even so, they do fall from time to time. Healed bones are very commonly found in the cadavers of feral gibbons and siamangs.)

A clue emerged one day as to why the lesser apes were poor learners at least in the test situation that had been designed for the experiments. A gibbon repeatedly touched the front of one of the Plexiglas bins as though to feel the slight abrasions on its surface. This observation led to a study in which irrelevant visual cues were introduced into the test situation. This was done by placing a piece of half-inch wire mesh into each bin so as to be visible either in front of or behind the objects to be discriminated (fig. 6). The irrelevant cues, if in the foreground, disrupted performance of even those great apes and monkeys that had highly developed learning sets. But if they were in the background (behind the objects to be discriminated), there was no disruption in performance. We also found that various species overcame or learned to disregard the irrelevant foreground cues as a function of how arboreal (tree-dwelling) the species is in the field. The more arboreal a species, the more disrupted its performance was by the introduction of irrelevant foreground cues. They also had greater difficulty in learning to ignore such cues. It was as though they had visual attention mechanisms which brought their attention to things most proximal or close to the eyes. In the forest, such things might constitute threats to eyes, hence things to note and to avoid.

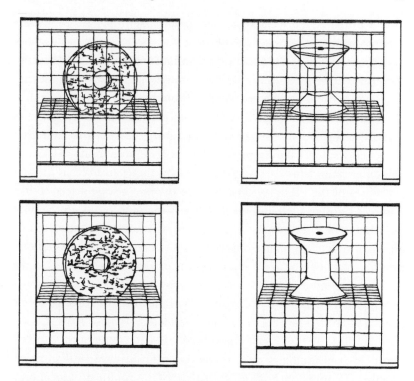

Figure 6. The Plexiglas bins as modified so as to exaggerate irrelevant foreground or background cues (upper and lower, respectively). The more arboreal the primate form, the greater the cost to members' abilities to learn when irrelevant foreground cues (one-half-inch mesh wire) were present. Irrelevant background cues had no effect (after Rumbaugh and McCormack 1967). Copyright © Karger/Basel.

One gibbon was selected to confront many problems in which irrelevant foreground cues were in place. A criterion for success was established for each problem. With the cues absent and with bins configured as in prior learning-set training, the gibbon did very well—92 percent on trial two of a block of discrimination problems. Thus it was apparent that the test situation was not as "fair" to all species as I hoped that it would be. Having each subject learn the initial red circle vs. red square did not establish reliably for all species that the objects within the Plexiglas bins were the targets to which they should attend. A better method of measurement—one that would not be sensitive to the kind of ecological niche occupied by each species—would have to be developed.

Comparative psychologists had long recognized the probability that results might be biased by differences in species' motivations, perception, strength, and preferences for various foods that served as reinforcers for correct choices in tasks. Although the data from the learning-set experiments were not totally uninterpretable, it was clear that the test situation had been grossly unfair, particularly for the gibbons and siamangs. Because of their strong natural tendency to attend to things closest to their eyes, these apes surely had been trying to learn of the differences defined by slight differences they perceived in the appearances of the Plexiglas bins. Because the bins always stayed to the subject's right and left and because it was the objects within the bins that had to be discriminated regardless of whether they were placed in the right or left bin on a given trial, it was impossible for the gibbons and siamangs to be correct and to get the prized food more frequently than 50 percent of the trials if they were trying to discriminate or solve the problem on the basis of appearances of the fronts of the bins. Being rewarded only 50 percent of the time over a long span of trials (3,000) can significantly discourage the subsequent development of learning set in squirrel monkeys; they become significantly worse than naive monkeys (Rumbaugh et al. 1965). In light of this finding we can appreciate how the gibbons' learning sets were suppressed by the Plexiglas bins in which the objects to be discriminated were placed.

Although the animals were not food deprived and really didn't need the food obtained from the test situation, they nonetheless seemingly enjoyed the test situation and getting the special kinds of food for being "correct." (The foods that were used varied by each subject's preference—cherries, ice-chilled lettuce, raisins, apple slices, and so on.)

Discrimination Reversal Tests

A study with five lowland gorillas (*Gorilla g. gorilla;* Rumbaugh and Steinmetz 1971) provided important data for the development of a more equitable method of measurement of primates' complex learning skills. The discrimination-reversal experiment entailed a long series of two-choice discrimination problems, each problem consisting of a pair of randomly selected objects that were new to the subject. One of the objects was randomly selected as the one to be "correct" (its selection resulting in food) for the first several trials—seven or thirteen. Then, without any signal or warning, that object would become incorrect, and after ten trials the problem was terminated and a new one initiated. Thus the subject had to learn to reverse its selection of objects in midstream, at an unpredictable point. The ability to be flexible, to learn rules, and to transfer what has been learned from one problem to the next were taken as indexes of ability on the part of the subject for complex cognitive operations.

On average a primate got nine trials to learn and then nine trials to reverse its choice before beginning a new test with different choices. A striking finding was that apes' performances on the training trials predicted very accurately their performance on reversal-test trials (fig. 7). Regardless of whether the percentages of choices correct on the acquisition trials were achieved with seven or thirteen trials per problem, a high positive correlation exists between those percentages and those attained in the reversal-test trials. But because this similarity did not hold for all other species, a new testing technique was suggested.

Several of the great apes, and in particular those who had excelled in learning-set training, did as well if not better on the reversal trials than they had been doing on the prereversal trials! By contrast, squirrel monkeys—a diminutive South American monkey with a relatively large brain but a rather smooth cortex—characteristically did worse on the reversal trials than they had been doing on the initial trials of each problem.

Thus the discrimination-reversal type of problem can be viewed as a transfer-of-training task. In that task, the subject had an opportunity to learn about the values of the two objects on the initial trials of each problem. Then, with the reversal of cue values, it had an opportunity to transfer that learning to a similar, yet different situation—one in which the test objects were present but in which the subject had to be flexible and alter its choice if it was to get any more food for the duration of that problem.

Qualitative Shifts from Quantitative Increments

From this perspective, many of the great apes, particularly those that had done well on learning-set training, were positive transferers; by

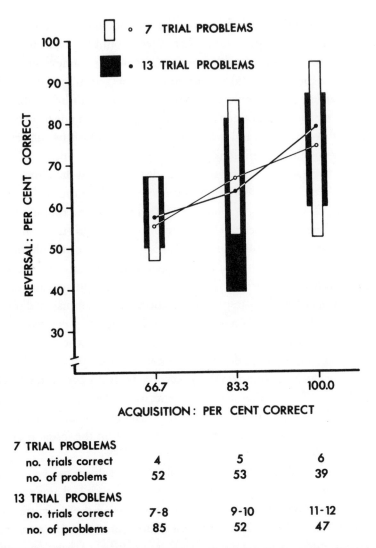

Figure 7. For five young gorillas *(Gorilla gorilla gorilla),* their transfer of training percentages correct (for example, reversal percentages of choices correct) was highly correlated with how much they had learned during acquisition (baseline) training—regardless of whether they had seven or thirteen trials per problem (Rumbaugh and Steinmetz 1971). Copyright © Karger/Basel.

contrast, monkeys characteristically were negative transferers. This finding was of high interest because evolution of brain complexity is seen as a continuum—from small to large and from relatively simple to increasingly complex. Transfer of training also is seen as a continuum, ranging from very negative to very positive. (Transfer of training refers to whether learning a given task helps or interferes with the learning of another task. Negative transfer is dangerous in driving cars, flying planes, and so on, where foot pedals and shifting mechanisms vary. By contrast, when changes are minor and adhere in shared principles, positive transfer dominates and facilitates the safe operation of each of a variety of cars, planes, and so on.) A shift from negative to positive transfer is a qualitative change. In its relation with brain complexity, we have perhaps one of the stronger observations in support of the position that quantitative changes (in this case, brain size) can result in qualitative changes in performance (in this case, quality of transfer). This relation has been anticipated by a number of scientists; the one most influential to my thinking was Nissen (1951).

Data from vervet monkeys and ring-tailed lemurs illustrate the point. A successive discrimination-reversal task was designed in which after every fifty-one trials the cue values of the two lighted panels were exchanged. Performance from the last twenty trials of each set of fifty was calculated as the performance level that existed just prior to the exchanging of cue values for the lighted panels, and the twenty trials following the reversal (not counting the reversal trial itself) constituted reversal-test trials. The data are presented in summary form in figure 8. As the vervets did better and better just before the reversal of cues, their reversal test performance increased—evidence of positive transfer. By contrast, as the lemurs did better and better just before the reversal of cues, their reversal test performance decreased—evidence of negative transfer (Rumbaugh and Arnold 1971). The vervet brain is substantially larger than is the lemur brain. With the quantitative enhancement of brain came a qualitative difference in the transfer of learning. This was one of several sets of data that pointed the way to the development of a fairer test of primate complex learning and transfer abilities.

In still another analysis (Rumbaugh and Pournelle 1966), when squirrel monkeys were matched with macaques or apes with reference

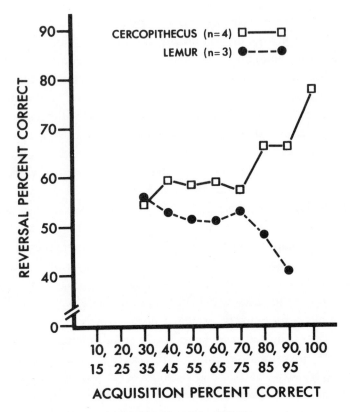

Proportion at each Acquisition Level:
LEMUR: 0.0 0.3 5.3 19.0 31.0 22.6 11.3 7.3 2.6 0.3
CERCOPITHECUS: 0.0 0.0 2.0 8.2 23.7 19.2 11.7 10.5 11.5 13.0

Figure 8. As vervets (*Cercopithecus aetheops,* an African monkey) and ring-tailed lemurs (*Lemur catta,* a prosimian) excelled on a discrimination learning task, their reversal test performance varied substantially and qualitatively. With increased learning (baseline) the vervets' test performance improved, but for the lemurs it dropped sharply. The amount learned in interaction with species determines reversal test performance and whether it is positive or negative (Rumbaugh and Arnold 1971). Copyright © Karger/Basel.

to percentage correct on the acquisition or training trials (84 and 85 percent correct, respectively), the squirrel monkeys did not equal the performance of the macaque and apes on the reversal test (76 and 86 percent, respectively). Conversely, it was determined that when squirrel monkeys were matched with apes or macaques for percentage correct on reversal test performance (76 and 77 percent, respectively), the squirrel monkey group had to have done substantially better on the acquisition or training trials than the apes or macaques (84 and 73 percent, respectively).

For the next several years I worked on the refinement of a procedure based on discrimination learning, one that would first take the subject to one of two levels of task mastery through the use of complex criterion-based training schedules. Schedules of training were worked out to take the subject to either the 67 percent correct level or to the 84 percent correct level, at which point the food-values of the test objects were reversed for the next eleven trials. The schedules of training yielded generally no or very low correlations between trials to reach criterion and subsequent transfer performance. Accordingly, latitude was allowed per individual and per species in trials to learn, though testing of transfer of learning was limited to a small and set number of trials. Ten or more problems were so given using the 67 percent criterion before similar testing continued at the 84 percent criterion. Only subjects that had extensive discrimination learning histories were used in the study.

The two training levels brought the subjects to the precise levels of mastery intended before reversal of cues for transfer-of-training assessment. On the first reversal trial, the one on which either the 67 percent or the 84 percent level of training was attained, the apes were correct at appropriate levels of "correctness" (about 30 and 15 percent, respectively). The training regimens were not just different operations; they brought the subjects to different levels of learning before the transfer-of-learning test trials. When the apes of the San Diego Zoo were tested and compared with monkeys, we found that the apes quite frequently improved in their transfer of training as the amount of training was increased from 67 percent to 84 percent responses correct, and that, by contrast, the monkeys generally did worse. For the apes, increased "knowledge" (being trained to 84 percent rather than only to 67 percent correct) served to further enhance transfer of training efficiency.

Species differed in their transfer-of-learning skills. Although rhesus monkeys did remarkably well, the others did not. Other than rhesus, monkeys notably did not transfer an increased amount of learning with the same efficiency or effectiveness as did the apes. Talapoin monkeys, the smallest of the Old World monkeys, provide a striking example. They are very poor at transferring learning to an advantage and also have relatively limited learning and memory capabilities (Rumbaugh 1973). Monkeys did not transfer the learning with the same efficiency or effectiveness as did the apes. For the monkeys (talapoins, in particular), increased "knowledge" led to a disproportionate decrease in their transfer-of-training skills.

Figure 9 presents transfer index data for an array of primate groups, representing more than 120 primates. The overall correlation between efficiency of transfer and brain size and complexity is r=0.79 and is highly significant. The transfer index is the best single predictor of individual rhesus monkeys' learning proficiency on a host of other tasks (Washburn and Rumbaugh 1991a). Accordingly, it may be viewed as an approximation of an intelligence index for primates.

Transfer index values for the gibbons were relatively uninfluenced by an increase in the criterion for learning before the reversal of cues. In this and in every other test in which gibbons served as subjects, they confounded expectations. They never performed as apes and they never performed as monkeys. They were a group unto themselves!

The group of squirrel monkeys did remarkably well, but any excitement regarding their excellence is tempered by the fact that they were the very best learners out of a colony of more than sixty such monkeys. I was hopeful that some species constant would restrain their excellence in this new test procedure, but that hope was not supported by the data. A random selection of monkeys from the colony would, in all probability, have provided a much less impressive performance for them.

And Then, Qualitative Differences in Learning

Another test procedure was designed to explore more definitively whether the nature of the learning process changed as brain complexity increased. Was the learning process one that tended to shift with brain evolution from rather simple habit formation to one that provided for the learning of rules and of relations between stimuli? If so, such a shift would help account for the marked differences in the learning and transfer skills of apes and monkeys.

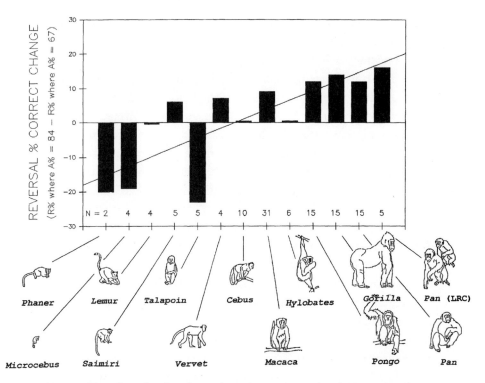

Figure 9. Transfer index data for twelve primate genera (total $N = 121$) and one group of language-competent apes. The ordering of the species from left to right is in general accordance with the size and assessed complexity of their brains. The vertical axis defines percentage change on test trials as a result of increasing the primates' pretest achievement level on each of a long series of problems from 67 percent to 84 percent correct. The increased learning enhanced subsequent test performance for the great apes but compromised it for the small-brained, small-bodied primates (with extra neurons $r = 0.79$; with brain weight $r = 0.84$; with body weight $r = 0.88$; and with brain volume $r = 0.82$; Rumbaugh 1995; *Phaner* and *Microcebus* data were provided by W. Cooper and E. Visalberghi, respectively). Copyright © New School for Social Research.

A series of studies with several groups of prosimians (primitive, small-brained primates), monkeys, gibbons, great apes, and children produced a rather orderly set of findings in support of that shift. The data were obtained by giving each highly experienced primate subject training until it reached a criterion of nine out of ten trials correct, a level higher than that used during prior transfer index testing. This higher criterion was necessary because of the overall excellence in learning abilities of the subjects.

The transfer index reversal test can be described in shorthand by using a distinct letter for each available choice and plus and minus signs to indicate the correct and incorrect choices, respectively. Thus in the basic reversal trial, $A+ B-$ becomes $A- B+$. That reversal test condition pattern was carried forward as one test condition in this experiment. The subjects' transfer of learning performances was compared with two other test conditions that entailed the substitution of test objects. In another condition, the stimulus that had been initially incorrect but had just become the "correct" one on the first reversal test trial was replaced on the second test trial by a new unfamiliar stimulus: $A+ B-$ during training became $A- B+$ on the first test trial, but then a new object, C, was substituted so that the condition became $A- C+$ on the second and following reversal test trials. The remaining condition entailed substitution for the stimulus that during criterion-based training had been correct: $A+ B-$ during training became $A- B+$ on the first reversal test trial, then C was substituted so that the condition for the remaining test trials became $B+ C-$.

The logic for the substitution held that if the pretest criterion had been achieved through basic stimulus-response habit learning, then transfer of learning should be most difficult in the condition that paralleled the transfer index test condition. In this condition, the subject would have to extinguish its habit of selecting the initially correct stimulus, which had just become the incorrect one on the first test trial. It also would have to overcome the acquired tendency not to select the initially incorrect choice because that choice had never been positively reinforced. Both of these processes take time and trials and thereby would have impeded test performance.

By contrast, quite different dynamics were introduced for subjects as they encountered the two other test conditions, both of which entailed replacement of stimuli. If on the second test trial the initially incorrect stimulus, B, was replaced with a new correct stimulus, C, the subjects would not have had to overcome their reluctance to select B. Their preference of stimulus A would have had to be weakened, however, for choice of it had been reinforced during training trials. But choice of the new stimulus $C+$ would be uncompromised, in that it

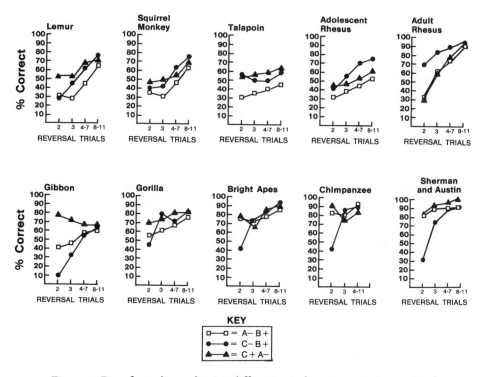

Figure 10. Data from the qualitative-differences-in-learning experiment reveal an increase in performance associated with enlargement of the primate brain and, more important, a gradual shift from associative to relational learning processes. The lemurs through the adult rhesus evidence associative learning. The group of gibbons are attracted initially to whichever stimulus is new on the test trials. The groups of apes find all three conditions of equal difficulty, hence are argued to have learned relationally about the training and test objects (Rumbaugh 1997). Copyright © Paul H. Brooks Publishing Co.

would have no history of not being rewarded with food if selected; choice of it was reinforced promptly. In the remaining condition, if A+ was discarded and replaced with C− after the first test trial, the subject would only have to overcome its reluctance to select B. This condition did away with the need to weaken or extinguish the habit of selecting A, which was no longer present. Figure 10 presents a summary of the three test conditions.

The critical data for analysis came from the relative performance levels within species on these three kinds of test trials. How correct they were otherwise is of secondary interest. All of these subjects had extensive histories of discrimination-learning research, and thus were viewed as primed to give their very best to the tasks involved.

Our frame of reference, which posits that large and complex brained primates should be likely to employ a comprehensive and relational mode of learning rather than one of stimulus-response habit formation, supports the prediction that they might find all three test conditions of equivalent difficulty. The basis for this prediction was that all necessary information was present in all three test conditions for the subject to select the stimulus-to-be-reinforced on all but the first reversal-of-cues test trial (A− B+), which was unannounced. Subjects could do well with the following strategy: if on test trials, stimulus A is present, don't choose it; if B is present, choose it (Rumbaugh and Pate 1984). By contrast, the smaller-brained primates were expected to benefit by way of accuracy of choice on either or both of the test conditions that entailed the deletion of one of the two original stimuli and substitution thereof with a new and unbiased stimulus, C.

The data were in strong support of these expectations. The performances of smaller-brained primates (in particular, small monkeys) supported the assumption that they were essentially stimulus-response habit learners. By contrast, the apes did equally well on all three tests conditions. Although of secondary interest, as species were ordered in terms of brain complexity, accuracy levels on test trials became higher—though not so high as to define a ceiling effect, which would have made them only speciously of equivalent difficulty. Two language-skilled chimpanzees, Sherman and Austin (Savage-Rumbaugh 1986), did best of all in terms of overall accuracy, a suggestion that language might help mediate the complexities of relational learning.

The rhesus macaques afford special information. Essock-Vitale (1978) found them to differ significantly from the associational mode of solving discrimination-reversal problems. Their pattern was more complex than the talapoin monkeys and lemurs but not as complex as that of the great apes. The best assessment offered here is that macaques are reluctant relational learners. They certainly are good at transferring what they have learned, but only with a great deal of experience do they become relational learners (Washburn and Rumbaugh 1992a).

So, a Large and Complex Brain Does What?

All of the studies conducted support the conclusion that a large brain with an elaborated cortex does, in fact, serve to enhance learning, to provide for complex learning processes, to enhance transfer of learning skills, and to provide for not just stimulus-response learning but also a mediational or rule-based learning process. Such changes, clearly defined in the data from experiments of primates—both human and nonhuman—place wands in the sands of time, wands that serve to approximate the course whereby we, as a species, have become the intellectual giants that we are.

But being so smart is not all good. One might argue that human intelligence has evolved far beyond reasonable bounds and is too destructive. Notwithstanding, we humans are here. We're going to have to work at it harder and more creatively to sustain the life-giving and -bearing processes of the planet.

8

Interesting Events
at the San Diego Zoo

Learning to manage the young apes in what had been the monkey-eating eagle's cage was quite a challenge. One story, selected from many, will make the point.

While a young orangutan, Roberta (age four), was being moved from her cage to the test one for her daily testing, there was one millisecond during which a sliding door to the outside remained closed but not locked. In that split second, that orangutan was transformed into a bolt of orange lightning. Contrary to the species' usual, slow-moving gait, this orangutan moved, and she moved fast! Out the door, over the fence, and over to a nearby television broadcasting tower! Then, up, up, and away, like a beautiful balloon, in the words of a then-popular song. She scaled that tower like it was a beanstalk going to the sun—but sadly for her, it wasn't.

Orangutans are at home in high trees. There was little fear that she would fall (though perhaps more in us than in her). But what about the antenna at the top of the tower? Was it hot? Might she be electrocuted? As she continued her climb, becoming a little orange sun, I (Rumbaugh) saw my newly established beachhead at the zoo being eclipsed. Regardless of injury to her, I had allowed an episode to occur that might have given me the gate: an escape of an ape. Visitors were everywhere enjoying the spectacle, but they could do nothing to help.

A keeper working with the nearby baboon and monkey cages heard our futile calls to the orangutan. He immediately grasped the problem, disappeared momentarily, and returned with a bottle of warm milk. He held it high and called, "Roberta, want some milk?" Perhaps even more quickly than she had scaled the tower, Roberta descended, jumped into the keeper's arms, and relished the milk as an orphan from a war-torn land might do. Although she was well fed in her new home, milk had been deleted from Roberta's diet. An opportunity to have it once again did the trick. I like to think that both the orangutan and my career were saved—by the bottle!

Albert Gorilla and an Encounter of the Worst Sort (i.e., He Won!)

When we started to test the adult great apes, ones never worked with before in our kind of research, we were understandably concerned about safety. Thus I designed and had built a test apparatus that would have done well on the beaches of Normandy or in Desert Storm. Behind a layer of steel, with bullet-proof glass-fronted bins in which to place our test objects, everything was in order, so it seemed.

What we had not anticipated was that the male gorilla, Albert, would take seeming umbrage at the device. He displayed his enmity time and time and time again, even several dozens of times within the course of each hour scheduled for work with him. His displays included high-pitched screams, chest beating, running, and slamming his doubled-up fists into the steel door designed to protect the device from exactly that kind of treatment. By the end of each session, my ears would be ringing and my adrenals exhausted. More than once I thought that he had loosened the bolts that secured the apparatus to the wall. Notwithstanding, I naively thought that across time he would come to enjoy pushing the bins and getting food for his academic efforts.

Not so. He was the poorest team player I've known. After several weeks of coddling him in every conceivable fashion, I gave him his first set of two objects between which to choose. On the first trial he was correct and took the food. All was going well. On the second trial he made

Figure 11. Albert, the young-adult lowland gorilla (age seventeen years; *Gorilla gorilla gorilla*) who smashed and sorely damaged the test apparatus (see fig. 12) when he had to shift his choice in accordance with the right-left placement of the stimulus object associated with food reward. Photo by Rumbaugh.

an error, for the correct object had moved to the bin on his left. On the third trial, again he made an error. Once again he chose the bin on his right. I tried to raise the steel door. He promptly broke out in perspiration, took one finger and slammed the door back down, whereupon he doubled his right fist and punched the bin on the right, the source of his frustration. I had locked the bin to protect it from such aggression, but

Figure 12. The test apparatus damaged by Albert *(Gorilla gorilla gorilla)* with a single blow from his right fist. The oil on his skin left the remarkable image of his fingers and fingernails on the glass. The apparatus consisted of two sheets of three-sixteenths-inch bulletproof glass framed in stainless steel. Photo by Ron Garrison, Zoological Society of San Diego.

when Albert's fist hit that bin, not only did the pin-lock break off, but the stainless steel bin itself broke free from its ball-bearing mounts. Welds were broken. Even more impressive, the double thickness of bullet-proof glass fronting the bin was shattered. Fortunately, Albert (see fig. 11) was unhurt. Figure 12 is an unretouched photo of the image that the oils on his hand left on the front of the glass. Careful inspection will reveal the outlines of his digits and fingernails, residues of oils on his skin.

I had been working with Albert daily for three months, but with that cup of tea, I thought I had better move on to other matters, all of which had to be accomplished within the next fifty years. Albert and I were getting nowhere.

I shut down the apparatus, went around to Albert, and said, as comfortingly as possible as only a beaten Ph.D. can say, "What's the problem, Albert?" Albert pursed his mouth, sat down, and slipped a fresh banana peel though the bars to me. I suggest that it was his way of saying, "It's nothing personal, but I just don't like this game!" I was touched by his gift, and gave him some food in return. Albert retired that day. It seems that the natural defensive role that should have been carried out in the jungles of Africa just couldn't let him compromise with the situation that my testing machine and I defined to him. Both it and I would have to go! And we did.

Albert never forgot me. Ten years later, he still could pick me out of a crowd of viewers. As soon as he saw me, his lips would puff, he would become tense, run back and forth, and then hide. He also would lace the air with that pungent odor peculiar to the male gorilla whenever he gets upset.

A Gorilla Baby Is Born at the Zoo

Albert, a reluctant breeder, did father one offspring while I was in San Diego. Separation from the females of his exhibit for several weeks seemed to teach him what life was all about. Nine months later, after he rejoined the females, a baby was born to Vila, and the baby was called Alvila. Hers was the seventh viable gorilla birth in captivity.

Vila was gentle and tender as a mother, but unfortunately she was not very competent. Still, she tried. With every whimper and scream from her baby, Vila would attend and do her best, but there were problems that would not go away; Alvila was weakening from lack of adequate care. The main problem was that initially Vila gave as much care to the placenta as to the infant and was satisfied to hold Alvila upside down as she attempted to comfort her. Finally Alvila was taken to Children's Zoo, grew up, and came to have babies of her own.

A View of the Zoo

Those were special, indeed exciting days of research at the San Diego Zoo. The apes were teaching us things that neither we nor others had known. The great apes clearly overlapped a great deal in their performances, so the belief of the time that the chimpanzee was the intellectual giant of the apes was probably not true. (That assumption may have arisen because of the relative availability of the great apes: the chimpanzee simply had been used in more studies than had the gorilla or the orangutan.)

The complex learning skills of the apes matured more slowly than those of the macaque monkey. The macaque monkeys did very well and sometimes surpassed the performances of the great apes. In accordance with the tendencies of arboreal primate species in nature, they tended to be distracted by irrelevant foreground cues. The more time they spent in trees, the more likely they were to be distracted by irrelevant cues in the foreground, but not in the background, that were presented along with the relevant cues of each problem.

Within limits, highly arboreal lesser apes, such as the gibbon, could learn to ignore irrelevant foreground cues. Once they had learned to do so, they approximated the great ape levels of achievement. Species have been selected differentially via evolution to perceive or filter out the cues of their environment. Quite possibly, highly arboreal primate species discern quite specifically the branches, twigs, and leaves, lest they jump to ones that cannot hold their weight or that threaten harm to eyes. The late J. M. Warren, of Pennsylvania State University at the time of his death, dubbed the specificity of cue perception an ecobehavior and wondered what structure of the brain provided for it. For the highly arboreal primates, it might be said that their visual bias for stimuli that are very proximal tended to keep them from seeing even the trees for the leaves and twigs. And a new and fairer test of complex learning was developed—one that I named the transfer index.

III

Studies of Ape Language
and Rational Behaviors

9

The LANA Project, 1971

The San Diego Zoo studies of apes and their abilities to learn how to learn, to transfer learning to an advantage, and to learn in terms of rules rather than a more constraining stimulus-response mode—all as a positive function of brain complexity—had made an important contribution. A large brain was the cost, biologically, of advanced cognition (Roitblat, Bever, and Terrace 1984). These laboratory studies revealed a positive relation between brain complexity and complex cognitive operations, findings that could not possibly have been obtained from research in the field given the limitations of present-day field methods. But the studies did not reveal *how* that advanced cognitive capacity was of adaptive value in the forests of Africa (home of the chimpanzee, gorilla, and bonobo; Savage-Rumbaugh et al. 1996) and of Borneo and Sumatra (home of the orangutan). That must be determined by field studies, not laboratory studies. Studies in the field would have to answer the questions—what was such advanced capacity used for, and why?

In the laboratory, the next logical step was to study ever more complex cognition in the apes and monkeys. Thus it was that the LANA Project (Rumbaugh 1977) found its way into the effort.

The director of the Yerkes Primate Center named all of the babies born to the colony. The name Lana may have been suggested by that of the beautiful actress of the mid-twentieth century Lana Turner. As moving as Lana Turner's beauty was, it paled next to the sterling achievement of Lana the chimpanzee—the first chimpanzee to prove the range of values of computer science as applied to an effort to teach her the basics of language. Even before we suspected just how well Lana would perform her daunting task, her name echoed the acronym for our effort—the Language ANAlogue Language Project. We would have been happy to achieve nothing more than an analogue of language from Lana's learning; thus we conservatively refrained from calling it language until much later (Rumbaugh 1977).

Lana Goes Hi-Tech

Although language research with apes has been approached from different perspectives and through the use of different methods of inquiry, a fundamental assumption of all of them appears to have been that language—whatever its requisites, processes, and functions might be—may not be a uniquely human attribute; certain rudiments of language may be discernible in life forms other than humans. It is only reasonable that in testing this assumption researchers have looked to the great apes as subjects for their research.

Although the LANA Project shared this assumption, it posed special questions: Is the cognitive capability of apes sufficiently advanced to permit them to interface in a meaningful, adaptive manner with state-of-the-art electronics? Could a chimpanzee learn a synthetic language and evidence sensitivity to the rules for word combination written for that language? On a gray, cold, rainy day in 1970, the basic plan for the LANA Project was conceived. Of course, the state-of-the-art technology of that day pales in comparison with that of the present—just as the most intriguing of today's technologies will seem primitive tomorrow. Science progresses on a carrier wave called technology, and innovations in apparatus establish milestones throughout the history of comparative psychology (Washburn and Rumbaugh 1992b).

We initiated the project with great enthusiasm, anticipating the several challenges of achieving a successful interface of great ape and computer. Would it prove a better way to study possible language skills of nonhuman primates? What significant insights might it contribute—about language, about apes, about humans? The main justification for studying language in a chimpanzee or any other ape is to learn something new about the nature and requisites of language. After all, because apes don't normally have language as we know and use it, if they learn any significant dimensions of language, then we may conclude that language does not rely on some mutation unique to humans.

As we have seen, the San Diego Zoo study had called into question the lore that the chimpanzee was the "smartest" of the apes—though that answer was not the reason for the effort. Chimpanzees, gorillas, and orangutans stood essentially equivalent in their complex learning abilities. We found no reason to declare a difference. Neither did we find any reason to conclude that there was a difference in learning ability between males and females.

So when the language project was undertaken, what species was selected? I decided to start with two apes, both captive-born residents of the Yerkes Regional Primate Research Center—one chimpanzee, Lana, and one orangutan, Biji. Both were about two years old, and we assumed that one would prove more promising even during the early days of the effort. Biji, true to the laid-back reputation of the orangutan, was more interested in seeing what happened than in making things happen. Lana, by contrast, was more active and, without question, gave the greater promise of the two apes. Yet the presence of Biji was obviously distracting to Lana. Biji was always clinging to Lana and otherwise distracting her as she attempted to interact with the computer-monitored keyboard that was devised for the project.

Historical Notes

Questions regarding apes' adeptness for language surely go back centuries. The word *orangutan* comes from the ape's description by natives of Borneo as a "man of the forest"; according to tribal lore, the orangutan will not talk, though it can, because if it did so it would have to go to work. The words for chimpanzee in some African languages were variations on "man of the bush." Such names suggest a recognition of ape's kinship with us—and possibly a facility for language. Early explorers wondered about the same possibility. In the eighteenth century, J. O. de la Mettrie (1748) speculated that although unable to speak, apes might master a gestural language, a possibility developed by Hewes (1977). Mettrie viewed language as the major division that set humans apart from beasts. He conjectured that if he were to try to cultivate that potential, he would assign to the chimpanzee the best teacher he could find. He also proffered that if one were to succeed in teaching language to an ape, the ape would become so gentle that it would no longer be "a wild man, nor a defective man, but he would be a perfect man, a little gentleman." Mettrie anticipated with some accuracy the abilities of young bonobos. As for Lana, no, she did not become a perfect gentleman—or even a perfect lady—but language certainly has had very positive and lifelong changes in her demeanor.

Chim and Viki

Early twentieth-century research into apes' language skills entailed efforts by Furness (1916) to teach an orangutan to talk, with no success. Furness reported, "I regret that I am forced to admit, after my several years' observation of the anthropoid apes, that I can produce no evidence that might disturb the tranquil sleep of the reverend gentleman" (Furness 1916, 290). Similarly, efforts by Yerkes (Yerkes and Learned 1925; Yerkes and Yerkes 1929) to teach Chim (a bonobo chimpanzee, though not yet identified as such) also failed. Yerkes had a hole put in the side of Chim's cage through which the researcher could pass a banana as he said, "ba, ba." It was intended that Chim would eventually make an association between the banana and that vocalization and would then try to say "ba, ba" as well. Chim did not do so, however, and after two weeks of twice-a-day training, both Yerkes and Chim are said to have lost interest. Notwithstanding, Yerkes's report included the speculation that if gestural communication rather than speech were used as the language medium, progress might be much greater. He also conjectured that chimpanzees would, indeed, have much to talk about if they could only master a language in which to express it.

Keith and Kathy Hayes worked intensively with the chimpanzee Viki in order to get her to talk. At best, she gave whispered approximations of "mama," "papa," "cup," and "up." She failed to use the "words" with high levels of reliability and gave little or no evidence that she understood what those four vocalizations referenced.

Notwithstanding, the Hayeses (Hayes 1951; Hayes and Hayes 1951, 1952; Hayes and Nissen 1971) lauded the cognition and intelligence of Viki. They recognized her and other apes as having all the requisites to thought characterized as "abstract, symbolic, conceptual, rational, insightful, and foresightful." They viewed the apes as culturally but not neurologically deficient. That view is apter today than it could have been at the time of the Hayeses' research. We now know that an ape exposed to advanced human culture while young and raised much as a human child becomes a symbolizing, creative, responsive, attentive, remarkably cooperative, highly imaginative, and accomplished being—probably not unlike some of the early precursors of humans.

Washoe and Nim

In the mid-1960s Alan and Beatrix Gardner (Gardner and Gardner 1969, 1971, 1998; Gardner, Gardner, and Canfort 1989) of the University of Nevada began a study based on Yerkes's suggestion that manual signing might be a more productive medium for studying language skills, if extant, in the chimpanzee. The Gardners' subject was Washoe, named after the county where the University of Nevada is located. Washoe was feral born and probably about one year old when she entered the Gardners' research program.

Washoe learned a large number of gestural signs of American Sign Language for the Deaf, or Ameslan. She learned best if her teachers manually molded her hand and fingers into the correct configuration and then move them through space (Fouts 1973). Early reports indicated that she appeared to extend use of her Ameslan signs rationally and to combine them into what might be called primitive phrases.

Project Washoe's contributions were profound and numerous. The project provided the initial evidence that a chimpanzee might acquire something similar to words of an active human language. Washoe left unanswered a number of questions that remain areas for research. Although she formulated many strings of signs, she gave no critical evidence of trying to produce sentences. The signs were all individually relevant to the context. Her competence in comprehending signs seemed never to equal her facility in producing them. Notwith-standing, Washoe was a trailblazer, as were those who worked with her in this historic effort to ascertain the efficacy of two-way communication between ape and human.

In a study methodologically close to the Gardners', Terrace trained a chimpanzee to use sign language and to communicate with a team of caregiver-researchers. Although Nim Chimsky learned to produce many signs, Terrace concluded that these were imitations rather than true linguistic symbols (Terrace et al. 1979; Rumbaugh and Savage-Rumbaugh 1994).

Sarah

Also in the mid-1960s, David and Ann Premack, then of the University of California, Santa Barbara, started work with a chimpanzee named Sarah (D. Premack 1970, 1971, 1976; A. Premack 1976; Premack and Premack 1983). David Premack and a colleague attempted initially to get Sarah to "speak" by using a joystick to activate and control the sound productions of a system. That approach was abandoned and re-placed by a system that employed plastic chips, of various colors, shapes, and sizes, on a magnetic board; each piece was intended to serve as the functional equivalent of a word.

Whereas the Gardners were interested in determining whether or not two-way communication might be established between chim-panzee and human, David Premack was interested, from a behavioral perspective, in the functional analysis of language. The Gardners assid-uously avoided saying that Washoe's signs were language, though they did argue for the size of her "vocabulary" and "grammar." Premack, from many perspectives, appeared to take the language capacity of the chimpanzee as a given, and so did the Gardners—a bold, even risky, assumption.

Premack's approach was to define the basic operations of lan-guage and then to define training procedures to teach them. He viewed language as a simple set of operations, and his techniques were more consonant with traditional laboratory procedures than were those of other investigators of that era. The chimpanzee Sarah was trained on a discrete-trial basis, with limited options for response and expression.

Only to the degree that those options were available for her to arrange on the metal board could she "speak." By contrast with Washoe's use of Ameslan, Sarah's access to a lexicon was a consistently limited set of options. Although Sarah's linguistic options might have been relatively limited, Premack contributed significantly to theoretical perspectives of the character and the basic behavioral and cognitive operations of language. In the final days of Premack's work with Sarah, he concluded that she did not have language—a conclusion stimulated by Terrace's conclusion that Nim's signing was primarily imitation of what he had seen others sign in recent minutes. Notwithstanding, Premack persisted in maintaining that Sarah's training had contributed uniquely to her ability to learn and to solve problems, a conclusion with which there is no reason to quarrel. Here we would conjecture that Sarah's symbolizing skills were honed during her intensive training and that those skills enhanced her generalized learning skills, as with Harlow's learning sets. Premack's most significant theoretical contribution may have been that of theory of mind: can an ape infer the knowledge state of another agent, human or chimpanzee? That question has had great heuristic value, and though the research has been controversial, it tends to support an affirmative answer.

In addition, long and systematic studies of dolphins by Herman, of an orangutan by Miles, of a gorilla by Patterson, of parrots by Pepperberg, and of sea lions by Schusterman have contributed major insights into the potentials for language and cognition of animals. (For a review of animal language research see Hillix and Rumbaugh 2003 and the recommended readings in this volume.)

Lana

The LANA Project was a team effort with colleagues from the Yerkes Regional Primate Research Center (Harold Warner), from the University of Georgia (Ernst von Glasersfeld and Pierro Pisanni), and from Georgia State University (Josephine V. Brown). None of us had great confidence that any ape could master meaningful language skills. At the time, we lacked confidence that the reports of the Gardners and Premacks in fact reflected processes of the chimpanzee that were homologous (essentially the same in process as well as in form and origin) to language in humans. We would be satisfied with defining a meaningful and helpful *analogue* to human language in a life from other than human. Notwithstanding our conservative stance on this matter, we were highly motivated to assess a chimpanzee's ability to employ language.

I mused, Why not use a computer? Why not have a system that would be monitored by a computer? Why not have the computer and its software assume responsibilities for detecting and recording, for future analyses, all "language" behaviors of the subject? Why not have the computer's software written so that it could take a naive subject—ape or child—and bring it systematically from no language to some language by enabling it to gain increasing control over events of an environment via keyboard operations?

To explore these ideas further, I needed to talk with someone who could tell me more about what computers could and could not do. I phoned Hal Warner, the biomedical engineer of the Yerkes Center. He kindly stopped what he was doing to come discuss the ideas that were racing about my office.

We had to define some specific way to inform the computer what the subject, initially an ape, was "saying." The computer could not intuit such a happening, even had we called it HAL. It needed a precise digital input. How could that be done?

The computer was a PDP-8, the size of good-sized clothes closet, with eight kilobytes of random-access memory, a minuscule fraction of the capacity of the laptop computer on which we write this book. Even so, it represented, in the early 1970s, a great advance over its predecessors that occupied a whole room. This computer was an important requisite to the tactics of the LANA Project. But it was the keyboard we designed that made possible the success of our research into apes' language skills—continuing now into the third millennium.

Progress universally depends upon good ideas, and the conceptual design of a keyboard has to be an exceptionally good one. From 1971 to the present, the keyboard has served first to advance language research through comparative studies with apes, and then to advance language intervention for children whose mental retardation sorely constrained their language learning and expression. And the keyboard had to be specially designed and engineered to withstand vigorous use by an ape.

We reasoned that we could use a keyboard of some kind. After all, typewriters had a long history in our culture, and Geoffrey H. Bourne, then the director of the Yerkes Center, had an old standard upright typewriter that he had obtained from someone interested in the language capacity of dogs. The typewriter had very large keys—and only a few of them, allowing room to enlarge them. Perhaps we could have the ape spell out words. Clearly, though, it was ridiculous to believe that we could teach any creature to spell out words if the creature had no concept of what a word was, what its function was, and how it could be used in combinations with other words to achieve social communications. So we discarded that notion with something bordering on disgust.

Why disgust? Because the idea was a reflection of the old! It had nothing new to offer, and only new ideas might provide us with the breakthrough for which we were reaching.

We probably would have mused on the automatic bank teller machine and the phone information server, but these devices were not then in use—at least not in Georgia. Similarly, touch-sensitive monitors were not then available or even known to us. Buttons on elevators served as interface allowing the passenger to communicate a destination floor, but they were only electrical controls of a switching system. What was our option?

"Well," I thought, "why should a key, even on a keyboard, be looked at as only an element (a letter) of some 'word' to be produced? Why not have each key be a word?" Each key would be embossed with something that would serve as a word. I was then concerned that if each word had a constant location on a keyboard, the subject might come to respond only to the locations of keys rather than to the symbols that were to function as words. The keyboard also had to have several unique attributes, not the least being that it would have to be expandable so as to give the subject access to as many keys as there were words learned—and to be learned.

The resolution to this problem came shortly. In contrast to the fixed locations of keys on a typewriter keyboard, our keyboard would be designed to allow keys to be relocated, ensuring that the subject would have to attend to the symbol embossed on each key. (The concern about the apes attending perhaps exclusively to locations of keys had its origins in the research with the apes and monkeys at the San Diego Zoo. Choice of location, rather than object per problem, deterred markedly with the learning and achievement rates of several subjects.)

But could such a keyboard be engineered and built with our resources? Yes, Hal assured me. Each key could be precision milled so that it could be put in any location on our keyboard, and the new location of each key would be defined to the computer through use of patch panels. Patch panels ensured that the computer registered the same response when a particular symbol was pressed, irrespective of its location of the keyboard. Using these patch panels entailed the plugging of literally hundreds of wires from a jack that led from a given key's location on the keyboard to another jack that, to the computer, always received the signal from the key whenever it was activated by the subject. It proved to be a tedious task to shuffle the keys' assignments on the keyboard, for every time it was done, all wires had to be connected anew. Notwithstanding, it was done—and it worked! (Well, it worked well enough. True to form, even our precision milled keys and plate for the keyboard were not total replicates, and some keys would "stick" when moved to some slots on the keyboard.)

Each key was made of Lucite and was seated in its slot on the keyboard so that when it was pressed, a circuit was completed that told the computer, in effect, "Be alert, someone just said 'banana'!"—or any of hundreds of other symbols used through the years.

We also included the option of backlighting keys so as to reinforce some, but not necessarily all, symbols for Lana. Thus a selected vocabulary might be used from time to time in experimental tests or instructional programs on special topics. We designed the system so that each key, appropriately pressed by a subject, would gain additional brilliance to signal to the subject that the key had been activated. It also became apparent, in due course, that Lana repeatedly pressed keys to produce both the increased brightness and the sound of the microswitch that closed with each depression of a key. The feedback was of significance to her learning and performance.

The actual appearance of the word symbols to be embossed on the keys was Charles Bell's insight. We had used small (2 inches $\times$ $2\frac{1}{2}$ inches) rearview projection screens for portraying both digits and pictures to primates for the automation of tasks used in earlier years at the San Diego Zoo. Each projector had nine small lights and lenses that focused upon a small rearview ground-glass screen. Activation of each light, in turn, resulted in the projection onto the screen of the film image positioned in front of that light. Our concurrent insight was that we could activate those lights in combination. By so doing we would, with only nine elements, construct a large number of patterns. What patterns? What could the ape see and discriminate? I knew from the literature, as well as from my own research, that anything that was discriminably different to us would also be readily discerned by an ape.

In conference with other colleagues, we rapidly selected a number of "stimulus elements" (parallel lines, a rectangle, an X, a circle, a triangle, a midscreen wavy line, and so on) which could be projected one on another so as to compose new patterns (fig. 13). Ernst von Glasersfeld, the linguist for the project, proposed that they be called lexigrams (1977).

How could words be used in combination? How would our computer of limited capacity "know" whether words produced in combinations "made sense"? Von Glasersfeld proposed that a grammar—to be called Yerkish—be written. The several interesting dimensions of Yerkish are recounted in the book that we subsequently did on the LANA Project (Rumbaugh 1977).

Unfortunately, many reports of the early days emphasized the language devised for the project and celebrated the significance of Yerkish. But it wasn't really the language that was important. Along with the computer and keyboard, the language was but a method of inquiry that made it possible for us to conduct language research with a nonhuman primate in ways otherwise not possible.

The use of Yerkish in the research ended when, about 1976, continued programming support for the language ended. Although at the time we regretted the termination of Yerkish grammar, it proved long-term to be a fortunate development. Yerkish grammar was criticized as being "finite state"—meaning that only specific options were appropriate given the prior structure of a series of lexigrams—and though that was not literally the case, the grammar was also called too unlike our own to be of significance to our understanding of language. Although Yerkish enabled us to make important early steps, it was best

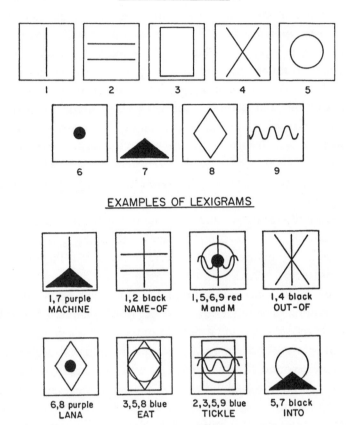

DESIGN ELEMENTS

EXAMPLES OF LEXIGRAMS

| 1,7 purple MACHINE | 1,2 black NAME-OF | 1,5,6,9 red M and M | 1,4 black OUT-OF |

| 6,8 purple LANA | 3,5,8 blue EAT | 2,3,5,9 blue TICKLE | 5,7 black INTO |

Figure 13. The lexical elements which, generally in combination, were used to compose the lexigrams on the row of projectors above Lana's *(Pan troglodytes)* keyboard. When Lana pressed a key, a facsimile of the lexigram on the key's surface was composed by a PDP-8 computer, then projected onto a ground-glass screen through the selective activation of twelve lights, each with its own lens. Nine lenses had film of the lexical elements shown in this figure, and three of them had film of primary colors. Various background colors for the lexigrams were composed by the addition of color from three primary colors. The amount of each color needed was controlled by the computer (von Glasersfeld 1977). Copyright © Academic Press.

abandoned for the long term. In its stead, another grammar was introduced—English! And that "new" grammar has served our long-term interests well, as reflected in the grammatical accomplishments of Kanzi chimpanzee.

Our deliberations included frequent return to a basic question: How might research into the possibility that apes might be capable of language be advanced objectively and in a manner that might be of benefit to children and young adults who, for various reasons, have difficulties in learning and using language? At the very least, even if our ape were to learn no language, perhaps our technology might make a positive contribution to work with children and language-compromised adults.

The Training of Lana Begins

How were we to get Lana interacting with the keyboard so that she might learn of the control which its use would give her over her life? We had intended to teach Lana language by differentially selecting and shaping, through Skinner's operant conditioning procedures, her responses at and to the keyboard. It didn't work; nothing happened. Days passed, and Lana was nourished not by the fruits of her work at the keyboard but by her rations at the end of each day given freely to ensure her health and vigor. We reluctantly asked Timothy V. Gill, a skilled behavior technician, to interact with her in her room-size cage of Lucite. Once that decision was implemented, progress promptly began and Lana began to learn her lexigrams and how generally to use the keyboard (fig. 14). The approach was not unlike that used by any parent or teacher who would set about to instruct a child in the use of, say, an electric piano or mechanical puzzle.

Lana watched intently and learned rapidly. Although progress was surprisingly rapid, I remember my disappointment: we were not going to have automated language learning by a chimpanzee working alone in a computer-monitored environment through use of a keyboard. The effort promised to be, and has remained, labor intensive. The dream of having an ape learning language in a computer-controlled environment might never be achieved, for language learning seems to require social interaction, social commerce, and the negotiat-

Figure 14. Young Lana *(Pan troglodytes)* at her keyboard (Rumbaugh 1977). Photo by Frank Kiernan, Yerkes Center.

ing of behaviors—not just the manifestation of operants and the pursuant contingencies. The lesson Lana taught us early on regarding the need for social interaction for language to be learned in any manner has stood to this day.

We began training Lana how to use the keyboard, through a blend of operant conditioning procedures, modulated by the view that a child's first word is, in fact, a phrase that has been abbreviated to a single word. Thus when a child says "cookie" to its mother, it might be viewed as trying to say, "Mommy, would you give me a cookie, please?" The use of one word, *cookie,* in this case might be holophrastic—a whole phrase in one word. We presumed that we might be able to teach Lana something that approximated what the normal child is thought to do when it begins to use single words to convey a complex request.

Accordingly, the stock sentence "Please Machine give M&M period" was selected for initial training. The sentence was one of several that would serve reliably to give Lana access to various foods, drinks, kinds of entertainment, and social company. The words "Machine give M&M" were tied together electrically so as to activate the entire string whenever Lana depressed any of the keys. The word *please* was not used to teach her manners. Rather, "please" was our gloss for the key that, when depressed, signaled to the computer that a request was being formulated. Also, the *period* key was used with no intent of teaching Lana punctuation. Rather, it was the key that, when depressed, signaled to the computer that the "speaker" had completed a sentence. The computer then determined whether or not the string of lexigrams adhered to the rules of the Yerkish grammar. If it did, the computer activated the appropriate dispenser, and Lana got that which she asked for—whether it was a specific food, a movie, a slide show, or a view out-of-doors, for which the computer would furl a curtain that covered the window.

Initially, only five keys were available. To receive a reward Lana had to press *please* first, then any of the three keys, *Machine, give,* or *M&Ms,* and then *period.* The five keys were in a row, right in the middle of her keyboard. After she became skilled in that procedure, we separated from the string the word *M&M.* Now Lana had to press *please,* then *Machine* and *give,* then *M&M,* and finally *period.* At the end, she pressed the lexigrams—"Please Machine give M&M period"—skillfully. It was easy to do, because they were ordered from left to right in that sequence (fig. 15).

Next, these five lexigrams were distributed about her keyboard. Lana now had to attend to the configurations of the lexigrams on each key's surface and selectively press them in turn. In the next stage, the *M&M* key was deleted and in its stead were substituted any of a number of things that might be dispensed by a device controlled by the computer.

Progressively, *give* was supplanted by *make,* and *Machine* was supplanted by the names of people who were present to attend to the process, and so on. By making these substitutions, we taught Lana a number of stock sentences, each of which was as solid as the dollar used to be when it came to getting such prized foods and drinks as Coke, bread, water, orange juice, primate chow, banana, or apple, or entertainment, such as a movie, a slide show, a few bars of her favorite rock music, a visitor, or a view of the outdoors.

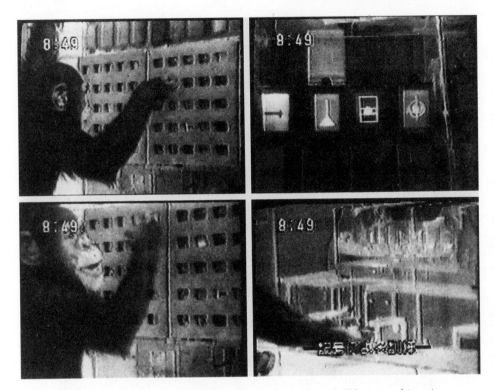

Figure 15. Lana getting a M&M by typing at her keyboard, "Please machine give M&M." Photo by Frank Kiernan, Yerkes Center.

By learning these language-relevant skills, Lana gained increased control over the events of her world. And she seemed to enjoy it! She certainly learned how things worked. If someone pointed to the slide projector, for example, Lana would ask, "Please Machine make [show] slide period," whereupon the projector was turned on. In the same way, if some one pointed to the tape deck, Lana would form the stock sentence, "Please Machine make music period." Those, and only those, specific sentences produced for Lana the specific conditions "requested."

We had reason to believe that Lana was somewhat at a loss when the keyboard was turned off or taken out for repair. She was relatively inactive at those times and always got excited when the keyboard was about to be turned on again for usual operations. Characteristically, she would give the chimpanzee barks of excitation associated with amusements and good food.

Lana also had to learn a few nonlanguage behaviors which, in human parlance, might have been termed manners. Each such behavior showed us that Lana was learning far more than the basics that reinforcement would have instated.

It was undesirable for Lana to urinate just anywhere in her Lucite room. So Tim set about to condition Lana to urinate in one specific spot—in a pan. Lana adapted quickly to this routine. She rapidly learned not to deposit all of her urine at one time. It was a commodity that, tendered in small amounts, would increase her haul of M&Ms. Thus she began to urinate just a bit, get an M&M, urinate a bit more, get another M&M, and so on. But despite even the best of management on her part, eventually she had nothing more "to give" for another M&M. At such a moment Lana came forth with a novel alternative to urination. Out of urine and desirous of another M&M, she turned around and spat saliva into the pan!—then looked expectantly for another M&M, which, indeed, she deserved and got.

Although humorous, Lana's compensatory and innovative behavior merits a serious word of comment about learning. In a strictly operational sense, Lana was rewarded for the response of urination—a specific motor pattern. What Lana learned, however, was something more like, "One has to put some liquid into this pan if one is to get a prized M&M." What we think we are "teaching" through the selective administration of reinforcement of responses and what the subject really "learns" might be quite different. Thus Lana's observed compensation when she had voided all urine is remarkable and makes a statement about the essence of primate learning when a complex and intelligent brain is "at work." We'll return to this topic in a more systematic way when we explore the topic of emergent behaviors, in relation to respondents and operants.

Lana's Reading and Sentence Completion

As Lana became proficient in producing her stock sentences, she became increasingly sensitive to whether she had successfully depressed a key. If a key she selected failed to become brighter and to produce a microswitch "click," she would press the key again and again, until it signaled a successful operation.

It was also observed that Lana learned that *period* served as an electronic eraser in addition to its intended function of ending stock sentences, a requisite for the computer to evaluate the acceptability of the sentence. From time to time Lana made errors in producing her stock sentences. Thus, for example, she would begin a sentence, "Please open Machine" when she meant to say, "Please Machine make window open" to get a view of the outdoors. Apparently she discerned that it was wasteful to try to complete such erroneous stock-sentence stems. Nothing could be done to salvage them. They would never work. It would be best to get rid of them. But how to erase them? Lana learned to use the period key because whenever it is used, what has been produced before is removed from the keyboard. Furthermore, the period key reset the keyboard for reuse in a moment. Thus Lana had good reason to learn to use the period key whenever she made and noticed an error in the production of a stock sentence.

To test this skill experimentally, we designed a study whereby we, and not Lana, would produce the stems of all of Lana's sentences. Such stems might be only two or three lexigrams long, or they might lack only the last word of a stock sentence. Some of the stems were grammatically constructed, whereas others were invalid. The invalid, hence useless, stems were in error in a limited sense: only one lexigram was out of place. We wondered whether Lana would perceptually differentiate correct from incorrect sentence stems. Would she, in other words, correctly complete valid sentence stems and appropriately erase invalid sentence stems through use of the period key?

Lana's performance in this experiment was outstanding. So adept was she that we wrote an article titled "Reading and Sentence Completion by a Chimpanzee" (Rumbaugh, Gill, and von Glasersfeld, 1973). Clearly we used *reading* and *sentence completion* metaphorically, but the metaphor was a powerful one. Without any targeted conditioning, a chimpanzee had on her own learned to discern whether or not sentence stems formulated by us were valid. With better than 90 percent accuracy she promptly erased useless sentence stems with the period key but completed accurately those stems that were valid. We found her skill to be both intrinsically interesting and of scientific significance. Again we found that Lana extended the boundary of what she learned well beyond our intent as she was reinforced by correct productions of stock sentences. Lana was innovative and clever in her novel behaviors.

Learning Names of Colors and Objects

Thirty-six objects were used in a new study designed to determine whether Lana might learn both the names of objects and their colors, and then whether she would answer a unique array of questions accurately. Boxes, shoes, bowls, cups, balls, and cans were used, six of each: one black, one blue, one orange, one purple, one red, and one yellow. These objects, then, made up a set of training materials for Lana to learn names of things and their colors.

Lana was first taught that various things had names. When asked "What name of this?" she learned to respond with the correct word-lexigram to M&M candies and a slice of banana. Correct response was rewarded with something other than the M&Ms or banana. Thus she essentially was labeling or naming the objects. Although to do so with the first two items selected for that training was a considerable challenge for Lana, the skill once mastered generalized readily to the naming of other objects that she had obtained through use of appropriate stock sentences addressed to her computer-monitored keyboard: ball, slices of apple, pieces of monkey chow, bread, and a glass of juice. She could get these items whenever they were available in the dispensing machines, activated by the computer.

She then was challenged to learn the names and the colors of the new set of thirty-six objects. Thus she would be asked, "What name of this?" or "What color of this?" Next she was asked to give either the name or the color of each item used, for example, "What color of this shoe?" or "What name of this that's red?" In subsequent tests with three or more objects present and with each object a different color (a red shoe, a purple can, and a yellow bowl, for example), Lana was about 90 percent correct in answering such questions as "What color of this bowl?" or "What name of this that's purple?" As the number of items in the display was increased, Lana took more time to respond and did so somewhat more accurately.

Lana extended her color discrimination skills to objects for which she had no name, and on some occasions she creatively named an object for which she had been asked only to give the color. For instance, when the object was a student's ill-formed yet basically rectangular handbag of deep purple and Lana was asked, "What color of this?" she typed, "Color of this—," and then hesitated. Only after looking long and hard at her keys, she continued, "—box purple." She named the purse quite accurately as box-shaped—though she had not been requested to do so—and then gave its color accurately.

Lana's ability to classify specific values of colors from Munsell color samples also was measured (Essock 1977). She used her lexigrams to tell us about how she saw various shades of six colors by labeling them red, green, blue, yellow, and orange. And what she told us was that she saw the world of color as though she were one of us.

Lana's Innovation

We had hoped that once Lana had learned her stock sentences she would modify their form and occasion for use so as to solve novel problems. This she did. We had been planning ways in which we might eventually be able to have at least elementary-level conversations with Lana, about things that were of basic interest to her. Understandably, we were impressed when Lana initiated the first conversation. On March 6, 1974, after seeing Timothy V. Gill drinking a Coke in the area just outside her room, Lana generated a new sentence: "? Lana drink this out-of room period." Tim opened the door and shared his Coke with her. She then was returned to her room.

Once the Coke was gone, Tim called me and I reminded him that Lana knew the name of Coke. With a fresh can of Coke, Tim was asked to position himself once again in Lana's view. If Lana again asked to drink "this" out of her room, Tim was to query her, "Drink what out-of room?" When Lana first saw Tim with another Coke, at her keyboard she typed, "Please machine give Coke." There was, however, none in the machine. She then typed, "Please Lana drink Coke this room." Tim answered "no." Within the minute she typed, "? Lana drink this out-of room." Tim replied, "? Drink what." And Lana's response was, "? Lana drink Coke out-of room." Tim replied "yes," and

Figure 16. Lana points to projected images of M&Ms and a ball, after asking, "Please machine make slide" (Essock et al. 1977). Photo by Frank Kiernan, Yerkes Center. Copyright © Academic Press.

let her out of the room to have the Coke. After a few sips, she was re-turned to the room and, again, made her requests to drink the Coke "out-of room." The entire episode, beginning with the second can of Coke, lasted only four minutes, evidence that she knew what she was about and did it well. The significance of this exchange is that Lana combined sentences and parts of sentences in novel ways and did so quite appropriately.

Did Lana literally understand the question, or did she just try something different, given that her first request had not been effective? We will never know, but we had learned that Lana would stay with a topic (in this instance the topic was getting Coke) and would alter her formulations at the keyboard in appropriate ways. We were under-standably encouraged.

Another particularly important conversation took place two months later: the first occasion on which Lana asked for the name of something she wanted. The object that Lana clearly wanted was a box that held M&M candies. She had seen Tim put the candy in the box, but she had not yet been taught the lexigram for *box*. She clearly was asking for the container when she typed, "? Tim give Lana this can." Tim, through his own keyboard, replied "yes" and gave her a can, an empty one that contained no M&Ms. Lana returned to the challenge and asked, "? Tim give Lana this can." Tim replied that he had no other can to give her. Lana then asked, "? Tim give Lana this bowl," where-upon Tim said "yes" and gave her an empty bowl. Then, as though Lana thought that another person might be more helpful, she asked, "? Shelly." Shelly was not there to help, and Tim replied, "No Shelly." Lana again typed, "? Tim give Lana this bowl." But before Tim could even begin to tell her that he had no bowl to give her, Lana used the period key to erase her request and then typed, "Tim give Lana name-of this." Tim replied, "Box name of this." As though grateful, Lana replied, "Yes," then continued, "? Tim give Lana this box." Tim gave her the box, and Lana got her M&M candies. Her name requesting continued next with a new vessel, a cup, and she succeeded as before.

On another occasion, Tim held a sliced orange for Lana, one of her preferred fruits. Lana knew the color, orange, but had not yet learned that the fruit held by Tim had that same name. He queried, "? What color of this." Lana replied, "Color of this orange," which cer-tainly it was. Tim confirmed, "yes." Lana then asked, "? Tim give cup

which-is red." Tim said "yes" and gave her a red cup, which she discarded. Lana then asked, "? Tim give apple which-is green." Tim
replied that he had "no apple which-is green." Lana then promptly requested, "? Tim give apple which-is orange." Tim responded with
"yes," and again Lana ran to the door to get the prized orange.

On several other occasions Lana used her sentences in novel ways
to solve problems of which persons present were unaware. She would,
for example, direct a person's attention to a vending device that wasn't
working by first asking the person by name to "move behind room,"
which put the person into proximity with the malfunctioning device.
Then Lana would use a stock sentence that normally would have activated the device. That series of events served to make clear to the person
present what Lana's problem had been: a malfunctioning vending device. This kind of application of her keyboard skills occurred many times
and served to document that Lana's language learning was well beyond
the limits intended by the specifics of the early training given her.

At times, Lana posed questions to herself and then answered and
complied. For instance, she would be seen at a distance to type at her
key-board, "? Lana groom," to which she would respond "yes" and
then groom herself. From learning to ask technicians to "move behind
the room," she apparently inferred that she could ask them to move
"things"—food—to the location of the vending devices. After various
approximations to that kind of request, she made the complete statement, "? Tim move milk behind—." Tim responded with the query, "?
Behind what," to which Lana responded, "? Tim move milk behind
room."

Offered a Fanta orange-colored drink but not having a specific
name for the drink, Lana asked for it as "the Coke which-is orange." As
we have seen, Lana formulated "apple which-is orange" to ask for an
orange. She also labeled a cucumber as "banana which-is green" and an
overly ripe banana similarly as "banana which-is black." These formulations are consonant with the reports by Fouts (1973, 1997) that Lucy
called citrus fruits "smell fruits," radishes were "cry hurt food," and
watermelon was "drink fruit" and "candy drink." Patterson (1977,
1978) reported that Koko, her lowland gorilla subject, coined appropriate names as well—terming a ring "finger bracelet," for example.

Lana has always had a taste for coffee and has been innovative in
requesting it. Her attempts to obtain it have afforded us with more

than two dozen documented efforts that include the following—? Brody move coffee to Lana; ? Lana drink coffee; Please Machine give coffee to Lana [or to me]; Please you give coffee to me; ? Tim give coffee cup; ? Tim give coffee to Lana; ? Tim give Lana cup of coffee; ? You give coffee out-of room; ? You give coffee to Lana; ? You give coffee to me; ? You give cup of this; ? You give Lana coffee; and ? You give this which-is black. We do not argue that Lana understood the grammatical nuances of these various efforts, but she clearly tried various means across time to get what she wanted (Pate and Rumbaugh 1983).

Cross-Modal Perception

Lana also demonstrated that she could declare two objects as "same" or "different" even when she could feel one object by hand but not see it and could see the other object but not feel it. For chimpanzees generally, this skill is a difficult one to achieve, but Lana learned in only twenty-nine trials what she was to do. When Lana knew the names for the test objects, she did best of all. This was the first evidence that for Lana her word-lexigrams were, indeed, semantically meaningful and were useful in making choices more accurately than when the materials were familiar but without known names.

Years later, other studies conducted by Sue Savage-Rumbaugh with the chimpanzees Sherman and Austin (Savage-Rumbaugh 1986) revealed even more advanced symbolic cross-modal perceptual abilities. In her experiment, the subjects were shown a series of symbols (for example, word-lexigrams) and then asked to select from a bag of various objects the specific object indexed by each lexigram. In this case, the symbolic cross-modal perception was demonstrated: the name of each object was sufficient for Sherman's and Austin's correct choices, thus providing solid evidence that the object's names served as meaningful representations for things even though they could not be seen (Savage-Rumbaugh, Sevcik, and Hopkins 1991).

Obstreperousness?

During the early days when the Cold War was beginning to thaw, we were visited by a delegation of Russians. Members of the delegation

were eager to see Lana, and we were equally eager to have them see
Lana do well. Tim began the session:

> TIM: ? Lana make window open.
> LANA: Lana want Tim give M&M.
> TIM: No.
> LANA: Lana want Tim Give M&M to Lana (a para-
> phrase of her previous statement).
> TIM: No. Tim want Lana make window open.
> LANA: No.
> TIM insisted: Yes.

Lana started to respond, "You—" but was cut off by Tim, who next insisted, "Lana make window open." Lana then replied, "Yes," but did
nothing. Lana resumed, "? You—," but Tim cut her off once again and
forcibly told her, "Make window open." Lana this time replied, "No."
Tim insisted, "Yes." Lana next requested, "Lana want Tim give cup of
juice." "No," responded Tim, "Tim want Lana make window open."
Lana responded, "No. Lana want Tim make window open." At this
point for reasons not clear, Tim capitulated and dutifully typed in the
sentence, "Please machine make window open." For the record, Lana
got nothing—neither her M&Ms nor juice. (Nor did she give Tim
M&Ms!) The Russians laughed with great pleasure. Lana had won the
contest. The Russians then jokingly offered to all of us that everything
was all right, that we needn't consider this event yet another international incident.

On a more serious note, what Lana did was quite remarkable: she
insisted that Tim do what Tim was insisting that she do. She simply
wouldn't do it! In addition, her demeanor was a nervous one; whenever
she tried to turn the tables on Tim, she became slightly more nervous.
We couldn't help but form the impression that she knew that she was
annoying Tim—and very much enjoyed doing so.

Lana's Production, Lana's Comprehension

These kinds of observations—and they were gleaned by the dozen
during several exciting years of research with Lana—made Lana ap-

pear quite skilled in language, given that she was a chimpanzee. As we
have seen, Lana was quite good in using and modifying stock sentences
in the face of novel challenges. She did so very productively, generally
getting what she was after. Notwithstanding, there were limitations in
Lana's skills.

Along with other researchers with apes at that time, we started
with teaching production skills (use of Ameslan, plastic chips, lexigrams) and assumed that comprehension was a companion of competent symbol use. It wasn't. Lana's comprehension, so far as we could
tell, was limited to "stock questions": "What name?" "What color?"
"What color of this [item name]?," and so on. She never gave indica-
tion of understanding novel requests, be they presented by word-lexigrams or by speech. True enough, Lana and all other chimpanzees can
behave as though they understand speech, as long as the speech is presented as part of a familiar event in a familiar context. Saying, "Lana,
give me your bowl," will probably result in her retrieving a bowl from
her cage. But in that situation, Lana has a number of supportive cues,
the verbal request being only one. If day after day she is asked to retrieve her bowl and is given some rewarding compensation for so doing—such as praise or a morsel of special food—she will learn to produce the bowl promptly upon request. Chimpanzees can learn a
number of scripts of this kind, each one being appropriate to different
contexts.

Not until research began with Kanzi in the early 1980s did it become unequivocally clear that, yes, a chimpanzee is capable of understanding not only individual words of human speech but novel sentences of request as well. But that story must await another chapter.
That said, it recently has been very clear that Lana's learning of word-
lexigrams was "for keeps." After more than twenty years, during which
time Lana had neither seen nor used many of the lexigrams that were a
part of her original keyboard system, she was presented again with
these lexigrams and asked to label various foods, colors, and objects.
Lana showed remarkable memory for those lexigram names, and she
identified a majority of the presented items with the correct lexigram
on the first trial (Beran et al. 2000). Lana selected the correct lexigram
from trial 1 for five of the seven lexigrams that she had not seen, indicating that she had "forgotten" only two of those lexigrams in twenty

years. In addition, in fifty trials with other lexigrams for which Lana had learned new referents during that twenty-year period, she was correct forty-six times when presented with the referents she had originally learned. It is quite remarkable that Lana was able to differentiate revised versus original assignments of the lexigrams and supports the interpretation that for her, the word-lexigrams were, indeed, words with symbolic meaning. Their meanings, though surely somewhat different and more circumscribed than they are for us, were sustained despite other training, some of which entailed redefinition of the lexigrams.

From our work with Lana we became confident that, within limits, she shared a common sensory and perceptual world with us and that it had been possible to build a variety of a linguistic bridge through the employment of the system and methods we had conceived. Without question, it was Lana's readiness to learn and her predilection to extend her skills beyond the bounds of specific training that permitted the project to succeed beyond the conservative boundaries and views with which we began the effort. Lana's data made it clear that she was well beyond the bounds of basic training, basic stimulus-response training, and the expectations of traditional perspectives of learning. Subsequent to the LANA Project, every other ape with which we have worked has made it clear that they develop new skills and project their learning in creative ways to new levels of achievement—ones traditionally thought to be unique to humans.

10

The Assembling of Language
Sherman and Austin

In her book *Ape Language: From Conditioned Response to Symbol,* Sue Savage-Rumbaugh (1986) provides a detailed account of the research with the chimpanzees Sherman and Austin. Her effort is best known for the demonstration that chimpanzees can coordinate their social and problem-solving efforts through use of learned symbols. A second research finding is from many perspectives more important scientifically. That finding was that the apes can categorize lexigrams in terms of whether each stands for a tool or for a food. We shall cite only some benchmarks of that study program, those that bear most directly upon our interest in learning of animal intelligence.

Requests, Names, Comments—and Comprehension

Savage-Rumbaugh (1986) differentiated among request, naming, comment, and comprehension. One can teach an ape to use the correct lexigram or to make the correct manual sign for each item that is manually displayed to it. If one then gives the item to the ape whenever it responds correctly in this kind of procedure, is the ape requesting the item, naming the item, or commenting on the item? And does the ape learn each item's name and thus comprehend another's naming and requesting that item? One might argue that the chimpanzee comes to know the names of things through such a procedure, but such a conclusion can be very misleading. The basic questions are: How do we know when the ape knows that the lexigram or manual sign used for a given item is a symbol that functions as a word that stands for it even in its absence? How do we know when the ape is using a lexigram or manual sign as a basic operant, in which case no symbolic function or semantic basis for the ape's behavior should be inferred? In other words, the food or object offered might come to serve as a discriminative stimulus through operant conditioning procedures and might serve to elicit a response of pressing a specific key. Indeed, whether the animal "knows" anything about the semantic meaning of the lexigram on the key being depressed remains unknown unless other assessments are made. As discussed many places in this book, animals can learn much more than what we intend or anticipate. What do apes learn when so taught?

Sherman and Austin had learned to select the appropriate lexigram that served as the name for each object, being awarded the object named. Now Savage-Rumbaugh set about to teach her apes the names of things and that naming an object need not mean that that object will be awarded to them. Instead, they got another item (for example, a bit of preferred food).

Initially, Sherman and Austin seemed confused by such training. They didn't get the object for which the appropriate lexigram-embossed key had been pressed, as they had in the past. Rather, they got something else; for them, it seemed to be a nonsensical procedure. Eventually, however, they learned to respond appropriately. Thus they were able to request things whenever they wanted them and, on the other hand, they were able to name objects, foods, and items portrayed in pictures either spontaneously or on request.

Comprehension was "encouraged" in a variety of ways. We say "encouraged" or fostered because although one can shape and reinforce motor responses, one cannot put in place a symbolic process or capacity in that way. To be clearer on this important point, one can influence the kinds of concepts that animals will learn, but whether or not animals can learn concepts at all is beyond the power of instruction and reinforcement. To form concepts is something afforded by the design and operations of a brain, and quite possibly there are species whose brains do not support the formation of concepts. One can teach a bird where to fly, but not that it can, indeed, fly. Similarly, whether a chimpanzee can literally understand what is being conveyed to it by lexigrams was an empirical question.

Sherman and Austin were encouraged to comprehend lexigrams in a variety of ways and contexts. In one procedure, one of the chimpanzees was taken into a separate room where he saw a teacher place a prized food or drink—an apple, for example—in a vacuum bottle or thermos. The chimpanzee then was taken to another room where his cohort was waiting. At the keyboard the first ape had to announce to the second what had been placed in the thermos. The second then had to ask for the item by formulating the sentence "Give apple." Only attention to and comprehension of what had been declared as the contents of the container could lead to obtaining it. The container was then opened. The presence of the apple affirmed correctness of symbol used by both chimpanzees, and, consequently, both got to eat shares of it. Thus comprehension was encouraged as the chimpanzees had to attend to each other's lexigram communications. That the announcement of what was in the container was meaningful was assured by having the ape select a picture of the item as well. The ape "knew" what he had declared, and the cohort would confirm that he, too, understood what had been announced by comparable test procedures.

Perhaps the need to communicate accurately in this kind of situation became clear when the keyboard was turned off and could not be used. In its stead, labels of foods and cans were strewn on the floor. Without training, Sherman or Austin picked up the appropriate label and handed it to the other so as to convey the contents of the thermos. There seemed little doubt but that they did intend to communicate, and were not just mechanically going through a routine.

A variety of more complex situations were employed as well. For example, one of the chimpanzees would be allowed to see a favorite food or drink put into one of several metal boxes, which was then locked with a specific tool—among them, a wrench, a key, a lever, and a magnet. Each box, once closed, could be opened only with the correct tool. Sherman and Austin were highly motivated to learn the names of their tools so that they could extract the prized incentive from a box. Once extracted, the food then had to be shared so that each was rewarded for his role. But only one chimpanzee saw the box into which the food was placed, and only that chimpanzee knew which tool was needed to open the box. That chimpanzee had to request the necessary tool of the other chimpanzee, which had in his possession the tool chest that contained all of the tools. The chimpanzee with the tool chest had to comply with a request conveyed through use of lexigrams on a keyboard. If the chimpanzee with tools provided something other than the one requested, the ape making the request would reaffirm his request by pointing at the word-lexigram.

The Chimpanzee on TV Is Me!

Sherman and Austin also learned that the images on a television monitor might be of themselves! Austin in particular was inclined to make faces and watch his image either in a mirror or on a monitor as he adorned himself with wigs and paint.

Austin always had a fascination with his throat—a place normally not accessible to one's own view. He discovered that if he opened his mouth very wide and got it as close as possible to the camera's lens, he could see quite a bit of his throat on a monitor. Quite remarkably, he also apparently concluded that the quality of the picture of his throat might be improved if it but had more light. His solution?—to shine a flashlight into his mouth while at the same time trying to get his open mouth as close as possible to the lens of the camera (fig. 17). All the while he was looking at the monitor to see what kind of view he was getting. Such innovative behaviors emphasize the importance of the integration of learning and behaviors when we look for antecedents to creativity in chimpanzees as well as in humans.

Sherman's and Austin's comprehension was also fostered by a project in which they could view on a monitor an array of foods and drinks in a distant room. To get the foods and drinks required substantial coordination of skills and behaviors. The rule was that one of the two chimpanzees had to "request" an available item. The second chimpanzee was then to get the one requested by his cohort. The consequence? They came to do quite well on the test, but what do you do when you forget the items listed on a board in the kitchen—items that

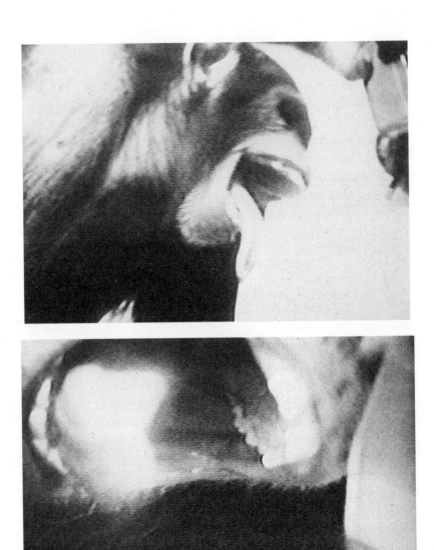

Figure 17. Austin *(Pan troglodytes)* uses a flashlight to illuminate his throat, which he views on the monitor. Photo from videotape by Sue Savage-Rumbaugh.

you are to bring from the store? You go back and take a second look. That's exactly what Sherman and Austin did. If the chimpanzee whose task it was to retrieve the food or drink forgot what he was supposed to fetch, he would come back, look at the keyboard once again to see what item had been requested, sometimes tap on it as though to make that image "stick in memory," then turn and be on his way. It is important to note that each did this on his own initiative.

Because the specific foods and drinks available in the distant room changed without notice, it was necessary that the chimpanzees attend closely to the picture visible on a monitor, that the requester ask only for items that were available, that the retriever attend to the item that his cohort requested (setting aside a preference of the moment), that the retriever remember the item requested as he made his way to the distant room, that he then select that item and no others, and that he then return to the room where the trial started in order to share the item with his cohort. Quite a heavy responsibility and load on memory, it would seem. Notwithstanding, the chimpanzees seemingly enjoyed the challenge and fulfilled expectations with about 90 percent precision or correctness (Savage-Rumbaugh et al. 1983).

Keyboard Comprehension

Sherman and Austin also had their comprehension honed in a task where they were to give the experimenter an item requested from a large array. They could do this almost without error as long as the request made of them was through the use of the keyboard. They could give the experimenter the item requested whether it be "the real thing" or a picture of the item requested. They did very poorly, however, if asked by speech.

Through the course of this project, a remarkable thing happened. Both Sherman and Austin began to take over the role of the experimenter. Each would "ask" for an item at the keyboard, then hurriedly pick it up and hand it off as if the experimenter had asked for it. Unless kept from doing so, the chimpanzees would continue until the array had been exhausted. Initially this usurping of the experimenter's role was seen as something of a nuisance. It certainly interfered with the intended procedure. But then it was recognized that the chimpanzees were "announcing" what they were going to do in the near future. One also might say that they were making a "statement" about their intended behaviors or that they were making a "comment" about what was about to happen.

Their "statement" skills, as we shall call them, were capitalized upon for the purposes of still another study. In this new study one chimpanzee would be sent to an area where he and he alone could view an array of foods and drinks that were subject to change every trial. On his visit, he was to select covertly the item that he "wanted." Next, he returned to a room in which the experimenter and the other chimpanzee waited at a keyboard. The returning chimpanzee then had to announce at the keyboard what it was that he would select if he returned a second time to the area just reviewed. The first chimpanzee then went back for a second time and was permitted to select one item. (His behavior was monitored by camera, and he was admonished to take only one food or drink if he tended to "sweep the tray.") The chimpanzee next carried the item back to the experimenter. Only if the selected item was the same as the announced item were the chimpanzees allowed to share and consume it. That the items of the array changed randomly across trials precluded the possibility that the chimpanzees just exhausted a list of all foods and drinks that they knew. The item had to be there on a given trial for anything else to go right. The chimpanzees returned with the item announced at the end of their first visit to the display with better than 90 percent accuracy.

The significance of Sherman's and Austin's spontaneous use of "statement" or "announcement" behaviors merits special attention. Surely they heard their human companions say what it was that they were about to do or what was about to transpire, but how could chimpanzees deduce that they, too, could do the same thing? To do so was highly complex. Then, too, how can one account for such behaviors unless one posits at a minimum a process of integration of skills that were acquired one at a time across the course of weeks of experience? How do the appropriate skills become sequenced, organized, and executed? How, in short, do they become integrated? Clearly, to integrate multiple behaviors would serve a variety of adaptive purposes and functions. To be able to do so surely entails symbolic operations that in our own selves we unabashedly call thinking. Had Sherman's and

Austin's brains enabled them to think with symbols, the meanings of which had been defined through months of patient training and experiences afforded to them by Savage-Rumbaugh's team? We believe that Sherman and Austin were indeed thinking, and that their thinking was made possible by the working of a complex brain that has learned many complex skills, which can become integrated by the natural operations of that brain. Learning to use symbols to communicate in social interactions might well have been the catalyst that enabled their brains to integrate learned skills knowledge and to think in terms of them.

In common parlance, if we saw children doing what Sherman and Austin did, we would conclude that they had some understanding about the whole script or scenario. Impatient for things to start or to go as fast as they might wish (or eager, perhaps, to play the role of the teacher), Sherman or Austin did what he anticipated the teacher would do—ask for an item by name at the keyboard. He empathized with the teacher's role in that task. That he then complied with his own request (as teacher) suggests that he knew the boundaries of the roles to be played by himself and also knew the structure and boundaries of the role to be played by the experimenter. (And to the credit of the humans present, they soon concluded that it was best to let Sherman and Austin "do their thing," a thing that turned out to have substantial scientific value.)

Food and Drink Sharing

A related observation was made in another situation. Sherman and Austin were taught to share tools and foods, as we have seen. Provided with an array of foods and drinks, one chimpanzee was to request a food or drink and the other was to comply with the request. If the request was for an item present and if the item "served" was the same as that requested, then both chimpanzees got to consume the favorite food or drink.

But what happened when Austin either didn't know the correct lexigram or failed to request anything? Impatiently, Sherman, whose role it was at the time to serve and not request, took Austin's hand. He then gingerly directed Austin's index finger to the appropriate key on the keyboard and then pressed it so as to activate the key. Having directed Austin's request, Sherman had broken no announced rule. He then hurriedly served a portion to Austin, while selecting for his own palate the larger portion. And on several other occasions, Sherman would forcibly orient Austin's face to the keyboard as though to get him to make a request, any request, for something to eat or drink that was available at the time on the table. Is there any real reason to doubt but that Sherman inferred that Austin simply was not task oriented and that in order to get food, within the boundary of rules, Sherman had to innovate and implement a way of pushing his cohort into performing his task? For Sherman to use Austin's finger to press the key for an item on the table was nothing short of incredible. Apes not only see themselves as cause-effect agents, they appear to assess very accurately what other chimpanzees and humans are and are not about. Neither Sherman nor Austin would agree with Tomasello's arguments to the contrary (Tomasello 1999).

Sherman's behaviors of this kind tell us a great deal about what it is that the chimpanzee knows and can experience. In this instance, the chimpanzee expects specific events to transpire and can become impatient if procedures don't go smoothly. When that occurs, the chimpanzee is perfectly capable of being highly innovative, evolving and executing clever and competent problem-solving tactics. These are prime examples of Emergents that will be discussed in detail in a later chapter.

In the tool tasks (fig. 18), where one chimpanzee asked another for a specific tool in order to extract food from a puzzle box, from time to time the chimpanzee with the tool chest would "vend" the wrong tool. In those situations, the requester would ignore the tool and ask anew or do something else—like throw the incorrectly vended tool on the floor and go tap on the keyboard where the lexigram for the tool requested was located. Things had to go right—or they did not go at all well! This was true especially for Sherman.

Sherman's insistence that things go well was epitomized in his insistence that he and he alone could finish his last trial for the day on a counting task. It was about 9:40 P.M. The day had been spent with NHK, a science film company from Japan, and was being finished with some late evening shots of Sherman.

Sherman just couldn't get the trial done correctly. He tried again

Figure 18. Sherman and Austin *(Pan troglodytes)* ask each other for specific tools on the table. Tools were needed to access food from various boxes and containers. Whichever ape sat nearer the keyboard would request a tool through use of the appropriate key. The ape to the right would give it to his cohort. They also shared foods in this same manner, with one chimpanzee asking for any food or drink on the tray and the other serving a portion of that food to his cohort. The one serving generally took the larger portion for himself. Photo by Sue Savage-Rumbaugh.

and again. Everyone wanted to quit—except for Sherman. He became more and more frustrated across the course of about ten minutes. Finally, Sue intervened and actively tried to show him what to do by placing her finger on the monitor so as to indicate the correct answers. Sherman paid no attention whatsoever. He would do it on his own or not at all. Finally, after about ten more efforts, Sherman recognized that he was about to complete the trial correctly, and he started to vocalize happily as he was about to make his last choice of numbers. And he was correct! Everyone celebrated. Not only did the incident portray his independence, it showed that cuing by Sue was not welcome.

Figure 19. A schematic portraying how Sherman and Austin used a monitor to guide their hands to the location of a banana slice that was stuck on the backside of a plastic sheet (Menzel, Savage-Rumbaugh, and Lawson 1985). Copyright © 1985 by the American Psychological Association. Reprinted with permission.

Spatial Problem Solving by Mirror and Television

Sherman and Austin were taught that banana slices were stuck on the side of opaque plastic that faced away from them. The only way that they could be obtained was by reaching through a hole and feeling about for them until locating them. This they learned very quickly (fig. 19). With the aid of a mirror and then television, the apes could see where they were reaching on the opposite side of the sheet of plastic. They made immediate use of the information so availed to them. Next, the fruit was deleted and a dot of ink became the target. The dot moved about randomly across trials, so only by looking at the hand's movement via the mirror or television could the chimpanzee make contact with it. Contact resulted in reward. Although the image on the monitor was reversed as in a mirror and inverted, the chimpanzees compensated in various ways so as to make the image useful to their efforts to touch the dot of ink. Within the first one hundred seconds of Austin's first exposure to the inverted image, he spontaneously turned his rump to the monitor, looked at it through his legs, with his head inverted, and almost immediately made contact with the target. The apes also tested the prevailing condition by waving a hand through the portal and observing its movement on the monitor. When there was a real-time, hence useful, image paired with one that was a replay of an earlier session, hence not useful, the handwaving enabled them to determine which was the current portrayal. These innovative solutions to the novel challenges presented by E. W. Menzel and his associates (Menzel, Savage-Rumbaugh, and Lawson 1985) are taken as strong support for the contention that apes keenly assess the aberrant demands of novel situations in ways so as to find solutions to them. In striking contrast to studies with chimpanzees (Gallup et al. 1971), work with rhesus and other macaques indicates that they are unable to benefit even from specific training that would assist mirror-guided movements of their hands (Held and Bauer 1974).

Categorization

Perhaps the most definitive data that support the argument that the word-lexigrams for Sherman and Austin had accrued lexical meanings come from a study in which, in the final test, the apes classified up to seventeen lexigrams as exemplars of either tool or food (Savage-Rumbaugh, Rumbaugh, Smith, and Lawson 1980). Initially, the apes were taught to assign three foods and three tools to two separate bins on the basis of their category membership (as food or as tool). The objects were next replaced with photographs and then lexigrams (see figure 20), and the bins were supplanted by two new word-lexigrams, one glossed as food and the other as tool. In the final test, with 16 lexigrams for Austin and 17 for Sherman, the chimpanzees were shown the lexigrams and asked to label, and hence categorize, those lexigrams as either a food or a tool (Savage-Rumbaugh et al. 1978). The lexigrams used in this final test were known to Austin and Sherman from months of previous work, but none of them had been used in the present study. To

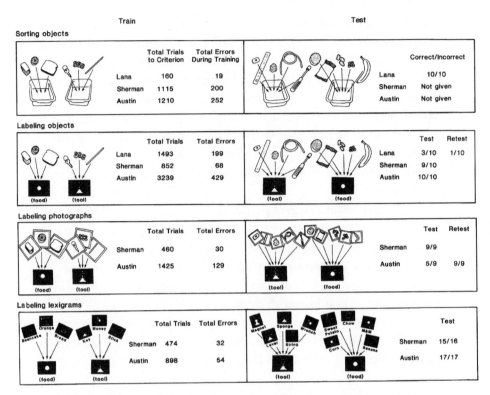

Figure 20. Sherman and Austin learned to categorize seventeen lexigrams as "tools" or "foods" through the course of training that used only three foods and three tools. The figure illustrates the nature of the training and testing and the results per stage of the experiment (Savage-Rumbaugh et al. 1980). Reprinted with permission of the American Association for the Advancement of Science.

categorize the lexigrams correctly in this test the chimpanzees would have to use some form of representation for each lexigram as it was presented. Austin made no errors. Sherman made one error, labeling a sponge as food. A sponge was used to soak up drinks from otherwise inaccessible places, and hence sponges were, from our perspective, a tool. That said, Sherman sucked the juice so avidly from them that he literally ate one or two a day. Thus, for him, it might be reasonable to accept his characterization of the sponge as food.

The research with Sherman and Austin served to encourage the referential use of symbols to obtain specific foods and tools. Tools were used to obtain foods otherwise not available. Through specific teaching efforts, Sherman and Austin learned the difference between naming and requesting foods and other items. Spontaneously, they learned to comment on what it was that they were about to do, whether that action was with a training program or otherwise. The apes came to attend very carefully to one another's use of the keyboard to communicate specific information and requests in a way they otherwise would not have been able to do.

The project with Sherman and Austin served to validate continued research with apes to the end of better understanding language. Without reasonable question, their accomplishments corroborated the principle that apes can learn the referential meanings of arbitrary symbols and use them to communicate so as to solve problems cooperatively.

11

Kanzi!

Science begins with systematic observation, yet most scientists look for theory, perspectives, and hypotheses to be empirically tested in research programs. To have theories and hypotheses worth testing, we need observation. At times, we believe that we are progressing on the basis of relevant observations only to find years later that they were inappropriate and diametrically opposed to those that should have been followed.

Without exception, investigators who have undertaken studies of ape-language skills have set out to teach their subjects through use of such devices as hand signs, plastic tokens, or lexigram-embossed keyboards. The tacit assumption seemingly went something as follows: "Apes obviously don't naturally learn or acquire our language system. If they could do so, someone would have spoken with a chimpanzee by now and would have learned of its private life, its fears, its desires." Researchers assumed that if apes have a potential for language, it is latent, and that if it is to be developed, it must be systematically instructed and reinforced by formal training. Work with the bonobo Kanzi proved those assumptions untrue. Kanzi was the first ape to manifest significant language skills that were acquired through the course of day-to-day living experiences. His comprehension of lexigrams preceded his competent use of them, and both comprehension and use were acquired without formal training. Similarly, his comprehension of both single words and their use in novel sentences of request established new standards for an ape in acquiring substantive language skills and doing so in a manner that paralleled that of the human child—with comprehension established before the productive use of word-lexigrams.

A Brief Biography

Kanzi's mother is usually said to be Matata, a female bonobo brought into the United States from Zaire (now the Democratic Republic of the Congo) on a loan-lease agreement by Geoffrey H. Bourne, director of the Yerkes Center when the transaction took place in the mid-1970s. A small group of bonobos had been brought over for biomedical research—which, fortunately, was never conducted. Later, Matata was assigned to our language project, primarily so that she could be cared for in a more gentle manner than was otherwise afforded laboratory chimpanzees.

Bonobo females frequently let others hold their newborn infants. Laurel, a bonobo from the San Diego Zoo, was at the Yerkes Field Station for breeding, and she gave birth to a male. Matata has a temperament given to domination over other females. So when she indicated to Laurel that she wanted to hold her newborn—Kanzi—Laurel obliged, though somewhat grudgingly. Matata took Kanzi to her breast, where he clung—along with Matata's own infant, Akili. Try as Laurel would to get her baby back from Matata, she failed.

Matata raised both infants and raised them well. Kanzi, of course, knows nothing of his lineage, other than that Matata is "his mother" and she must be treated accordingly. That includes not breeding with her, though biologically that would be advantageous for the propagation of captive bonobos.

The feral-born Matata was perhaps five or six years old when she was brought into a captive setting. Surprisingly, Matata was a poor student in the ways of the Western world: they simply did not afford her the opportunity to use the knowledge and skills that she had mastered in the wilds of her native land. It wasn't that she lacked intelligence; rather, she just seemed unable to learn New World technology and symbols.

But out in the woods, Matata was highly perceptive and skilled. She could snatch a rabbit attempting its escape, discern which reeds had insects, and hear the subtle sounds of others in the woods. Sue always kept her on a long lead so she wouldn't venture off on her own. Matata was generally cooperative while walking through the woods, but given a chance, she would snarl her lead around branches and small trees, seemingly to annoy Sue. Sue, being the smarter of the two, observed that it was when she let Matata just sit for a long period of time that those agonizing expressions of intelligence were likely to come forth. She also observed that Matata could not simultaneously walk and think up mischief. Whenever Matata's eyes started to dash about the limbs and nearby brush and logs, it was time to get her moving again.

By contrast, in language mastery Matata was at best a borderline failure. Her learning was transient. She couldn't even master the reliable use of ten word-lexigrams with which to request items. Notwithstanding, efforts to teach her were sustained. We did not know that they were destined to fail. The methods that had worked well with Sherman and Austin were ineffective when applied to Matata.

It was in the early 1980s when Matata came to the Language Research Center with Kanzi. When Kanzi was two and a half years old, it was time to separate him from Matata long enough for her to be sent to the Yerkes Field Station to be bred again with Bosondjo—a male who also was part of the long-lease agreement with Zaire.

Because of the stress separation imposes upon both mother and infant, especially if they can hear each other, Sue had been unwilling to try to teach Kanzi language apart from Matata. He had been present while Matata was "in class," but by and large the youngster simply made a nuisance of himself throughout each teaching session; he had received no formal language instruction. Kanzi was overactive. He always had to be doing something. If nothing else, he would spin on one foot, or do flips, or just run about.

But when Matata was sent away for breeding, it became immediately clear that Kanzi had been learning in her language class. He immediately demonstrated that he understood most if not all of the lexigrams that were in Matata's program. And he could do things with those lexigrams that indicated that for him they functioned symbolically, as representations of things not necessarily present. He could ask for each object to be given to him through use of the appropriate lexigram. He could "name" each object—and be satisfied with a bit of food or drink other than the object at hand. He could "announce" that he was going to get a certain food from the kitchen next door, and do so.

Lessons from Kanzi

So impressed was Sue with Kanzi's language skills that she decided that there would be no more formal language instruction. This represented a radical shift in research tactics, but one that made all the good sense in the world, despite its violation of tradition and convention. Why have we and others been trying to *teach* language when under certain conditions the chimpanzee can *learn* or acquire language on its own?

This first lesson taught to us by Kanzi was groundbreaking. The acceptance of the "fact" that language skills are foreign to chimpanzees clearly did not rely on any observations of what happens when an ape is reared in a language-enriched environment where all communications and events are consistent, logically structured, and hence predictable. That, of course, had not been done, but had it been done, it would have been unlikely to entail the use of lexigram-embossed keyboards as with Matata, in Kanzi's presence.

The lexigram keyboard permitted the caregivers to coordinate its use while concurrently saying the word glossed for each lexigram used on the board. With each sentence uttered by caregivers, Kanzi saw lexigram-embossed keys pressed as he heard words. The act of a human pressing a lexigram whenever its equivalent is spoken may serve to help the subject to sort out or parse individual words from the speech stream. To give an example, when a teacher said, "Kanzi, let's go to A-frame and get some Coke," she or he would depress, in turn, the keys for Kanzi, go, A-frame, and Coke as they were spoken. With those word-lexigrams being used in combinations with others across a variety of situations, it provides the opportunity for the subject to learn the specific referent for each one.

And it wasn't many months before people at the lab who worked with Kanzi came to believe that he was understanding spoken English. We have had many chimpanzees do things that led us to believe that they really understood speech, but in controlled tests, they failed to do so. Stringently controlled tests were lacking in earlier work by the Hayeses with Viki and by the Kelloggs with Gua (Kellogg 1980; Kellogg and Kellogg 1933). By contrast, when Kanzi was tested for his speech comprehension, positive results were strong and clear.

For these tests, a booklet held, say, three photographs or three lexigrams. One of them would be a match for a word which Kanzi would hear through his earphones. Earphones were used so that the person who held the booklet for Kanzi would not know what word was presented. After Kanzi heard a word, he would gesture for the booklet to be opened. He then would touch a lexigram or picture, as the case was on a given trial. The examiner then would look at a small white card, turn it over, and learn for the first time what the word was that Kanzi was to have heard. If the lexigram or photo was appropriate to the word, then Kanzi was verbally rewarded and given food or drink. Kanzi was never deprived for any of these or other tests. Food and juices were used as reinforcers simply to enunciate the fact that he had done well.

Some readers will say, "Oh, yes, my dog does that kind of thing. He'll bring my slippers, or his bone or ball or whatever I ask for by name. So what's different about Kanzi?"

We know that dogs can retrieve specific objects as requested, but whether or not they can do so on the basis of speech alone remains unclear. But Kanzi can point to the correct photo or lexigram in his test booklet when the words he hears are taped recordings, digitized speech, and synthesized speech sounds. Electronically generated speech can lack human intonation and quality. Nonetheless, Kanzi can interpret its meaning. Kanzi also points to the correct referent (photo or lexigram), and he can name objects and ask for objects and activities through use of his lexigrams. He performs these types of tests well even with native speakers of Japanese, who spoke English for purposes of tests.

All of that said, there is no reason that I can see to argue that dogs or other forms of animal life might not be capable of learning to comprehend words as standing for things that are not necessarily present in time or space. I would and do expect, however, that the potential of apes in this regard is greater than for any other form of animal life.

The "Naturalness" of Kanzi's Language Learning

That Kanzi (fig. 21) spontaneously learned the meanings of literally hundreds of lexigrams and spoken words merits special attention. By "spontaneous," we mean that Kanzi learned without specific training. He learned by living, by growing up in an environment in which lexigrams and speech sounds were important for the achievement of communication that could not otherwise be accomplished. He also became adroit at making sharp pieces of flint by observing Nick Toth do so (Toth et al. 1993). Kanzi then used the chips of flint to cut ropes and pieces of hide so as to be able to access incentives not otherwise available to him.

Children learn their language "spontaneously" in the same sense. True, their vocabulary can be expanded by special effort—and so can Kanzi's. With the human child, the comprehension of speech that it hears occurs much earlier than its ability to speak—and such was the case with Kanzi. With the human child, speech emerges without special training. With Kanzi, his comprehension and use of lexigrams emerged without special training. For the first time in the field of ape-language research, an ape manifested a pattern of language acquisition that was typical for the normal human child. He was not encumbered by experimenters trying to teach him things as had been done without exception in all previous ape language research.

Characteristically, apes have been introduced into language studies only after they reached a certain age. Gardner's (1969, 1971) Washoe was estimated to have been one year old. Premack's (1976) Sarah was even older. Lana was about two years old when serious work with her commenced. Exceptions are found in the Gardners' second generation of chimpanzees. Some of them were much younger and might yet manifest the advantage thereof, as they are in the research program of Roger and Deborah Fouts (Fouts 1976; Fouts and Fouts 1989; Fouts, Fouts, and van Cantfort 1989).

Of special interest is the rearing as a human infant of Terrace's chimpanzee, Nim (Terrace 1979), for many months before it entered

Figure 21. Young Kanzi came to comprehend human speech and to comprehend the meanings of lexigrams and how to use them with no formal training. He learned by observing the training of his adoptive mother and by day-to-day experience. He also learned how to knapp flint so as to obtain a sharp-edged piece with which he could cut ropes and leather to access prized incentives. Generally, he held the cobble in his left hand and the hammer in his right, as portrayed here. Language Research Center.

sign-language training. Terrace's final interpretation of Nim's production of signs was that they were not language. Yet it has been said by those who worked with Nim that he did understand a good deal of speech. Because no systematic record of his speech comprehension was made, however, the validity of the impression remains an imponderable. If it is true that Nim understood speech, then why it was not studied by Terrace is of interest. The emphasis of that era was, however, on "production"—that is, the use of gestures, lexigrams, and plastic tokens to reward "speech."

Savage-Rumbaugh is no longer persuaded that production, or even speech, is as fundamental to language as is comprehension. The arguments for this conclusion include the observation that the normal human child comprehends a substantial number of words and phrases well before it talks at all, let alone in sentences. The conclusion also rests on the obvious fact that one literally has nothing to say until he or she first knows (comprehends) words and their meanings. To speak in the absence of comprehension is nothing more that the productions of the neighborhood automatic bank teller machine or of the subway mechanism that warns, "Please stand away from the closing doors." To be taken to task thus by an automated "speaker" is both impressive and somewhat insulting, but it is not to be construed in the same sense as an admonition from a fellow (human) passenger on the train.

Kanzi's comprehension skills, acquired through living, not through special training, would have had a grand and constructive impact upon comparative psychology and studies of language had he lived, say, fifty years ago. An observational base like the one we now have would have told us: Don't set about to teach language to a chimpanzee! Rather, raise the chimpanzees in different ways, each of which approximates patterns of child rearing, and then study differences in groups' language abilities (Lyn and Savage-Rumbaugh 2000). Kanzi's database would have made clear that the road to the chimpanzee's potential language skills is not paved with good teaching methods. Rather, it may be paved best by a milieu that approximates the norm for child rearing. A primate brain that is as complex as that of an ape's or human's will extract from early experiences those that pertain to language and will organize them into a structure that will provide for an unending process whereby language is acquired.

Kanzi's Sentence Comprehension

"Kanzi, can you give Karen some cereal?" "Kanzi, can you make the doggie bite the snake?" "Kanzi, can you put your collar in the freezer?" "Kanzi, can you put the paint in the potty?"

These kinds of questions serve to exemplify more than six hundred novel sentences of request that were given to Kanzi and to Alia, a young girl whose mental age was an estimated two to two and a half years by the completion of the study. None of the sentences had been practiced or modeled by a human. The purpose of the study was to determine the general boundaries of Kanzi's abilities to comprehend novel sentences as revealed by his behavior. Alia's response to the questions was to serve as a means of calibrating Kanzi's performance.

Alia was especially qualified to fulfill her important role in this study. Her mother, Jeanine Murphy, had worked extensively with Kanzi during his earlier years. Jeanine had about ten years of experience working with the various chimpanzees of the LRC and knew in detail the procedures for use of the keyboard in interaction with young chimpanzees.

When Jeanine and her husband, David, started their family, we considered it a great opportunity to initiate a long-term comparative study in which one or more of her children would have the benefit of working with the LRC keyboard in addition to other aspects of normal rearing. Such experience with the keyboard was established by reserving a home on the LRC's grounds for Jeanine's use with her children in the afternoons. The children were not treated as chimpanzees, of course, but whenever weather permitted, Jeanine would take them on walks about the LRC and into the woods in a manner that approximated similar activities with chimpanzees. The children took their keyboards on these walks and were given the opportunity to learn of lexigrams in addition to learning about communication through the use of speech and pictures. The children were never discouraged from speaking. They were reared as normal children in every respect but had the additional opportunity to learn how word-lexigram symbols might be used to communicate where words otherwise might fail them.

Initially, the statements of request were "just given" under the natural conditions of the day. More specifically, initially both Kanzi and Alia were just asked to do certain things that they had never been asked to do. They had never been told, for example, to "make the doggie bite the snake." They knew of real dogs, for the center had two massive elkhounds. Kanzi knew of real snakes. He had seen several in the forest, and their appearances reliably served as an object lesson regarding danger at hand. For Alia, snakes were toys and pictures in books. Furthermore, neither Kanzi nor Alia was instructed that a toy snake was to be responded to as a make-believe snake and that a toy doggie was to be responded to as a pretend dog. Nonetheless, Kanzi's and Alia's responses to the questions posed about snakes and dogs made clear that they saw their representations at hand as elements to be incorporated into their attempts to comply with the request (figs. 22 and 23).

By definition, a novel sentence of request can be given but once. After that, it is a familiar request, and previous experience can alter a subject's behavior. In other words, only the subject's attempt to fulfill the request when first posed can or should be used to infer comprehension.

With both children and young apes it is important not to let tasks, especially new tasks, become too hard too quickly. If that happens, the subject will simply quit, at least for a while. If the challenges remain too hard, the subject will have nothing more to do with it. It is a child's way—and an ape's—of avoiding failure experiences. Not infrequently, children and apes will become preoccupied with doing other things or will become troublemakers if they don't achieve reasonable levels of success.

To avoid such eventualities, Sue phased in controlled test procedures gradually. Initial statements of request posed to the subjects were made face to face or with the subject's back to the speaker. Only as the subject learned that being asked to do new things was something of a game did Sue place herself behind a one-way vision door, through which she could see Kanzi but Kanzi could not see her.

Another critical step that Sue included in the testing procedure was that the subject was never wrong. If the subject promptly carried out the request presented, it was profusely praised with such statements as "That was really good, [Kanzi/Alia]!" or "Good job!" Chimpanzees and bonobos, like children, enjoy praise. The subjects were also rewarded with bits of prized foods or cups of preferred drinks, but

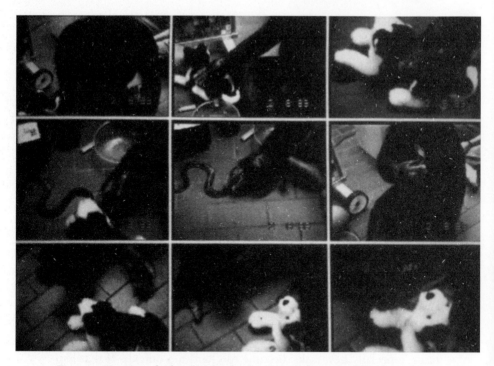

Figure 22. Kanzi is asked to "Make the doggie bite the snake." He finds the toy snake, opens the dog's mouth, inserts the snake, then closes the dog's mouth. Language Research Center.

because neither was deprived of foods and drinks, the reward food and drink probably carried limited incentive. After all, Kanzi frequently voluntarily stopped eating in order to do the next trial; it seems unlikely that he worked in order to get more food.

If Kanzi had difficulty in complying with a request, Sue would repeat the question and then, if necessary, pose it in a different manner. Alia's mother, Jeanine, did the same for her. Whenever Kanzi or Alia still failed to complete the novel request, he or she would receive direct assistance. Sue or Jeanine would come out from behind the mirrored screen and model the requested behavior. Kanzi and Alia were always treated with care and respect and never given any reason to believe that they had failed or had disappointed their mentors. To be scored as correct the subject's fulfillment of the request had to promptly follow a single presentation. Only partial credit for compre-

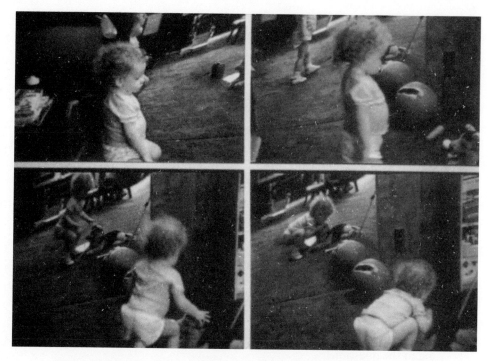

Figure 23. Alia when asked to "Make the doggie bite the snake." Whereas Kanzi inserted the toy snake into the toy dog's mouth, Alia clearly misunderstood and bit the doggie herself (Savage-Rumbaugh et al. 1993). Reprinted with permission of the Society for Research in Child Development.

hension was given if the subject responded correctly to a reworded question.

On each trial, many objects were randomly placed in front of Kanzi and Alia. Generally there were at least five objects and as many as eighteen. Some objects were placed near places known by name to the subject—the bedroom or outdoors, for example. The objects were randomly selected and moved about frequently so that both Kanzi and Alia had to search for the object or objects mentioned in the next sentence of request. Duplicates of certain items were also present, with one being, for example, on the floor in front of the subjects and the other being in the bedroom or outdoors. Such duplication was necessary for certain kinds of questions that asked the subject to do something with an item designated by its location. For example, the request

"Kanzi, go get the telephone that's outdoors" would be made when there was also a telephone indoors, so that Kanzi's ability to comprehend statements regarding location could be assessed.

The first two hundred sentences of the study were given under conditions not strictly controlled; but more than four hundred sentences were given in tightly controlled conditions. In controlled trials, the mentor was out of view. Furthermore, any other person in the enclosure with Kanzi had to listen to loud music through headphones so that he or she would not hear the questions posed and provide inadvertent cues.

Practically all test trials were taped, then scored. Everything that was said to the subject and every response by the subject became part of the transcript. It was thus possible to categorize the subject's responses according to various parameters. Did the question posed, for example, require that the subject take the specified item to a location or to a named person in the area? What assistance was offered by the mentor if prompt compliance with the request was not forthcoming? What apparently unrelated behaviors did the subject engage in while responding to the question?

Several types of sentences were given to Kanzi and Alia. Type 1a took the form "Put object X in/on transportable object Y"—for example, "Put the ball on the pine needles." Type 1b was the same except that the subject was to put an item on a nontransportable object, such as the stove. Type 2a requested that the subject "Give/show object X to animate A"—"Give the lighter to Karen." In type 2b the subject was asked to do the same with two objects; type 2c asked, for example, that the subject "Give Linda a hug"; and type 2d asked the subject, for example, to "Get Linda with the [toy] doggie." Type 3 requested that the subject do action A on object X (with object Y)—for example, "Knife [cut] the sweet potato." Verbs used here were *bite, eat, feed, hammer, hide, knife* (cut), *open, play, slap, squeeze, throw, wash,* and *vacuum.* Type 4 announced information upon which the subject might or might not act—for example, "The surprise is hiding in the dishwasher." Type 5 asked the subject to "Take object X to location Y" ("Take the snake outdoors"), or to "Go to location Y and get object X" ("Go the refrigerator and get a banana"). In this type of question the subject might also be asked to get a specific object from a specific location—for example, "Go get the carrot that's in the microwave." In type 6 the subject was asked to make animate *A* do something to a specified recipient—"Make the doggie bite the snake." Type 7 consisted of eleven sentences that did not fit into one of the other categories.

We detail the variety of sentences in order to make clear that the task before the subjects was neither simple nor predictable. They had to listen carefully so as to decode the request and carry it out. "Get the ball that's outdoors" might well require that the subject ignore or step over a ball on the floor inside. The scoring system was complex; however, to receive full credit the subject had to fulfill the request on its first presentation with no rewording.

From one perspective, syntactical comprehension and translation into action is more complex than translation from one natural language to another because there often exists no one-to-one translation between a word and an object or between a word and an action. Translating a sentence like "Can you feed your ball some tomato?" into another language is relatively trivial. Translating it into action is more difficult because it requires conceiving of an object, a ball, as something other than something that bounces and can be hit or thrown to others. The ball must be redefined conceptually as something that incorporates capacities of a human or another ape, including in this case the ability to consume food offered to it. Attending only to the key words of this sentence—*tomato, ball,* and *feed*—fails to resolve ambiguities both syntactic and semantic. These words might suggest that one should eat the tomato and the ball, actions not encoded in the complete sentence, "Can you feed your ball some tomato?" Kanzi's response to this novel sentence of request—he had never been trained to do that with his ball—was to take a morsel of food and literally try to insert it into the mouth of his pumpkin-faced toy ball (Savage-Rumbaugh et al. 1993, 99). He also responded appropriately to "Give me the ball and the hat," though he gave only the ball, and to "Put the ball in the hat." In the second of these sentences, ball and hat were syntactically related and not just conjoined as they were in the first of these two sentences.

Kanzi also handled remarkably well a substantial set of requests in which the words that constituted the requests were the same but the meanings were reversed. For instance, he carried out appropriately the novel requests to "Pour the juice in the egg" and "Pour the egg in the juice." Only his understanding of meaning encoded in the syntax would enable him to respond correctly, given that he had not otherwise been specifically trained with each sentence. Both requests were given in the same context and shared the same three words—*pour, egg,* and *juice.* He correctly carried out seventy-one of eighty-eight (81 percent) different sentences of this type, somewhat better than Alia's score of 64 percent (fifty-three of eighty-three). Dolphins have demonstrated similar sensitivity to word order (Herman, Kuczaj, and Holder 1993). The purpose here is not to claim that an ape is a better learner of language than a child but rather to make clear that Kanzi's understanding of novel sentences of request were competitive with that of a precocious $2\frac{1}{2}$-year-old child (see Bates 1993 for a commentary on this project).

To dismiss these remarkable accomplishments as mere instances of slot-grammar, in which only one word is changed in a sentence otherwise held constant, is neither fair nor adequate. Such an explanation serves only to deny the basic lesson defined by the procedures and data from a comprehensive, well-controlled study.

On the lighter side, at times, Kanzi would assume a puzzled expression when he heard a really bizarre request and would seemingly ask for reaffirmation of the request. For example, when asked to "Put the melon in the potty"—a freshly cleaned portable toilet—he stood up, put his hand on the melon, then paused. Only with affirmation of the request, "Put the melon, the melon in the potty," did he do so (Savage-Rumbaugh et al. 1993, 184). (Some time later, when asked to "take the melon out of the potty," he curiously sniffed it while complying with the request.)

Clearly, the production of language cannot be competent without comprehension of language. Children acquire language first in comprehension. Only later on do they talk. Kanzi's comprehension, coupled with his competent use of the keyboard, indicates that language both received by him and used by him was replete with meaning. In his combined use of lexigrams and gestures, Kanzi evidenced reliable consistencies reminiscent of grammar. Some of the rules that summarize these consistencies were of his own innovation, whereas others appeared to be modeled after the rules of others who worked with him (Greenfield and Savage-Rumbaugh 1993).

Kanzi set a new standard of achievement in acquiring substantive language skills. He acquired them spontaneously—without formal training—through the course of day-by-day living. As is the natural course of language acquisition for the human child, he came to comprehend the meanings of word-lexigrams used by others before he "talked"—that is, before he used them to initiate requests, to comment on things, and so on. He was the first ape to comprehend the complexities of novel sentences of request, spoken to him by an experimenter in a highly controlled test situation.

The perspective of Kanzi's achievements and their meanings are captured succinctly by Domjan (2003, p. 384):

> Kanzi's performance provides the best evidence available so far that a nonhuman mammal can acquire sophisticated linguistic skills. Kanzi acquired a substantial vocabulary and also showed evidence of syntax in language production. In addition, he mastered some of the flexibility of language. He could understand differences in meaning created by different word orders and new messages created by combining familiar words in unfamiliar sentences. The language sophistication of Kanzi proves that many important linguistic skills are not uniquely human attributes. Thus, these findings vindicate Darwin's belief that seemingly unique human abilities and skills do not reflect a discontinuity in the animal kingdom. (For a discussion of the broader philosophical implications of this research, see Savage-Rumbaugh, Shanker, and Taylor 1998.)

Anyone who doubts that Kanzi's skills are language should try to use language while refraining from use of skills that Kanzi mastered.

IV

Investigating Rational Behaviorism Across Species

12

Asking Questions so That Animals Can Provide the Right Answers

Why have chimpanzees and bonobos succeeded in demonstrating use and comprehension of language where other animals have failed? How have they learned to understand symbols (including, in some cases, human speech) as referential, functional, shared vehicles for the communication of comments, questions, requests, and other meanings? The answer to these questions is multifaceted. No doubt, these successes reflect the marvelous complexity of the great ape brains, the ingenuity and dedication of the teams of scientists and technicians who provided appropriate early social interactions, and the shift in research focus from one of production to one of comprehension, language-structured rearing, and enculturation. Additionally, and pertinent to the present chapter, chimpanzees' and bonobos' success in language acquisition and use likely owes a debt to the invention of the keyboard as the medium for nonvocal linguistic communication. That is, an answer to the theoretic question "Can apes learn language?" was inextricably woven with the practical question "What is the appropriate technology for ape language research?"

The point here is that the same marvelous brains, raised in the same language-steeped culture, with the same research focus on comprehension, may not have produced the same corpus of results without the insight of using a keyboard-mediated, computer-based, manual, interactive language system. Of course, this is speculation (although the history of ape-language projects supports it), as we can never and would never go back and try to teach Lana, Sherman, Austin, Kanzi, Panzee, Panbanisha, and the other apes without the use of the lexigram keyboard. This keyboard, which has itself undergone major changes across the years with developments in technology, still affords a ready and common medium for apes and humans to communicate. It requires a discrete and objective response and thus eliminates the ambiguities and subjective biases that may constrain sign language. It is interactive and immediate, producing auditory feedback and immediate changes in the environment where appropriate. Although keyboards can be cumbersome and cluttered, making them less ideal than speech, they were an excellent innovation for ape-language research and seem likely to have been pivotal in permitting our apes to argue on their own behalf for their language capacities.

Asking Questions Can Constrain the Answers

Similarly, one might wonder why the notion of Emergents did not appear earlier in the psychological literature. Why is it possible to posit a Rational Behaviorism now, in contrast to the radical behaviorism that characterized comparative psychology through most of its history? Why did it take so long to accumulate phenomena like those discussed in this book that cannot be explained by the classical behavioristic concepts of respondents and operants?

Again, part of this answer can be found in changes in apparatus. The dominant apparatus of the twentieth century, the operant chamber or Skinner box, served to constrain the field to findings consistent with associative forms of learning. The Skinner box is ideally suited for isolating individual variables for investigation, for controlling extraneous influences on behavior and for manipulating specific stimulus or reinforcement consequences. In the attempt to identify the simple laws of behavior, behaviorism proscribed an apparatus and paradigm that generated laws of simple behaviors. No one can deny that an organism learns stimulus-stimulus or stimulus-response-consequence relations when only these associative mechanisms are available. But the possibility that animals might learn more than associatively was not even considered, much less measured. History has made clear the limitations of these associative mechanisms for explaining complex forms of cognitive behavior that are beyond the scope of the lever press or the pigeon's peck.

The constraints on research, and thus on theory, imposed by the operant chamber call to mind an earlier behaviorist apparatus that similarly shaped the nature of findings. Thorndike tested cats in puzzle boxes, chambers with multiple potential mechanisms of escape. The correct method for escaping the puzzle box could not be found by insight, reason, or other emergent method; that is, the cat within the box could not see, and thus could not possibly know, how to escape the box. The puzzle box could only be learned by trial-and-error; consequently, it is unsurprising that Thorndike found that cats learn only by trial and error.

It is certainly true that cats learn (in puzzle boxes and many other contexts) by trial-and-error. Rats, pigeons, people, and other organisms certainly learn from the consequences of behavior. Dogs, people, and other organisms are certainly influenced by reliable stimulus-stimulus relations. But we cannot assume that all learning is associative just because learning is associative when it is constrained to be so. We cannot infer that all behavior is simple just because simple behaviors have been extensively studied.

The advent of computers provided more to psychology than a new jargon and a new metaphor for cognitive theory (although both of these contributions were important). Computers provided a new apparatus, and a plethora of new research paradigms, that yielded the opportunity for emergent forms of behavior: learning that was silent, that was complex, that was unreinforced, that was—in a word—emergent. The literature of fifty years ago was replete with studies of the laws of work. The contemporary literature continues to include such studies, but also features examples of behavior that transcends operant or respondent explanation, and that challenges one to accept a Rational Behaviorism.

Thus the shift in research findings with the development and implementation of language keyboards illustrates an important and general principle for science: research results are always constrained by the methods (including the apparatus) used to produce them. The history of psychology, and particularly of comparative psychology, is rife with examples of paradigm shifts with the emergence of new technologies. These paradigm shifts were made not only in terms of the common research procedures used within the discipline (as when Skinner's operant chamber became the prescribed tool for studying learning) but also in terms of the theoretical conceptions and limitations that were held for particular animals (as in the way that the cognitive abilities of apes have been redefined by the lexigram-keyboard). Nowhere is this statement better illustrated than in the history of research with rhesus macaques and other monkeys.

Spatial Discontiguity

Consider for example the fifty-year literature directly and indirectly treating stimulus-response spatial discontiguity in macaques. In testing that employs the Wisconsin General Testing Apparatus (WGTA), if the naive primate subject is to execute its choice using a button or similar device that is even slightly distanced—spatially discontiguous—from the object "chosen," learning is profoundly handicapped if not precluded. That is, the animals choose correctly 50 percent of the time on trial 1 (because they have no choice but to guess), but they also perform near chance on trial 2 and subsequent trials. Learning of each two-choice problem is retarded, and the "win-stay, lose-shift" relational strategy does not emerge. By contrast, if the subject executes its choice of objects by displacement of an object, even naive rhesus monkeys normally learn quickly and proficiently. That is, the animals will learn to displace the positive (rewarded) object in order to obtain a reinforcer and will avoid the negative (unreinforced) stimulus. Indeed, as we have seen, the monkeys will adopt a "win-stay, lose-shift" emergent strategy on trial 2 of each novel pairing of objects.

This finding, which was replicated in numerous studies, led to the conclusion that rhesus monkeys could not resolve situations of stimulus-response spatial discontiguity. Rather, the monkeys appeared to attend only to the area near their fingertips. Monkeys sample from the area around what they touch, and fail to notice the stimuli to be discriminated unless those stimuli are directly contacted (Meyer, Treichler, and Meyer 1965). This finding is reminiscent of the failure of rats to learn two-choice discriminations until Lashley introduced the innovation of a jumping stand, which permitted the rats to respond directly to the stimulus cards.

The compromise in learning by monkeys under conditions of stimulus-response spatial discontiguity resisted numerous experimental attempts to draw the monkeys' attention away from the response locations and toward the stimuli to be discriminated. In study after study, monkeys failed to learn at normal levels when the animals were required to respond to locations apart from the stimuli to be discriminated, unless extensive and systematic shaping was used, in which the response locations were gradually moved from the stimuli.

It was against this corpus of data that we proposed a new testing apparatus for research with rhesus monkeys. Earlier, the chimpanzees Sherman and Austin had demonstrated the untutored ability to respond to computer-generated stimuli by manipulating a joystick after just a few minutes of demonstration by Sue Savage-Rumbaugh (1986). Indeed, they elbowed their way into position so that they could deny her the use of the joystick and use it themselves. They seemingly understood what the task was all about. This finding was taken at the time as another manifestation of the chimpanzees' sophistication and intelligence. No one at the laboratory thought that rhesus monkeys would be similarly able to master skilled use of the joystick on computer tasks.

Nonetheless, along with a team of scientists at Georgia State University, we set out to discover whether rhesus monkeys could learn to respond to computer-graphic stimuli by manipulating a joystick or similar response apparatus, anticipating extensive experimental benefits if they could. The capability would provide great opportunity for enrichment of the monkeys' lives and even greater opportunity for research into their cognition. But our hopes were tempered by that fifty-year literature on stimulus-response spatial discontiguity. It appeared unlikely that the monkeys would attend to the screen and learn about the stimuli when the response device, the joystick to be manipulated, was about eight inches away—and the pellet cup was even farther away from both the joystick and the screen. According to the results of numerous careful studies, the monkeys could not be expected ever to master control of a computer-graphic cursor by manipulation of the joystick.

Fortunately, the rhesus monkeys had not read the literature. Within a few hours of having access to the computerized test system— computer, monitor, joystick, dispenser, and a curriculum of training software—the monkeys were moving the cursor into contact with computer-generated target stimuli. At first, the animals simply wiggled the joystick randomly, whereupon they received a reinforcer for that activity. Quickly and systematically they came to move the joystick so as to control the cursor with precision, directing it into targets of decreasing number and size. Not only did the monkeys learn quickly those psychomotor skills necessary to "touch" a computerized stimulus with a cursor (without physically touching anything close to the computer screen). They were also able to learn two-choice discrimination problems with computer-generated stimuli. Eventually, they evidenced trial-2 learning-set formation—the emergence of the "win-stay, lose-shift" strategy—at a rate and level comparable to the published reports for monkeys tested with a traditional Wisconsin General Testing Apparatus (WGTA) with no discontiguity of the stimulus, response, and reward locations. Quite serendipitously, we had automated the WGTA, an effort that had frustrated researchers for decades, for though clever systems had been devised, none of them had enabled high-level learning-set formation. The understanding of the parameters of learning-set formation and concept formation in rhesus had been the goal of researchers for years. Research had been compromised by lack of an automated WGTA.

Our results suggest that rhesus monkeys' learning was consistently compromised by the structure of the WGTA rather than by a cognitive limitation of the species itself. When rhesus monkeys are tested with the computerized test system, the animals learn at levels that are normal or better despite spatial discontiguity. Rhesus monkeys are not constrained to attend to and sample stimuli from the vicinity of their fingertips, except (for unknown reasons that should be the subject of additional inquiry) when tested on versions of the WGTA. Indeed, test-wise rhesus are able to negotiate a separation of several inches

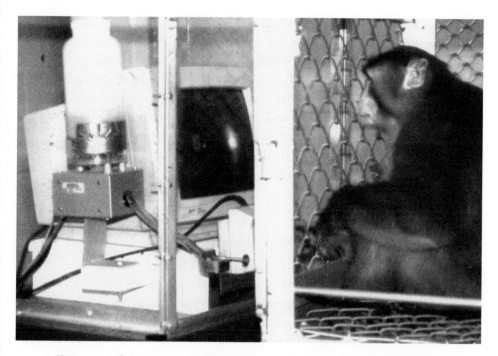

Figure 24. The Language Research Center's Computerized Testing System (LRC-CTS), with an adult rhesus monkey manipulating the joystick (lower right of monitor) so as to maneuver a cursor on the screen. Language Research Center.

between the image selected and the target "button" on the monitor. Even if the "buttons" are moved around on the screen and positioned so that the subject must move the cursor away from the image selected in order to chose it, the effect is trivial upon the rhesus monkeys' accuracy of choice. In fact, rhesus monkeys have led a revolution of sorts since the development of the computerized test system (also known as the Language Research Center's Computerized Test System, or LRC-CTS; see fig. 24). Many of the cognitive limitations that had previously been demonstrated for the species have been overturned by new data from the computer-task paradigm. Gamelike software versions of many of the classic tests from comparative psychology have been written and introduced to the monkeys. These include tests of discrimination learning, matching-to-sample, oddity-from-sample, transfer index, mediational paradigm, delayed response, sameness-difference, delayed matching-to-sample, conditional matching, and stimulus equivalence (see Rumbaugh, Richardson, et al. 1989; Washburn, Hopkins, and Rumbaugh 1989; Washburn and Rumbaugh 1992b).

Additionally, many classic cognitive tasks (for example, visual search, Stroop, serial-probe recognition) similar to the versions used in research with human adults and children have been written and introduced successfully to the monkeys. On the basis of data from these tasks, we now know the qualitative nature of rhesus monkeys' cognition to be much more similar to that of humans than was previously believed.

Relational Learning

As we have seen, an important qualitative difference that can be observed across primate species is the distinction between species that learn associatively and those that can also learn relationally or mediationally. That is, some primates (namely the prosimians and many small-brained monkeys) appear to learn discriminations primarily, if not exclusively, by associating stimuli with responses and outcomes. Indeed, these forms of conditioning characterize learning by all organisms to some degree; many changes in human behavior can easily be traced to operant or respondent learning. Humans and the great apes, however, also can become excellent learners of relations. That is, they can escape the bonds of stimulus-response associationism and respond on the basis of emergent, generalized patterns of events that may never have been directly reinforced. They also generalize and even reverse prior learning to a leveraged advantage.

When tested with a WGTA, rhesus monkeys initially tend to be associative learners. With time and training they become skilled in forming learning sets, and their transfer index scores rise above those of other monkeys, though not as high as those of great apes. Furthermore, they transferred learning positively, as do humans and great apes; however, when tested in the paradigm designed to assess for associative versus relational learning, in the conventional WGTA situation rhesus monkeys remain burdened by associative learning proclivities. That is not to say that they are not relational learners at all. When they were tested extensively with the computerized test system, rhesus monkeys clearly demonstrated the ability for relational or mediational learning. But they simply are not as adept at relational learning as the great apes can become. Although quantitative differences are still evident in the learning performance by rhesus monkeys, great apes, and humans, these data demonstrate qualitative similarities in learning among the species.

Predictor-Operator

In order to use nonhuman animal models of human behavior, we must identify the domains in which findings from monkeys do not generalize to performance by humans. One such area, according to some researchers, is the ability to capture and track a moving target. U.S. Air Force researchers examined monkeys' performance during a pursuit tracking task. They reported that monkeys, unlike humans, appeared not to try to anticipate where the target was going. Rather, the monkeys responded at each moment to the current position of the stimulus, whereas humans uniquely performed as predictor-operators, biasing their tracking response in accordance with the anticipated future movements of the target.

Rhesus monkeys have now been tested on a number of computerized tasks requiring responses to moving stimuli. In these tasks, monkeys have consistently tended to respond to where a target is going, not just to where it is or has been. That is, rhesus monkeys are also predictor-operators, although the accuracy of their predictions differs quantitatively from that of humans. Although humans are better at the tasks, both human adults and rhesus monkeys move to intercept a predictably moving target rather than just chasing it around the screen, and both "fire" a ballistic "shot" across the screen at an angle that approximates the optimal path of intersection with the moving target. The differences that were ascribed a qualitative nature when monkeys were tested with a different apparatus were clearly revealed to be quantitative in nature when the animals and humans were tested with the computerized test system.

Perceived Control

It's a fascinating truism, as robust in science as it is applicable in advertising and education: people love choices. Not only do people prefer to have options or choices, but their performance is improved on tests in which they have control or choice compared with those tests that are obligatory. Consider, for example, the answer a student might provide on an essay question. Research suggests that the student will provide a better answer to this question if allowed to select it from, say, three options ("answer any one of the following three essay questions") than if that same question were assigned to the student without options. Indeed, research on this topic has further demonstrated that it is not even critical that the person have actual control over which task or test will be administered; performance benefits are achieved any time the person perceives that he or she has options, choices, and control.

The perception of choices and of control over those choices is a higher-order awareness that may serve as one hallmark of intelligence. Until recent years, this was a capacity that seemed certain to be beyond rhesus monkeys. However, research with the computerized test system changed this perspective. A rhesus monkey can be given menus of icons, each of which corresponds to one of the battery of tasks that make up the monkey's repertoire. Selection of any icon, by moving the joystick to control the cursor, results in the presentation of some trials of the corresponding task. That is, if the monkey touches the MTS icon with the cursor, a series of matching-to-sample trials is initiated, and then the icon is presented again for further selections. Similarly, the monkey would pick the MAZE icon to receive the opportunity to solve two-dimensional mazes.

It is noteworthy that the monkeys learned to use this menu format (which we call SELECT) to gain access to the tasks. That is, the animals quickly abandoned the random selection of icons and began to show reliable preferences—to pick their favorite tasks most often, and their least preferred tasks less often. When the icons were changed to a completely new set of pictures, the same patterns of preferences quickly emerged. This development showed that the preferences were reliable and that the monkeys understood the meaning of each icon. This finding alone was surprising, in that it suggested that monkeys had learned symbolic representations for the task-icons.

Even more amazing were the results of the animals' performance on tasks that were selected from this menu format. The latency of responding, the speed of choice, the accuracy of response, and the number of trials performed were all improved when tasks were selected by the monkeys rather than assigned to the monkeys without choice. Even when the variety and the order of the tasks were matched between conditions, the monkeys performed significantly better on tasks that they had chosen than on the same tasks when assigned. The monkeys match-to-sample more accurately when they select the matching-to-sample task from a menu than when it is assigned to them by the experimenter. They shoot a moving target more accurately when they choose the LASER task from the menu than when the task is assigned. This result is made even more impressive when one remembers that the monkeys are never obliged to work on the joystick tasks. The monkeys have continuous access to the computerized test system and some task or tasks. They work when they want to work, rest whenever they want to rest, and receive a full ration of food each day whether they engage in task-directed activity or not. No animal in our laboratory is deprived of food or reduced in body weight for purposes of testing, and thus the monkeys are always free to work on computerized tasks whenever they choose. Because of this, we believe that we obtain performance data from the monkeys that reflect the times when the animals are most highly motivated to work—whether the tasks have been assigned to them or are available in the menu format.

Even given these conditions, the monkeys perform better when given control over the tasks on which they will work than when tasks are assigned without options. The availability of choices in this paradigm is an empirical fact, but the monkeys' responsiveness to these choices in terms of the significant alteration in their behavior under these conditions reveals that they do in fact perceive the choices. They perceive that they have control over the test situation, and, like humans, they perform better accordingly.

Not only do these data indicate a capacity heretofore undocumented for rhesus monkeys, but the data also help to address one of the theoretical debates that characterize the study of perceived control by humans. One explanation for the effects of perceived control is the speculation that people may be concerned about how their performance will appear to others, particularly on a task that was chosen rather than assigned. Although humans may indeed feel presentation pressures like this, they seem unlikely to account for the effects of perceived control because rhesus monkeys, which also show perceived control effects, probably do not experience any pressure or embarrassment regarding the evaluation of their performance by humans or other monkeys.

Asking New Questions

These areas of research illustrate, but certainly do not exhaust, the ways in which the computerized test system has changed our perception of the cognitive sophistication of rhesus macaques. The right technology, applied with the right training protocols, to the right species at the right time has afforded the opportunity to revisit many of the tried-and-true principles of comparative psychology. In this way, we can assess the degree to which the findings of literature are products of the apparatus used to produce them, much as the trial-and-error learning that Thorndike described was an unavoidable artifact of the particular puzzle boxes he used for studying the behavior of cats.

Of course, revisiting these previous studies with new paradigms does not impugn the original data. Cats did indeed learn by trial and error in Thorndike's studies, just as rhesus monkeys did indeed suffer from stimulus-response spatial discontiguity in numerous Wisconsin General Testing Apparatus (WGTA) experiments. The data from new paradigms serve only to constrain the generalization of these findings by reminding the field that observations may be influenced by the methods used for measurement. Doubtless, new technologies will be used someday to revisit some of the findings from joystick-based research using the computerized test system. In the meantime, we should remember the importance of establishing psychological principles from the convergence of evidence from different sources, different paradigms, and different species.

But the computerized test system has provided the opportunity to do more than replicate or even overturn previously published findings. Many new questions can be asked with computer-task paradigms that could not be accommodated by manual apparatus. Indeed, one real benefit of the computerized test system is that each monkey can produce more than two thousand trials, across tasks and conditions, each day. A researcher using the WGTA is hard-pressed to record even one-tenth as many trials daily, and can test only one animal at a time using the manual apparatus. In contrast, we sometimes have had more than a dozen rhesus monkeys working simultaneously on computerized tasks, each with a dedicated computerized test system, and each producing hundreds or thousands of trials each day.

The new questions that can be asked are not just a product of the monkeys' prolific work ethic, however. The computerized test system allows humans, apes, and monkeys to be tested on identical tasks and under consistent conditions. Consequently, many test paradigms that were developed for research with human adults and children can now be administered also to joystick-competent nonhuman primates. A few examples of these new vistas for research will illustrate the unsurpassed level of cross-species comparability that can be obtained with the computerized test system.

Competition

One look at the computer-game industry underscores the importance of competition to humans. It is an objective fact of life that nonhuman animals also compete—for example, for resources or for mates. What is unclear is whether monkeys *know* that they are competing—that is, whether they change their behavior under conditions of competition compared with conditions in which they are not competing or are cooperating. With the computerized test system (as with the computer-game industry), it is easy to put pairs of "players" into a competitive game. For example, we modified for two-monkey play the LASER task, in which manipulations of the joystick result in a ballistic "shot" of light being fired from a computer-graphic turret across the screen toward a moving target. Two turrets appeared on the screen, each controlled by one monkey, and the first monkey to hit the target with a shot received the reinforcer (a fruit-flavored chow pellet). This task was made available to the monkeys continuously, such that each day included times when only one monkey or the other was engaged in the task, times when neither monkey was playing, and times when both monkeys were shooting at the same target and vying for the same reward.

Again, the issue is not whether the monkeys were competing—

they were, by definition, whenever both were engaged in the task. The question was whether the monkeys would alter their response strategy because they were competing—would they behave as if they knew they were competing? The answer to this question was clearly "yes": both monkeys increased their rate of firing shots, at a cost to their accuracy, under competitive conditions. When a monkey was working on the task alone, the tendency was to hit the target in just a few accurate shots. When both monkeys were working on the same trial, however, each monkey exhibited a speed-accuracy tradeoff indicating that the goal was no longer "hit the target in few shots or little effort" but rather "hit the target first." The monkeys not only competed, but they knew they were competing and changed their behavior accordingly.

Attention

Over the past four decades, few areas of cognitive inquiry have received as much attention as the construct of attention itself. Beginning in the late 1950s and continuing to the contemporary literature, the study of how we select stimuli for processing (or block nonselected stimuli, or allocate mental effort to processing) has been central to cognitive psychology. As a consequence, the literature is replete with tasks, paradigms, and phenomena that serve to define attention. Humans are not unique in the ability to attend to particular stimuli, although research on nonhuman animal attention has predominantly followed the operant tradition of examining learning of multidimensional stimuli when one stimulus attribute (for example, color) is reinforced and other attributes (for example, pattern) are ignored. Although this research is interesting and important, it is difficult to integrate conditioning phenomena like blocking with the cognitive phenomena that anchor studies of human attention.

In recent years, however, rhesus monkeys and apes have been tested using the computerized test system on numerous attention tasks that originated in this human literature. From this research, we now know that monkeys engaged in visual search show pop-out effects, in which a target stimulus is located in the same amount of time irrespective of the number of nontarget stimuli in the array. These effects occur for the same stimulus features that produce pop-out effects for humans (searching for an *O* embedded in a field of *X* stimuli, for example, or searching for a *C* located in an array of *O*s). For visual searches with varied stimulus mappings (locating an *F* amid an array of *E, L,* and *T* stimuli, for example), the time required to locate the target increases, both for humans and for monkeys, as the search-set increases in size.

Similarly, humans and monkeys show comparable interference and facilitation on a numerical version of the Stroop task. In the classic Stroop color-word task, humans are shown a series of words and are required to name the print or display color of the words. If the words are color names that are incongruous with the print color (for example, the word BLUE appearing in red), naming time (saying "red") is slower than if the colors are congruous or the words are neutral. A similar effect can be obtained with humans in a numerical Stroop task: people take longer to count incongruous numerals (saying "four" when viewing the stimulus "5555") than to count neutral stimuli (saying "four" when viewing the stimulus "DDDD"). We also found Strooplike effects for numerical judgments by rhesus monkeys. The animals, which had previously been trained to respond on the basis of the value of Arabic numerals, experienced the same kind of response competition that characterizes human attention and executive function.

The monkeys' capacity for judgments of relative numerousness also provides one source of evidence for negative priming. Not only can monkeys select one of several competing stimuli (or stimulus attributes) on a given trial, but there is evidence that they "filter out" or inhibit the nonselected stimuli. That is, response time on any particular trial is altered by the stimuli that appeared on the preceding trial. If the target stimulus on a given trial was also the target stimulus on the previous trial, response time is faster than if the target stimuli are unrelated between trials. If, however, the target stimulus on a given trial was presented as the nontarget stimulus on the previous trial, response time is significantly slowed. The response to the new target (which was previously the nontarget) has been negatively primed—suggesting inhibition of the nonselected stimuli or dimensions that carries over between trials. Because humans also show robust negative priming effects under a variety of circumstances similar to these described for monkeys, these effects represent new evidence of the similarity in attention across primate species.

Through these and related studies, we have seen that monkeys, like humans, manifest the cognitive skills of focusing, scanning, shifting, and sustaining attention. Although numerous quantitative differences in these skills exist across species, the results from the computerized test system research indicate that what monkeys can do, they do in ways qualitatively similar to humans.

Uncertainty Monitoring

The inhibition, problem solving, planning, and monitoring required to perform some of these tasks takes the research into the domain of "executive function" (or prefrontal function, because these cognitive skills appear to be localized to the prefrontal cortex of the primate brain). These indirect studies of executive function are complemented by a series of experiments in which metacognitive abilities are directly investigated.

Studies of human confidence (or uncertainty) trace back to the earliest days of psychology. In that era of psychophysics, studies of perceptual judgments frequently permitted participants to rate their certainty about a decision or even to escape trials about which they were uncertain. From this beginning, however, scientists who were interested in metacognition came increasingly to rely on self-reporting, verbal and memorial stimuli, and circular definitions of uncertainty. (Participants rated their confidence lower on trials in which they were uncertain, and the degree of their uncertainty on these trials was measured by confidence ratings.) These methods have been heuristically and productively employed to produce a large and interesting corpus of data that correspond to literatures on human judgments of learning, metamemory, feelings of knowing, and uncertainty.

Although these methods are valuable for research with human adults, they are ill-suited for investigations with populations that are nonspeaking, developmentally disabled, or without a knowledge base that can be tapped by questions about which one may be uncertain. To examine the monitoring of uncertainty by nonhuman animals, for example, requires both a procedure for administering trials on which the animal is objectively uncertain and also a response option that allows the animal to indicate its uncertainty.

J. David Smith of the University of Buffalo and his colleagues have designed just such a paradigm for the computerized test system. Rhesus monkeys or apes are required to make a stimulus decision (whether a computer-graphic box is filled with exactly 2,950 illuminated pixels or fewer illuminated pixels). If the animal judges the box to contain the target number of pixels, it makes one response, and if the animal judges the box to be populated with fewer than 2,950 pixels it makes a second response. We can then titrate the number of pixels in the box to locate the threshold level for this discrimination—that is, to find the point where the animal is equally likely to make the target response as the nontarget response. This is an empirical point of uncertainty, the point in the stimulus continuum at which we objectively know that the monkey does not know how to respond.

Of course, many paradigms may bring a monkey to a place of uncertainty. Recognition paradigms, memory tests, same-different judgments, and judgments of relative numerousness all produce errors that may reflect uncertainty. What distinguishes Smith's psychophysical paradigm is that the monkeys also have a third response option: at any time, the monkey can choose to escape any trial—to clear the screen and to be shown the correct answer—by selecting this third response option. Not only does the task bring the subject to a point of empirically determined uncertainty, but it gives it an option for responding adaptively to that uncertainty, in that the monkey can avoid errors and maximize rewards by using the escape option on exactly those trials where it is uncertain. The question for this study was "Would the monkeys use the escape option on trials in which they are uncertain?" In broader terms, "Can the monkeys monitor and respond adaptively to their own uncertainty?"

Before learning the answer to these questions, consider the results obtained from human participants. Humans usually say that stimuli with about 2,950 pixels are the target. Stimuli with very few illuminated pixels are almost always identified correctly as nontargets, but the likelihood of responding "target" increases as the number of pixels in the box increases. Consequently, for every participant the probability of responding "nontarget" decreases across the stimulus continuum, the probability of responding "target" increases across this same continuum, and at some point these two reciprocal curves cross.

It is exactly at this point of crossover, this threshold for the perceptual identification, that humans are most likely to use the escape option. People seldom escape when few pixels are illuminated, because they know that these are nontarget stimuli. People seldom escape trials in which 2,950 pixels are illuminated, because they judge correctly these to be the target stimuli. However, around the threshold—the point at which we know (without the participant's self-report, although subjective reports confirm what we know from the objective measure) that the participant is uncertain—people are most likely to escape trials.

Monkeys show exactly the same pattern of results. The phenomenology of the uncertain response is comparable across species. The individual differences in the readiness to respond are comparable across species. Monkeys, like humans, reserve their use of the "uncertain" response for exactly those trials for which we know objectively that they are uncertain. Like humans, monkeys appear to monitor their subjective levels of certainty for these tasks and to respond adaptively to these subjective cues (see Smith, Shields, and Washburn in press).

In a series of experiments, Smith and his colleagues have shown that these uncertain responses are not dictated by objective cues, but rather stem from subjective states of confidence.

The general methodology—a task that brings humans or monkeys to a measurable point of uncertainty and also gives the participant a method for coping adaptively with uncertainty—has generalized to other tasks. Monkeys also show humanlike responsiveness to uncertainty in a psychophysical method-of-constant-stimuli task (a categorization task, for example), in a sameness-difference task, and in a serial-probe recognition memory task. In each of these tests, objective "escape" cues are unavailable, and yet the monkeys—like humans—do use the escape response, and use it on precisely those trials on which the organisms are uncertain.

It is difficult to imagine conducting this amazing series of experiments if it were not possible to test the monkeys using the exact apparatus, the computerized test system, that is useful in studies of human metacognition.

These few examples serve to illustrate how apparatus (or, more generally, the way empirical questions are posed) can shape the answers obtained. Many other examples can be provided, of course, spanning every decade and category of psychology. These examples are not restricted to instances in which computerized apparatus have been applied to old problems—although new technologies, or innovative applications of existing technologies, have an undeniable capacity to revolutionize a field. In part, this explains why scientists get swept up in the fashionable and seductive paradigms of any day (for example, the imaging technologies so popular in multiple areas of contemporary psychology). It is useful to remember that even these sexy, powerful, and popular paradigms—be they imaging techniques, manual apparatus, or even computerized test systems—have limitations that constrain the answers obtained. The strategy to be recommended is a convergent approach illustrated by recent work on primate laterality, which has included studies of hand preference versus skill on computerized measures (Hopkins et al. 1992) as well as on other behavioral measures (Hopkins and Pearson 2000) and physiological measures (Hopkins and Fowler 1998); tests of lateralization in perception (Parr et al. 2000) and production (Fernandez-Carriba et al. 2002); analyses of genetic (Hopkins 1999) and social (Hopkins and Fernandez-Carriba 2000) influences on lateralization; and imaging-based analyses of anatomical asymmetries (Cantalupo and Hopkins 2001).

The importance of convergent methods and findings for generating comparative psychological principles has been heralded elsewhere as well. Sternberg and Grigorenko (2001) emphasized the value of converging operations for unifying the fractured discipline of psychology. Any one methodology or operation reveals only part of the information about a psychological construct (Garner, Hake, and Erikson 1956). Synthesis and comprehensiveness (for example, within comparative psychology, between comparative psychology and cognitive psychology, or between the cognitive school of thought and behaviorism) can be found in the convergence of multiple methods, technologies, and perspectives.

These data combine to present a picture of the cognitive capacities of rhesus monkeys that is very different from the one that dominated the literature just a few years ago. Monkeys, although still different from humans and apes in important ways, possess a remarkable range of mental abilities that attest to the continuity between species in the primate family.

We have only begun to tap the potential that arises for studying the similarities and differences across primate species. What other principle that "we all know must be true" will be the next to fall under the weight of scientific inquiry renewed?

13

When Emergents
Just Don't Emerge

Should you conclude, in light of these findings, that monkeys tested with the computerized test system can do everything that chimpanzees can do—or everything that humans can do, for that matter? More broadly, is it possible that all of the so-called species differences that have been documented in the comparative literature are simply artifacts of the apparatus or paradigms used to ask the questions? These are empirical questions, of course; however, it is unlikely that all of the established species differences are artifactual. Although one can never prove the null hypothesis—the burden of proof for showing that a species does have some capacity is more clearly defined and attainable than the burden of proof for showing that a species does not have that capacity—findings that are consistent across multiple paradigms and convergent sources of information make a compelling case for some meaningful differences across the primate order.

I (Washburn) was taught a vivid lesson about species differences during graduate school by a fellow student, Bill Hopkins, now a professor at Berry College. To illustrate the difference between the cognitive abilities of chimpanzees and monkeys, Bill gave a paper surgical mask to the chimpanzee Austin. Austin, like the other apes and monkeys at the Language Research Center, had often seen human caretakers wearing similar surgical masks. Austin immediately imitated what he had so frequently observed. He placed the mask over his nose and mouth, and bounced playfully around the play yard. Austin even pulled the rubber band around his head to secure the mask before returning it upon request to Bill. Subsequently, Bill led me into the monkey laboratory and handed a similar surgical mask to Abel, the smartest of our macaques. Abel immediately took the mask, sniffed it, and began to eat it. We scrambled to retrieve the paper mask before it became part of the monkey's diet for the day. The contrast could not have been more clear: Austin saw the object as a mask and manifested immediately novel behaviors indicative of imitation and play; in contrast, Abel saw the same familiar object as something to be eaten. The chimpanzee responded as a two-to-four-year-old child might, whereas the macaque reacted as a human infant might.

This anecdote suggests species differences that have been carefully documented in varied research contexts. Whereas the previous chapter emphasized what monkeys can do and the influence of these capabilities on comparative psychological theory, the present chapter examines what is learned by what monkeys (apparently) can't do. This discussion can be divided into two sections: species differences (capacities that have been demonstrated for apes but not for monkeys) and meaningful failures (tasks on which monkeys have inexplicably failed to learn relationally).

Misbehavior of Organisms

Forty years ago, Breland and Breland (1961, 1966) published one of the most influential and widely cited papers in the history of psychology. The Brelands described examples of "misbehavior of organisms"—instances in which the behavior of an animal failed strictly to obey the laws of behaviorism. These observations included a variety of instances of so-called instinctual drift—behavior that follows strong instincts rather than the operant contingencies. Although the Brelands said little to help us predict when instincts would override operant contingencies, the notion of instinctual drift was an important contribution to the literature because it showed an unexpected limitation on behaviorist accounts.

Four decades later, we have begun to accumulate a number of findings that are curiously similar to those reported by the Brelands (1961). However, these new observations are not instances of instincts competing with operant contingencies. Rather, these so-called meaningful failures to learn are tasks in which the monkeys have failed to learn relationally but have instead been restricted to responding according to operant contingencies. We might call these behaviors examples of "associative drift" because they illustrate, in ways directly comparable to the limitations described by the Brelands, unexpected limitations on emergent forms of learning. For reasons that cannot at this time be described, stimulus-stimulus and stimulus-response-reward relations sometimes override and preclude more generalizable rule-based forms of learning, thereby resulting in performance by monkeys that is very different from that observed for humans or apes.

These meaningful failures are failures only in the sense that the monkeys did not learn what we wanted them to learn. That is, each monkey did learn something—each did complete many trials successfully and receive many reinforcers. However, each monkey could have learned a relational strategy for each task, a strategy that would generalize to novel trials and produce more efficient responding.

Of course, one might argue that these failures aren't truly meaningful. As we have seen, the literature is replete with examples of animals failing to learn in one context but then demonstrating a capacity later, when trained longer or in a different way. Although it certainly remains possible that future research will resolve these failures, we believe that each of these meaningful failures is indeed meaningful for various reasons:

> a. First, the monkeys have failed to learn despite extensive efforts—and high motivation—on the part of the researchers to help the monkeys succeed. Every reasonable effort was made to help the monkeys. Despite thousands of trials and many attempts at training, the monkeys failed to learn the relational response.
>
> b. These failures are consistent across the animals. Every monkey that was tested on these tasks failed to perform in the intended way—unlike tasks on which some monkeys

learn well and some monkeys learn poorly, resulting in failure only on average.

c. Finally, none of these failures was predictable. For each,
the monkeys had succeeded on a similar task that would
seem to require comparable cognitive skills.

Let us consider this list of meaningful failures and the corresponding
successes to see what they reveal about Emergents, operants, and respondents.

Mirror-Image Matching-to-Sample

Rhesus monkeys, like chimpanzees and humans, can recognize complex images that are presented to them. In a matching-to-sample format, a sample object or image is presented and the monkey—or other
animal, as the matching-to-sample task has been frequently used with
a variety of species, including humans—must select from two or more
choices the stimulus that is identical to the sample. Even with fine discriminations, monkeys can match-to-sample with high levels of accuracy, indicating that they see the world in much the same way that humans do. However, the monkeys are incapable of matching-to-sample
when the choice stimuli are identical except for left-right mirror image
(for example, b versus d, or > versus <). With these stimuli, which appear easily discriminable to human adults, the monkeys perform at
chance levels.

To appreciate how unpredictable this failure is, consider: Imagine putting the mirror-image stimuli b and d on the computer screen
in random positions and reinforcing each response to the "b" stimulus.
This variation on two-choice discrimination learning should be mastered rapidly by monkeys (with formation of learning set and good
reversal-of-training). Notwithstanding, after thousands of trials with
the same pair of stimuli and the same contingencies ("b" responses reinforced, "d" responses extinguished) the monkeys will still be at
chance, selecting "d" on half of the trials.

Why do the monkeys fail to use the generalized matching rule
with mirror-image stimuli? Why do they resort to associative tactics

(responding, for example, on the basis of position) rather than gleaning the relational response that would generalize to new stimuli?

Ballistic Predictions

Christine Filion conducted an interesting experiment as part of her graduate work at the University of Georgia. She wanted to determine whether monkeys could extrapolate movement. Specifically, she used a task in which a line (the ballistic trajectory) moved slowly across the screen in a straight line toward one of five small rectangles (the targets). At various points, the line would stop moving and the monkey was required to indicate which target would be hit by the ballistic trajectory were the movement to resume. That is, the monkeys were required to determine, by the trajectory of the line, at which target the ballistic trajectory was progressing.

Filion had numerous reasons to believe that the monkeys would succeed at this task. The animals had demonstrated the ability to shoot at moving targets on the computer screen. Not only were the animals good at hitting the target, but they could also abort errant shots well before the shot missed the target. Additionally, Filion, Washburn, and Gulledge (1996) later found that the monkeys could hit the target even if it moved behind a physical occluder (for example, a piece of opaque paper taped to the screen). This required the monkeys to extrapolate the invisible movement of stimuli based on the way it had moved when visible.

Nonetheless, the monkeys failed to learn the relational rule in the ballistic prediction task. They quickly learned which target would be contacted by the ballistic trajectory but failed to generalize when either the position of the targets changed or the position from which the point of origin of the ballistic trajectory was changed. Further analysis revealed that the monkeys learned stimulus-response spatial associations for each trial. This associative strategy served the animals poorly when novel probe trials were introduced with never-before-experienced positions. Why did the monkeys, capable as they are of learning relationally, nonetheless learn to respond according to stimulus-response (operant) associations?

Drawing

In a similar design, we tried to teach monkeys to reproduce simple shapes on the screen. A sample image (for example, a horizontal line, a vertical line, or a simple shape) appeared in the top half of the screen. The monkeys "connected the dots" at the bottom of the screen by moving the cursor (by manipulating the joystick, as in all of their tasks). Unlike usual conditions, the cursor left a "trail" behind it, allowing the monkeys to leave a residual line as they connected the dots.

If they connected the dots to produce the desired stimulus, the animals were reinforced. In this way, the monkeys quickly learned to produce the first stimulus (for example, a horizontal line), whereupon a novel probe trial was administered with a new shape (for example, a vertical line). All of the monkeys failed to produce this new shape on trial 1. Training proceeded with both of the first two shapes until performance reached a set criterion, whereupon a third target stimulus (for example, a diagonal line) was introduced. No monkey drew this diagonal line on trial 1. Training and testing continued in iterations following this procedure: trials to criterion with all familiar shapes, followed by introduction of a novel sample, followed by more training, then another probe, and so forth.

The monkeys quickly learned to draw each shape but consistently failed to generalize to new forms. That is, the monkeys solved the task on every trial using a "on stimulus X connect these dots, but on stimulus Y connect these other dots" associative strategy. The relational rule ("reproduce the shape") would have worked for every generalization trial, and would have resulted in more correct responses. Nonetheless, the monkeys learned associatively. Why?

Concentration

One of the most familiar children's games is called "the memory game" or a variety of commercial trademarks (including *Concentration*). The basic game involves pairs of cards, each bearing a colorful picture on one side and a nondescript surface on the back. These cards are shuffled and placed, picture side down, on a table. Players take turns flipping two cards to reveal the images. If the pictures match, the cards are won by the player and removed from the array; if the images are different, the two cards are returned to their original position picture-side-down. Thus players must remember an increasing amount of "what did I see and where did I see it?" information.

The concentration game would seem to be ideally suited as a task for the comparative investigation of visuospatial memory. Children routinely perform as well as or better than adults on the task, and it doesn't require language to explain or to play. Indeed, the monkeys learned to play the game, and performed hundreds of problems successfully. However, monkeys consistently perform more poorly than humans, and indeed more poorly than chance, on the task.

How can this be? Although the monkeys do seem to understand that the object of the game is to find pairs of matching images, they frequently repeat specific errors. For example, a monkey might turn over two cards to reveal pictures of a football and a tree. Then it might turn over two new cards to reveal a car and a tree. Ideally, the monkey should then immediately turn over the two cards bearing tree images. On some trials however, a monkey might make similar errors repeatedly (football, tree; football, tree; tree, football; football, tree; car, tree; football, tree; and so forth). If the monkey closed its eyes and wiggled the joystick randomly it could find the pairs more quickly on these odd trials.

The monkeys don't often repeat a string of errors, but when one does its performance becomes paralyzed for dozens or even hundreds of responses. Why would a monkey that can respond relationally become enslaved on some problems to associative cues for responding?

Other Tasks

Several other tasks could be cited that also illustrate meaningful failures to learn. In each, the monkeys could have responded according to a rulelike relational (and humanlike) strategy but instead were constrained by stimulus-response-reinforcement associations that could not generalize to novel trials. The question for current discussion is "Why?" Under what conditions do monkeys sometimes show emergent behaviors, and under what conditions do they manifest only operant or respondent forms of behavior?

Unfortunately, one answer at this time is "We don't know." Our analysis has revealed a number of commonalities across the meaningful failures (for example, they tend to require imagery or spatial representation), but so far these have not been conclusive (monkeys can learn relationally on other tasks like Laser that also seem to require imagery or spatial representation).

We have examined a number of putative factors that might contribute to these instances of associative drift without yet identifying the conditions in a convincing way.

Fortunately, another answer at this time is "It's an empirical question." Much as Breland and Breland (1961) were able to describe instances of instinctive drift, without specifying the exact conditions that would permit prediction of those "meaning failures of operant conditioning," we have reported some phenomena that reflect "meaningful failures of relational learning." Doubtless these descriptions will serve the heuristic purpose of stimulating research, and just as certain this research will reveal one day the reasons behind these meaningful failures.

Ape-Monkey Differences

The literature is replete with other competencies that are characteristic of humans and apes, but not of monkeys. Space does not permit extensive treatment of these topics here, but some can be listed in order to establish the research questions for the next few years.

Language

The language comprehension and production abilities documented in previous chapters have not been approximated by nonape species. Even for macaques, which are capable of relational learning, it appears that the disposition to learn associatively would prevent the acquisition of symbols that could be comprehended and used to communicate meaning in ways that are generalized, generative, and communicative.

Self-Recognition

One of the most active and controversial areas of comparative inquiry pertains to animals' ability to recognize their own reflections in a mirror. The ability to recognize oneself is usually assessed using the famous "mark test" in which a mark is placed surreptitiously on an animal's brow—a mark that can be viewed only in a mirror—and the animal is observed to see whether it touches the mark after seeing it in the mirror. A variety of ape species have passed the mark test. A chimpanzee, for example, recognizes its reflection in the mirror, or even uses a televised image of its face to explore areas not otherwise visible. Monkeys have never provided convincing evidence of recognizing themselves in mirrors. Rather, a monkey typically responds to the reflection as if it were another monkey.

However, we did report a finding that may qualify this statement. We found that monkeys, although they performed poorly on the mark test, seemed to recognize videotaped images of themselves. Rhesus monkeys were given the choice of working on computerized tasks for pellets only or receiving pellets and videotape reward. The videotape was of rhesus monkeys: themselves, their friends, or unknown animals of the same species. Although a monkey generally preferred not to watch the videotapes at all, it was significantly more likely to watch video of itself than of other monkeys (whether familiar or novel). How is it that the monkeys preferred their own faces on video if they could not recognize their own faces? This question merits further exploration with this new paradigm.

Tool Construction and Use

Cebus monkeys are noted tool users, both in captivity and in the wild. Other monkey species (for example, rhesus macaques) are notoriously deficient in tool-making and tool-use skills, at least compared with apes and humans. Gorillas, for example, have been found to use tools both in captivity and in the wild (Boysen et al. 1999; Parker et al. 1999). On the other hand, one could see the joystick as a tool for controlling a cursor. If this is true, then perhaps the tool-use and even the tool-making skills of nonhuman animals have been underestimated.

Imitation

Imitation has been extensively investigated in several ape species. Controversies still exist over what constitutes good evidence of imitation and what animals have achieved this evidence. Parenthetically, it is curious how imitation can in some instances be seen as psychologically primitive and a given (as in the conclusion that Nim's communicative signs were imitations), whereas in other literatures imitation is seen as psychologically complex and beyond the achievements of nonhuman primates. An exhaustive review of this literature is beyond the scope of this book (though fortunately, the literature has been subject to several excellent summaries elsewhere). For purposes of the present discussion, suffice it to say that language-trained chimpanzees at a minimum are capable of imitating the actions of others (for example, to open an "artificial fruit" or puzzle box; Tomasello et al. 1993), although they may not imitate as readily or as accurately as human children. There is no compelling evidence for imitation of actions by monkeys, despite several attempts to document such imitation (see review by Visalberghi and Fragaszy 1990).

Theory of Mind

Finally, we mention the large number of other paradigms subsumed under the rubric "theory of mind"—or, more specifically, responding to the mental states of others (Premack and Woodruff 1978). Studies of deception, teaching, imputed intention, and shared knowledge illustrate this research area—which again has been characterized more by contention than consensus. Although for some paradigms the evidence for theory of mind in apes is stronger (for example, Mitchell 1999; Menzel 1999) than for others (for example, Povinelli et al. 1990), it seems clear that the behavior of chimpanzees and other great apes is not so clearly influenced by the inferred mental states of others as is human children's behavior; however, apes are much more likely to pass theory of mind tests than are monkeys.

Human-Nonhuman Differences

In this book, we are reviewing a number of milestones of human intelligence that are also observed in nonhuman animals, particularly the large- and encephalized-brained apes raised from birth in a cognitively challenging and language-steeped environment. This is not to deny that there remain substantial qualitative and particularly quantitative differences between humans and nonhuman animals in psychological competencies. Many of these are the subject of ongoing scientific inquiry at research laboratories around the world. How will these studies alter our understanding of learning and performance across species, given how much has changed in the way we now conceive of apes and monkeys relative to just a decade or so ago?

14

Animals Count

In recent years the topic of numerical cognition has been the focus of one of the most interesting, productive, and contentious research areas in comparative psychology. The questions driving this research have ranged from "Do animals respond to the numerical attribute of stimuli?" to "Can animals count or perform elementary mathematical operations?" This array of research questions has intrigued many of the most active and influential researchers in our discipline, and comparative studies of numerical cognition have been a staple at some of the preeminent research laboratories in the world. These studies have included a wide range of animals, including pigeons, parrots, rats, raccoons, marine mammals, and various species of monkeys and apes. An equally diverse set of research paradigms have been employed in these studies.

Given this investment of creativity and effort and this opportunity for convergent findings, you might expect that tremendous strides have been made in answering the questions raised. However, the literature on numerical cognition has generally been characterized by more heat than light. The race to demonstrate various aspects of numerical competence first and best has led to many controversies but little consensus on the capabilities of animals to judge quantities, to count, to add, and so forth.

We started conducting research at the Language Research Center on the topic of numerical cognition in an attempt to avoid controversy. That is, we believed that the argument that the chimpanzees at our laboratory were using lexigrams symbolically would be strengthened if we could also show symbol use (in this case with numeric symbols) in what appeared to be a less contentious research area. As it has turned out, more than a decade later, the assertion that the apes have language skills is probably more widely accepted than the claim that they have counting skills.

Notwithstanding the controversy that surrounds research on numerical cognition by animals, it appears that several general conclusions can be derived from the literature. These conclusions derive from studies from multiple investigators, with multiple species, using several different research procedures. Our intention is not to present an exhaustive review of this literature; rather, we will highlight selected studies that illustrate well the summary principles. Numerous excellent reviews of the literature have been published recently, and interested readers are encouraged to consult these reviews for additional information.

Animals Do Respond
to the Numerousness of Stimuli

The first general conclusion from the literature corresponds to the question that has received the most research attention. Many researchers have attempted to determine whether animals can respond to the number of stimuli, in the same way that they obviously respond to other stimulus attributes like form, color, size, and position. The difficulty with evaluating this ability, however, is that so many other variables are linked to numerousness. Changing the number of stimuli that are displayed also can change the overall surface area, the density, the brightness, the overall pattern, and (with sequential displays) the temporal characteristics (for example, duration or rhythm) of the stimuli. The challenge to the researcher is to demonstrate that the animals are responding to number rather than to these related but nonnumeric cues. Additionally, the learning capacities of most animals are sufficient to permit conditioned responses to stimulus patterns that are familiar. That is, once the subject has been rewarded for responding in a particular way to, say, three stimuli, the burden for the researcher becomes demonstrating that subsequent responses are based on the "threeness" of the stimulus rather than on associations formed to a different element of stimulus on the basis of prior conditioning.

Although many research paradigms have been used to investigate this issue, the most common requires animals to make judgments of relative numerousness (Dooley and Gill 1977). An animal is shown two or more arrays of stimuli (for example, dots) and must pick the array with the most items. In some variations of this procedure, the animal must select the array with the fewest items. Either method is appropriate, because either allows the researcher to test the animal with a range of numerical values and to see whether the animal is sensitive to this stimulus attribute. But as the researcher's ambition is to determine whether the numerousness of the stimuli, rather than some other available variable, is the determining factor in the animal's choices, she or he must also try to control these confounding variables. For example, Roger Thomas and collaborators (1980) at the University of Georgia tested squirrel monkeys with cards on which various numbers of dots appeared. The size, closeness, and pattern of the dots was varied across cards, but the monkeys' task was always to pick from two choices the card with the fewer dots.

Thomas and associates (1980) reported that the monkeys learned to respond accurately to ratios up to seven dots versus eight dots, and that these judgments were based on the numerical attribute of the array. This finding has been replicated and extended—to other species, to other stimuli, to other quantities, and so on—many times. Most recently, Liz Brannon and Herb Terrace of Columbia University used a similar paradigm with rhesus monkeys. Brannon and Terrace (1998) described a series of careful controls designed to eliminate nonnumeric cues to which the monkeys might respond. Even without reliable cues from surface area, density, and pattern, the monkeys reliably selected the smaller of two arrays. They responded significantly better than chance, even on pairs of stimuli that had never before been presented. The monkeys could have responded accurately on these trials only if they were sensitive to numerousness cues.

Note that there is no evidence that the monkeys actually were counting in these tests—that is, that the animals enumerated the individual items in each array and then compared the results of this tabulation. Rather, the conclusion is that monkeys can make judgments of relative numerousness, and these judgments are not based on nonnumerical stimulus cues. Note also that one can painstakingly control, as Brannon and Terrace did, the extranumerical cues for responding, but it is impossible to control all of these cues simultaneously. That is, one can vary the size of the stimuli so that surface area does not increase as the number of stimuli increases; then, however, the density of the stimuli will change with number. When one controls density cues, overall size varies. Each manipulation of numerousness leaves some other cues on which responding could be based. It makes little sense to suppose that animals would use any other attribute or combination of attributes just to avoid the use of number, although some researchers believe that animals use numerical cues only as a last resort, when other more "basic" or more "prepotent" cues are unavailable.

Despite these complications, one actually can test for the ability to make relative numerousness judgments in a situation devoid of density, size, surface area, rhythm, duration, and complexity constraints. If one could replace arrays of physical stimuli (patterns of dots or shapes) with arbitrary symbols that represent each array, then animals could be asked to judge the relative numerousness of the quantities associated with each symbol without the cues normally provided by the quantities themselves. This is just the strategy employed in research with dolphins (Mitchell et al. 1985). The dolphins learned to associate various symbol items, each with a specific quantity of fish. For example, they might be given a choice between a hoop (associated with three fish) and a pail (associated with two fish) and allowed to choose whichever item they preferred. The dolphins were allowed to eat the quantity of fish associated with whichever stimulus they selected. Under these conditions, the animals were significantly likely to select the symbol associated with the greater number of rewards.

We conducted a similar study with rhesus monkeys, using numeric symbols that are even more typical of human experience. Monkeys were shown pairs (and ultimately, up to five) Arabic numerals and were allowed to pick whichever numeral they wanted. Numerals were presented as graphic stimuli on a computer screen, and the monkeys responded by manipulating a joystick to direct a computer-generated cursor into contact with one or the other numeral. The monkeys received the number of pellets, delivered automatically and arrhythmically, corresponding to the value of the numeral they selected. For example, if presented with the numerals 3 and 5, the monkey would receive three pellets for picking the 3 or five pellets for picking the 5. Across trials, the monkeys learned to select the greater of the two numerals—despite the fact that the monkeys were rewarded with pellets no matter what numeral they picked (except when they picked the 0). We reported (Washburn and Rumbaugh 1991b) that one monkey responded to never-before-seen probe trials (novel pairings of numerals that had not been used during training) without error, and replications of the study with additional animals revealed that the monkeys perform consistently and reliably better than chance on these novel pairings of numerals.

What does it mean that these monkeys can see an array of up to five numerals and then select them, in appropriate numerical order, from largest to smallest? Again, there is no evidence that the monkeys are literally counting the pellets delivered and associated with each numeral. But clearly the monkeys learned more than they had to in order to obtain rewards. That is, they received pellets after every nonzero response, and only the relative number of pellets provides a differential cue for the values of the Arabic symbols. Notwithstanding, the monkeys became very skilled at picking between the numerals in a nonrandom way. Did the monkeys learn that the numeral 5, for example, represents five pellets, so that they can perform the relative numerousness judgment task on the basis of a comparison of represented quantities in the same way that they would judge the actual quantities if they were visible? Or did they instead master a complex series of relative numerousness statements, learning for example that the 6 produces more pellets than 5, and 7 produces more pellets than 5, and that the difference between 7:5 is bigger than the difference between 6:5 (and so forth)?

This question echoes the classic contrast between the two meanings of the word *parsimony*, as in the statement that "scientific explanations should be characterized by parsimony." Morgan's Canon states that scientific explanations should not use a more advanced psychological ability to explain performance when a simpler psychological capacity will suffice. That is, one should not explain the monkeys' performance as requiring symbolic knowledge of absolute number, because the "matrix of relative values" explanation also fits the data without supposing complex cognitive ability. Conversely, Occam's Razor defines parsimony by indicating that we should avoid many-step explanations when just a few steps will suffice. According to this view, the absolute-knowledge view is the more parsimonious, as it requires that the monkeys only learn ten things (the amount associated with each numeric symbol), whereas the relative-knowledge view requires that the monkeys memorize a complex matrix of relations: "X is greater than Y by Z much."

Fortunately, the two views are also subject to an empirical test. Because the monkeys can make judgments of relative numerousness of Arabic numerals, and can make judgments of visible arrays of dots, we became interested in what would happen if we mixed stimulus types. If what the monkeys had learned was a matrix of relative values, then we would not expect them to know how to respond to a comparison between, say, the numeral 5 and an array of six dots. If, on the other hand, the monkeys know that the numeral 5 represents "five things," then they should be able to arbitrate trials like this in which the stimulus types are mixed. Georgia State University graduate student Jonathan Gulledge (1999) tested rhesus monkeys under exactly these conditions: monkeys made judgments between pairs of Arabic numerals, between pairs of dot arrays, or between mixed trial types (for example, eight dots:the numeral 4). Even on novel probe trials—the first presentation of each numeral:dot pairing—the monkeys performed significantly better than chance and just as accurately on these mixed trials as on the more familiar dot:dot and numeral:numeral trials.

These data indicate that monkeys not only respond to the numerousness attribute of stimuli, but they also learn the quantity that is represented by each numeric symbol. They can use this knowledge to respond accurately on never-before-experienced trials, even though the knowledge was not necessary in order to obtain pellet rewards.

Animals Can Perform Combinatorial Operations on Quantities

The relative numerousness task also provided a good basis for testing the ability of animals to combine quantities. What would happen if, instead of seeing two arrays of stimuli from which to pick the larger quantity, the animals were shown four arrays and given the sum of two of the arrays? That is, they could either receive all of the items in the pair of piles on the left or in the pair of piles on the right. To solve this task, the animals would have to do more than compare arrays of stimuli on the basis of numerousness. They must also somehow ignore the space between pairs of arrays and perceptually combine the pairs to determine the greater sum. That's exactly what chimpanzees proved able to do.

Sherman and Austin were tested at the Language Research Center using an apparatus that featured four wells, each filled with various numbers of candies. The chimpanzees could choose to receive the pair of candies on the left or the pair of candies on the right, and would receive the contents of whichever pair they selected. In a series of experiments, the chimpanzees were able to select the pair that netted the larger total quantity, even when nonnumeric cues were controlled and even when the single-largest or single-smallest quantity did not indicate which sum was greater. We referred to this ability to combine the quantities mentally and to select the greater total as *summation* (Rumbaugh, Savage-Rumbaugh, and Hegel 1987).

Summation can occur temporally as well as spatially. That is, chimpanzees can apparently sum across a sequence of presentations to select the greatest quantities. For example, Dr. Michael Beran, then a Georgia State University graduate student, dropped candies one at a time into opaque cups and allowed the chimpanzees Lana and Sherman to select which cup they wanted. On some trials, he would drop a few candies in the cup on the left and a few into the cup on the right; then a second experimenter would, without looking into the cups, drop a few candies into each cup. Finally, the first experimenter would drop more candies into each cup, again without checking the contents. Then the chimpanzees would pick between the cups, under conditions in which neither experimenter knew the exact number of candies in either cup or even which cup held more candies. To choose accurately, the apes needed to sum the number of candies, dropped sequentially and on separate occasions by separate experimenters, in each cup and then pick the cup with the greater total. The chimpanzees responded at accuracy levels significantly greater than chance for all pairings (up to a ratio of 7:8), although accuracy generally declined as the total numbers of candies became relatively high and the comparisons got very fine (Beran and Rumbaugh 2001).

In follow-up research, Michael Beran is examining the chimpanzees' ability to handle other combinatorial operations. What happens if you subtract candies from the cups? What if the cups are combined in multiplicative ways? The point of these studies is not to teach the chimpanzees arithmetic per se. Arithmetic is a complex set of rules for combining numbers, in much the same way that grammar rules govern the combination of words. Rather, we are interested in what the capacity to combine and manipulate quantities—in these ways that seem analogous to basic forms of addition, subtraction, multiplication, and division—reveal about the animals' knowledge and use of numerical information.

Animals Can Count

The title of this chapter is meant to be a play on words. On the one hand, we hope to have made the case that animals do count—that they matter, and that the consideration of their data is important for an understanding of constructs of human intelligence, learning, language, numerical cognition, and so forth. On the other hand, the title really is meant to be the answer to a question that has fascinated scientists and others since before the days of Clever Hans, the horse renowned early in the twentieth century for amazing counting skills that were later shown to be the result of cuing.

Counting is a specific operation for ascertaining the exact number of things or events—dots, tones, pellets, responses, alleys in a maze, and so on. It requires a mental or physical tagging of each individual item, the assignment of a different, order-invariant label to each tagged item, and the understanding that the label of the last tagged item also represents the cardinal value of the set of counted things. That is, counting is different from simply judging more or less, and is in fact different from judging the absolute number of things in an array. You may look at an array of three coins and know that there are three without counting them (a skill called subitizing). Literal counting requires enumeration of the items and the understanding that each tag in the enumeration ("one, two, three . . . ") represents not only that item but also the total number of items that have been counted to that point.

How then can one ascertain whether nonhuman animals are using counting as the mechanism for making judgments of numerousness? Two strategies have been employed to answer this question. First, all researchers interested in counting by nonhuman animals have tried to eliminate alternate mechanisms by which a task might be solved. Lacking a viable noncounting explanation, the researchers have concluded that their animals are counting. For example, rats can learn that the third alley and only the third alley of a maze is baited with food. Having learned this, they will enter only the third alley, irrespective of how much distance is placed between the alleys. Could they solve this task by a method other than counting?

Claims that rats can count have also been based on the interesting research of John Capaldi, Richard Burns, and others who study the speed with which mazes are run. In one version of this paradigm, rats find preferred food items at the end of a runway maze on three consecutive trials. The fourth trial is always unrewarded. Predictably, the animals run through the maze faster on the first three trials, which end in reward, than on the fourth that ends without incentives.

How is it that the rat knows, however, that it doesn't need to run quickly on that fourth trial? Given that each trial looks and smells identical to the rat—that is, until it enters the goal box—how could the rat keep track of the trials unless it was counting?

Researchers using this paradigm have carefully controlled all of the extranumerical cues that might be available and useful to the animals, and have concluded on the basis of their findings that rats can count (Burns, Goettl, and Burt 1995; Capaldi and Miller 1988). One downside to this paradigm is that the rats learn to count only to a single particular number; that is, a rat conditioned to count to three cannot count to two or to four. Recently, however, we've used the same type of task with monkeys solving computer-generated mazes. As the rats do, the monkeys solve the maze slower on trials that will be unrewarded. Unlike the task for the rats, however, we can easily indicate for the monkeys a specific number to which they should count, while varying the trial that will be unreinforced, by making the target stimulus the corresponding numeral. For example, if the target in the maze is the numeral 3, the monkeys will be reinforced on three consecutive trials, but if the target is 4 they will also be reinforced on the fourth trial. The monkeys show the predicted pattern of performance: They solve the maze significantly more slowly on the unrewarded trial (whether it is trial 4, 5, or 6). There is no way a monkey could know that the trial will be unrewarded unless it is counting the trials.

We noted earlier that there are two strategies for addressing the counting question, and some researchers have taken the second step of giving the animals the opportunity to show that they are enumerating, in much the same way we might do with children by asking them to count aloud. Sally Boysen of the Ohio State University, Tetsuro Matsuzawa (1985a, 1985b, 1990) of Kyoto University, and researchers at the Language Research Center have each played key and influential roles in this vein of research. Boysen, for instance, has documented tagging behaviors by her chimpanzees as they respond to quantities or the symbolic representations of quantities. That is, chimpanzees would touch or partition individual items in arrays presented in numerical tasks, producing behaviors that look very much like the tagging that children do when they count. These observations complement an extensive corpus of investigations in which Boysen and her colleagues have examined chimpanzees' counting and symbol use. For example, a chimpanzee might travel to one location in the laboratory and view a container with zero to three oranges; then the chimpanzee would move to a second and third site similarly baited with zero to three oranges. Finally, the chimpanzee would return to an array of Arabic numerals and indicate how many total oranges (one to four) had been observed in the three locations. Boysen's chimpanzee Sheba performed at better-than-chance levels on this "functional counting task" (Boysen 1993; Boysen and Bernston 1989), even in sessions in which the experimenter was blind with respect to the correct number of oranges that had been hidden.

At the Language Research Center, the enumerative abilities of the chimpanzees were even more explicitly investigated. Lana, then seventeen years old, was trained and tested over a period of months on a computerized task called NUMATH (Rumbaugh, Hopkins, et al. 1989, 1993). In this task, Lana was shown an Arabic numeral (1, 2, or 3) and was to bring the cursor into contact with a corresponding number of boxes on the screen. Thus she was required overtly to touch each stimulus to produce a set corresponding to the target number—but would she literally count (both enumerate and also stop at the appropriate quantity)? Each time she touched a box, she received feedback. An error was scored on any trial in which she touched more boxes than indicated by the target number, or in which she terminated the trial too early by returning the cursor to the target number before the appropriate number of boxes had been touched. Across versions of the task, the characteristics of the boxes to be touched, the nature of the feedback, and the positions of all stimuli were manipulated. In the final version of the task, Lana performed significantly better than chance on the task without visual feedback. She counted out the number of boxes appropriate to each target number, and did so with no feedback except for her memory of how many boxes had been tagged at each moment.

A different computerized task was used with Lana and the other chimpanzees at the Language Research Center. Sherman, Austin, Mercury, and Lana were tested on a task called ORDINALITY, in which the requirement was again to count out the number of boxes or dots corresponding to a target number. Counting was accomplished by moving Arabic numerals from an array into contact with the boxes to be counted out. In response to the target numeral 4, for example, the chimpanzee might use the joystick to move the Arabic numeral 1 to one box, to move the numeral 2 to a second box, to move 3 to the third box, to move 4 to a fourth box, and then to return to the target number to say "I'm finished!" Although the numerals had to be used in proper order, any box could be tagged. As with NUMATH, errors were recorded when the animal returned to the target numeral too soon, or when too many boxes were counted out.

To eliminate the chance that the chimpanzees were just sequencing the numerals until they reached the numeral that matched the sample, dots were also used as wildcards for some or all of the numerals. Thus an animal could also be tested with the target numeral 4 and required to count out four boxes, using only the dots to tag which boxes had been counted already.

This research is ongoing. At the time of his untimely death, Austin could count accurately to 4 on a version of the ORDINALITY task in which he had to select a quantity of dots corresponding to an Arabic numeral (Beran, Rumbaugh, and Savage-Rumbaugh 1998). We reported data for Lana and her son Mercury showing that their productive counting was accurate to 6 or 7 (Beran and Rumbaugh 2001), and it is reasonable to anticipate that they will continue to improve as the task becomes streamlined to allow quicker responses.

What Comes Next?

Questions remain about which is the best way to teach and to test for counting skills. Undeniably, the productive and receptive counting abilities that have been demonstrated by chimpanzees remain well behind those characteristic of even young children, although one could argue that these limits reflect the failures of researchers as much as constraints on chimpanzee ability. It seems reasonable to ask whether in fact there are limits on numerical cognition by animals. However, it also seems to be time to put some basic questions to rest and to move on to the next round of questions.

There is no reason to believe at this point that numerousness is a less salient stimulus cue than size, position, color, and so forth. The data reviewed here and elsewhere suggest that animals across a wide range of species do respond to the numerical attributes of stimuli— naturally, without specific training, and with ease and accuracy. Moreover, with specific training they can acquire knowledge about the quantities represented by numeric symbols (Rumbaugh and Washburn 1993). Monkeys and chimpanzees have demonstrated the ability to understand the meanings of these Arabic numerals, and can use them interchangeably with visible quantities in tasks requiring judgments of relative or absolute numerousness. Finally, we should move beyond the question "Can animals count?" to new questions pertaining to the nature of symbol knowledge and number-related thought. Indeed, Randy Gallistel and Rochel Gellman—two of the leading theorists in the field of numerical cognition, spanning both the comparative and the human-developmental literatures—have argued that all of the number-related phenomena discussed here and elsewhere show that all animals use a basic and nonverbal counting mechanism. So if we don't need to pursue further the question "Can animals count?" what should the next wave of research be designed to assess?

In a very real sense, the research area of animal numerical cognition has come full circle. It again parallels the ape-language debate that inspired us to begin research on counting. Just as we believe the question for the ape-language issue has changed from "Can an ape learn a humanlike language?" to "What does it mean for an ape to learn, at least at a basic level, a humanlike language?" we anticipate a rich future of research in numerical cognition designed to answer the question "What do numerical cognition abilities allow a monkey, an ape, or some other animal to do that it could not otherwise accomplish?"

V

Rational Behaviorism
A System for Instincts,
Respondents, Operants,
and Emergents

15

Brain Business
Cause-Effect Reasoning

Humans are given not only to thinking in terms of cause-effect reasoning, but also to dichotomous reasoning about what caused a given event. We are ever so prone to thinking that either it was Cause A or Cause B that brought about Event Z, when in fact there can be a large number of causal candidates. Also, the effectiveness of a given causal antecedent for an event might well depend upon its interaction with one or more other antecedents. The world and the events about us are not as a rule to be satisfactorily explained in terms of either-or thinking—but we keep on trying to do so. Good versus bad; we versus they; free versus captive; rich versus poor; family versus nonfamily, win versus lose, and so on—we never tire of our efforts to reduce complex matrixes to digital switches.

Our question here is "Do nonhuman animals reason in terms of cause-effect relations?" Both Pavlovian respondent conditioning (for example, Rescorla 1988a, b) and Skinnerian operant conditioning can produce grounds at least for us humans to think in terms of such relations. The unconditional stimulus of meat powder *causes* the dog to salivate. In a very real sense that is true, as long as a number of other conditions prevails. We must have a relatively healthy dog that is at

least relatively normal neurologically. Its salivary glands and neural ac-
tivating system must be functional, and it will help if the dog is hungry.
Thus meat powder alone is not a sufficient antecedent to "cause" the
salivation, and any number of other ingredients, including a weak acid
solution, will also elicit salivation. On the other hand, we are not so
readily inclined to conclude, once conditioning has been established,
that the conditional stimulus "causes" the salivation. Rather, it is more
likely that the conditional stimulus operates as a signal of something
that, in its own right, literally causes salivation. Only if we first view
the dog after conditioning has been instated might we think, rather
naively, that the conditional stimulus causes the conditional response
of salivation. Across time, however, we would find that presentations
of the conditional stimulus by itself (never again paired with meat or
other unconditional stimulus) loses its effectiveness. The conditional
response of salivation becomes increasingly weak and eventually disap-
pears. Under this condition we now say that the response has become
extinguished. Though extinguished, it has not been destroyed. Rather,
it has just lost its effectiveness.

This fact can be demonstrated by again having the unconditional
stimulus follow presentation of conditional stimulus. Even a single
presentation can revive salivation as a conditional response. It is as
though even a single re-presentation of the conditional stimulus and
unconditional stimulus activates the memory of the conditioned relationship between these two stimuli established during conditioning
procedures—and it probably does just that.

Although, as with Hume (1748), we are prone to think of causes
being invariably contiguous with observed effects, such is rarely the
case in the real world. Even the most certain of imminent events might
not occur. When they do not, we are always well advised to look for
one or more reasons why they have not.

Brunswik (1943, 1952) persuades us that there are "no sure things"
in the real world. Both we and animals are reduced to making guesses
about the validity of cues. Predictions are always subject to failure, yet
both humans and animals must predict correctly often enough to survive and attain goals. John Stuart Mill (1843) stated the obvious in his
argument that real organisms do not wait to discern what the single
condition is under which they are eaten and those under which they
are not eaten. Experience cannot afford all the information needed for

survival. Inferences, guesses, and risks must be taken in the interests of survival, but they don't always succeed. Scavenger birds that dash between lanes of speeding cars have no opportunity to learn by really serious mistakes. When one makes a serious mistake, it becomes the meat to be harvested by the next scavenger.

It is relatively easy for superstitions to develop in people's explanations of events. People use light switches dozens of time each day. Some were doing exactly that when New York suffered a massive power failure. And some of those using the wall switches in their homes or offices just at the very moment of the power failure actually believed that their turning of the switch caused the power failure. And some of them, in turn, felt very guilty for their having "caused" the failure. They did not, of course, cause the failure, but that did not preclude some "victims of logic" from viewing themselves and their use of the light switch as causal to the discomfort of the entire city. Perceptions of events can, on the one hand, lead to valid interpretations of events. Those interpretations can advance science and technology across time. On the other hand, invalid interpretations of events can lead to superstitions and perhaps to practices that, sooner or later, will be associated with the intended event. Dance the rain dance long enough, and it will surely rain. Droughts provide the occasion for many to be duped by those who, with their black powder and cannon and incantations, will cause the rain to come to a specific area in need of rain.

All causes precede their effects. Events associated reliably with one cause might or might not be brought about by another cause. Either a blow or a high-intensity sound can have the same consequence of breaking fine glass. Or one might argue that the blow and the high-intensity sound share a consequence that becomes the same glass-breaking cause: both induce vibrations that break the glass. Animals are unlikely to reason in such a technical manner. Still, respondent conditioning procedures, which demonstrate strongly that the conditional stimulus must precede the unconditional stimulus for conditioning to be likely to occur, can be taken to mean that animals have brains that selectively attend to flow of perceived events across time whenever they go about the business of learning the relations that pertain to their worlds. Backward conditioning, in which the conditional stimulus follows the presentation of the unconditional stimulus, is notoriously ineffective. When it does occur, it is unstable and likely dependent upon memory of traces that endured after the presentation of the unconditional stimulus, traces that were still viable at the moment of conditional stimulus presentation.

Jean Piaget (1930, 1974) was interested in children's perception of causality and concluded that they went through predictable stages. First they learn of the efficacy of their responses. Suckling on the mother's breast can abate hunger, yet the infant has no literal understanding of what causes what. It could never understand that its sucking on the nipple stimulates the mother's breast to make milk. Yet such is the case. Eventually across the years, the child, through its tenacious experimentation with elements of its worlds, discovers a great deal about cause-effect relations, first with regard to motor competence and eventually as structured by formal thought and language. Primates also move along the scale of cause-effect reasoning and logic defined by Piaget as they mature. Quite possibly, some of the apes even reach Piaget's final stage of formal operations (Antinucci 1969). Antinucci and his colleagues also conjectured that monkeys are probably incapable of mastering symbolic communication systems for which the great apes are known to be capable.

Lloyd Morgan's Canon and Parsimony

As we have seen, Lloyd Morgan's canon (1894) advanced the principle that one should never use a more complex framework of interpretation of behavioral phenomena than is necessary. In addition, explanations should be simple, in accord with the principle of parsimony. But a complex interpretation should be used if necessary to be both sufficient and correct. Indeed, Lloyd Morgan did not insist on the explanation being simple-minded, only on its being in keeping with what was necessary and defensible given what was or was not known about the intelligence of the subject at hand. He would not subscribe, for example, to the explanation of a car's speeding down the freeway by the simple account that "the turning of the car's wheels makes that possible." That is surely a simple explanation, but it is not sufficient to be satisfactorily correct. That level of explanation fails to account for the complex systems of mechanics, physics, and human performance involved. It is not sufficiently complex to permit an understanding of how the wheels are powered to turn and how the direction of the car is controlled. Neither is it sufficient to say that a rat, for example, presses a bar in a Skinner box because that response has been reinforced. What does it really mean to say that a response has been reinforced? To reduce that explanation to the operations of giving a pellet of food per bar press does not suffice.

With reference to animals' behaviors we might say that an animal mates or builds a nest because of instinct, here subsumed by the term *biological smartness*. But labeling behaviors does not explain them. Labeling serves at best only to direct us toward the kinds of analyses through which we might obtain a better (though never complete) explanation of behavior. Kuo (1967) did not like the term *instinct*. He thought it a lazy way to explain a behavior. Underneath all instinctive behaviors are complex neural and hormonal and releasing and guiding systems that support or enable the behavior. That said, we will find that the biological bases and parameters of instinctive behaviors both enable the behaviors and constrain them, in that they are not necessarily flexible when faced with the challenges of a changing environment.

Lloyd Morgan's canon has been so pervasively used in accounting for learning by animals that surely we have repeatedly thrown the baby out with the bath water. Take, for example, the effect that the unconditional stimulus has in Pavlovian conditioning and the effect of the reinforcer in operant conditioning. It can be and has been concluded that Pavlov's dogs salivated when presented with the conditional stimulus because during conditioning procedures the conditional stimulus had preceded the onset of the unconditional stimulus by a fraction of a second. Similarly, it has been concluded that a rat learns to press a bar because food pellets, thereby obtained through automatic vending systems, reinforce pressing of the bar. The change of behavior (salivation or bar pressing) has been equated with learning. Learning has been defined as a more or less lasting tendency to respond to a stimulus because of the history of reinforcement for specific responses. Simple? Yes. Correct and sufficient? No.

Cause-Effect Learning by Animals

Take, for example, a rat learning to traverse an elevated T-maze, one in which it must at each choice point turn either right or left, depending upon which turn leads on eventually to the goal box. In between choice points, the rat simply runs down a straight alley. Rats' learning of the way to turn at each choice point works backward from the goal box and forward from the start box. The several choice points in between or in the middle of the maze are the most difficult to learn, as indicated by error rates. The principle of reinforcement declares that what the rat learns is a series of right and left turns that eventually allows for expedient running of the maze. It runs fast on the straight alleys, slows down as it approaches a choice point, and it might even stop to look down both alleys before making a choice. This visual checking of options has been termed *vicarious trial and error* by Karl Muenzinger (1938). Muenzinger noted that the frequency with which rats employ vicarious trial and error at choice points increases as learning is in its critical stages of development. All of this said, rats learn far more than a sequence of right and left responses.

One now well-known psychologist told me (Rumbaugh) of a significant episode when he was a graduate student involved in training rats to traverse an elevated maze. As each rat left the start box of the maze, its speed of running would increase in the straight alley, then slow down as, at the first juncture, a left turn had to be executed. Failure to slow down would result in the rat's literally falling off the elevated maze. Yet with extended training, the day came when a given rat not only did not slow down at the first choice point, it ran faster and faster. When it reached the choice point, it made no attempt to turn left, as it had done dozens of time before. Instead, it skillfully leaped across the space that intervened between the first choice point and a straight alley farther ahead in the maze.

The rat had learned the overall pattern of the maze. Somehow it also had learned of its own motor capabilities to leap. On the eventful trial, the rat tested the hypothesis that it could span the distance, land, then scamper on the next choice point. It succeeded, and its success tells us that Tolman (1948) was quite correct in his argument that rats and other animals, including us, can learn cognitive maps of the environment and use them to define shortcuts and new paths of choice to get from one point to another (Ellen, Soteres, and Wages 1984). For Tolman, learning was based on the relations between stimuli and events of the subject. Thus even a rat might learn about what leads to what, and what can and cannot be undertaken or risked in the interest of efficient procurement of incentives (in this case, food at the end of the maze). Furthermore, rats seemingly develop expectancies about the quality of reward that they are to receive. Failure to have that expectancy confirmed can result in a diminution of performance in terms of accuracy and promptness (Crespi 1942; Krechevsky 1938).

A postscript: the graduate student who observed the shortcutting rat was a student of an ardent behaviorist who did not believe in Tolman's principles of learning. I asked him whether he told his professor of the behavior of the rat and how it adventurously leapt the span. "Of course not!" he said. (He had been reinforced for "keeping the faith.")

We have seen how Lana, my first chimpanzee subject in language learning (Rumbaugh 1977), was being conditioned by Timothy V. Gill to urinate in a pan so as keep her learning area cleaner. Each time Lana urinated in the pan, she was given an M&M candy, a prized reinforcer. Lana rapidly learned that peeing in small amounts netted the most M&Ms. Accordingly, her contributions to the pan grew smaller and smaller, and her receipt of M&Ms increased rapidly.

Contrary to conditioning theory, the response of urination, instrumentally conditioned from that perspective, did not become more vigorous and stronger. Rather, it became smaller and smaller so as to effect more reinforcers. It wasn't urinating that Lana learned; rather, it was stopping urination. Of course, she had to start it to stop it. That said, even the best effort to ration urination will result eventually in the bladder's being empty. When that happened, as recounted earlier, she turned around and spat into the pan, then looked expectantly, with outstretched hand, to Tim for another earned M&M. Clearly, Lana had learned that the task was not just to urinate into the pan. Rather, it was that putting liquid into the pan was "good," and if she could but do that she would receive an M&M. One cannot equate a contribution of spittle with one of urine unless one has made an inference regarding cause-effect postulations and what the task basically is about.

And what experimental evidence is there to extend support for this thesis? First, it should be noted that the novel and appropriate behaviors of subjects just recounted also serve in solid support of the theme here pursued: target behavior changes (maze running and bar pressing and salivation) seemingly brought about by reinforcement are not necessarily the sum total of what has been learned.

In recent years, we had need of developing a training procedure that would result in a rhesus monkey *(Macaca mulatta)* using a foot to

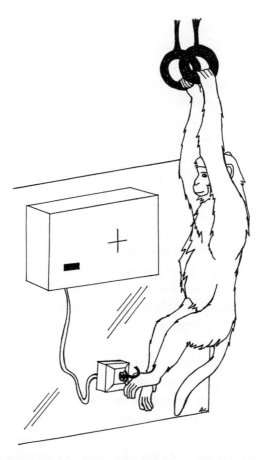

Figure 25a. A rhesus monkey *(Macaca mulatta)* was trained, using a foot, to control the movement of a cursor on a monitor so as to chase, then capture a target. After mastering the task, he was then for the first time permitted to use his hand to manipulate the joystick (see fig. 25b). Without hesitation, he used a hand rather than a foot, despite his reinforced training. His performance with a hand was better than it had ever been with his foot. He had learned "about the task," not specifically to use his foot—though that was the specific response rewarded throughout training. Language Research Center.

do a relatively complex task. The task was to control a joystick so as to skillfully bring a cursor into contact with an erratically moving target on a monitor. It took us six months to succeed in training the monkey to do so. The monkey was not allowed to use its hands in this task (figs. 25a and 25b). The monkey was required to pull down on each of two

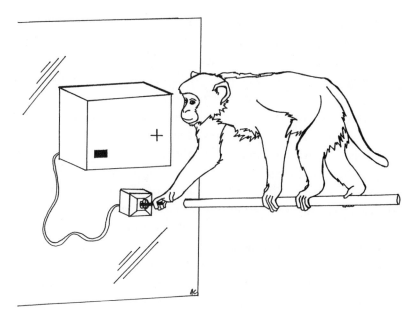

Figure 25b.

overhead rings to start the next trial. Only a foot could be used on the joystick. Once the task was mastered to a criterion of skillfulness, however, we gave the monkey the opportunity to use either of its hands to control the joystick if it chose to do so. What did the monkey do? Had it learned only about using its foot to do the task, leaving it naively incompetent to do the task with a hand?

No one predicted accurately the monkey's behavior. Some eminent psychologists predicted that the monkey would have to start all over, learning to use its hand as it had been conditioned to use its foot. Some predicted that substantial transfer of training from the foot to the hand would occur, that transfer would be positive and would assist perfection in use of the hand. A few predicted that the monkey would do well from the start, from the first use of its hand on the joystick. Everyone was wrong. The monkey was better with the first use of its hand than it ever had been with its foot! The monkey had learned first and foremost about the task: move the joystick so as to make contact with the cursor on the moving target. It had not learned that in this task one must use a foot because that was the motor system used during training.

The point is that, yes, reinforcement can serve to delimit what a subject does and how the subject does it. By selective reinforcement we could have required that the monkey use a foot and only a specific foot. Notwithstanding, that would not have kept the monkey from learning about the task itself. Our knowing just how broad the monkey's learning and comprehension of the task was in this situation depended upon us giving the monkey the opportunity to do it "his way." His way proved to be to use the hand—and with greater facility than even had been mastered in the use of his foot. The cause for success had nothing to do with a specific limb. Here we are reminded of Roitblat's (1988) proposal that cognitive action systems can be conceived of as having nodes that represent different levels of abstraction. The rhesus monkey's training probably generated one or more nodes that represented movements of the foot so as to control the joystick and to perform the computer-based task. Yet the monkey's brain went well beyond that node to establish higher-level ones that served to represent the training situation as a whole, the performance of which was not restricted to a single set of muscles or even to a single limb.

Reinforcement as Payment

Again there is apparent need for working toward an understanding of learning and behavior that goes beyond respondent and operant conditioning frameworks even for animals. Although there is no doubt that reinforcement increases the probability of a behavior's recurring, it does so, we believe, not because it stamps in any specific stimulus-response bond or habit or connection but because it is a resource that serves to meet needs, real or apparent. A reinforcer is really a benefit (pay) for work done. Reinforcement does not explain why an organism learns a relation between stimulus events; the patterns or relations are there to be perceived (learned), but reinforcement might provide a reason for the organism to care about the relation. Real needs such as hunger and thirst and an alteration in ambient temperature are profoundly affected by relevant rewards and reinforcements: they are benefits to the learner.

Apparently creature comfort, such as preferred sitting or sleeping area or the presence of a friend or mate, contributes to the quality of life. It is a benefit to the doer. House dogs don't really need close physical presence of members of the family, but as we all know, they certainly seek them out for general presence, if not contact and petting. Thus the benefit of what we have called reinforcers serves to attenuate real needs that must at some point be met if life and health are to be sustained. Benefits also can contribute to quality of life.

Another way of looking at the effectiveness of reinforcements in their control of behavior is that everyone "likes to be paid," be it for the work entailed in pressing a bar, for which food pellets are obtained, or in some other context of task and reward. And pay need not be just a medium for meeting survival needs. Pay can be money, privileges, control, social companionship, the opportunity to exercise or to hear music, or any of a variety of rewards.

Payment justifies work, but organisms tend inherently to be more lazy than they are ambitious. Given a chance, they will take the easy way to get what they need or want. If it takes less time to get the goal box, where food is to be found, or less energy to take a shortcut, they will figure out how that might be achieved. There is but one way that they can, in fact, succeed in "finding a better way," and that is through brain power.

Brain Power

Brains are metabolically very costly. They consume large quantities of blood sugars and are operational twenty-four hours a day throughout a lifespan. By contrast, muscles can achieve peak loads but cannot sustain them twenty-four hours a day. They, more than the brain, need rest and relaxation. Both the brain and muscles, however, are subject to fatigue and, indeed, exhaustion if they are highly activated for long periods of time.

How is the cost of a brain justified? For one thing, a brain is vital to the coordinated functioning of all systems of bodies, as exemplified by birds and mammals. In addition, they can reason. They can compute better ways of doing familiar tasks. They have been selected across eons for doing just that. They are not passively shaped by the pellets of food that drop into mouths of the bodies that carry them. Rather, brains receive selective input from the environment because of the sensory systems that are subject to great variation across species. Brains fa-

cilitate learning of certain kinds of things and make almost impossible
the learning of still other things. Brains will facilitate the conditioning
of nausea to tastes and food odors, but not to noises and lights (Garcia
and Koelling 1966). Conversely, brains will facilitate the conditioning
of pain to lights and noises, but not to the tastes and odors of foods.
The brain is constructively biased in the ways it facilitates or blocks
learning and performance. Brains are biased to enhance perception
and learning and memory and behaviors consonant with the ecological
niches for which various species have become adapted. Without those
qualities, their high costs could not be justified. Indeed, as the ecological demands placed upon a species diminishes, one finds relatively
small-brained creatures.

The brain, then, has a certain biological preparedness in its basic
design, structure, and function. The consequence is that the brain
takes certain givens from its history and certain givens of the here and
now and computes on a continuing basis, so it appears, what behaviors
are and are not possible. Of those that are possible, the brain computes
their probable efficiencies in terms of energy costs. All of this is to the
end that the prospects of survival are increased—with as much comfort and ease as possible.

Learning, we hold, is not the stamping in of stimulus-response
bonds or habits or behaviors. Rather, learning entails sensitivities to
salience. What constitutes salience? Events of several kinds, especially
those that entail the release of great energies (thunderstorms, volcanic
eruptions, trees falling, avalanches), or events that entail great surprise
or threat (unanticipated attacks, unexpected deaths of cohorts and
leaders). Salience also is inherent in a hungry creature's search for food.
Even slight cues of food become topics of great attention to a hungry
dog. Access to food is even more highly salient. Salience also is inherent in finding a more agreeable temperature condition when too cold
or too hot. To the degree that events are salient to the sensory and perceptual systems of an organism, they will be attended to and learned
about. Memories of them are subject to being stored. Conditioned
stimuli and other cues that are reliably followed by high-energy or important consequences, such as food, can become salient across time
and experience. We will pursue consideration of salience in learning in
the next chapter.

The brain stores memories, so it would seem, with some kind of logic so that memories are recalled in accordance with their relevance, or at least probable relevance, to the challenge of the moment. In ways not well understood, the brain then processes memories and perceptions in a manner that appears to manufacture new and creative relations among them, relations that might become analogues for behaviors, new and inventive behaviors. Were it the case that behaviors are limited to respondent and operant conditioning procedures, there would be no provision for a new behavior to come forth. But novel behaviors might well come forth as organisms must find solutions in desperate situations where no specific behaviors conditioned or perceived in the past will work. Necessity is the mother of invention, and the invention of behaviors might well depend, on the one hand, upon great and real needs that must be met—or, on the other hand, boredom to be broken.

Emergents

The novel, the creative, the inventive behaviors that we here are pointing to we have called and will call Emergents (Rumbaugh, Washburn, and Hillix 1996). The processes that underlie Respondent, Operant, and Emergent behaviors provide, in turn, for the acquisition of learning and behaviors that embrace the activation of the autonomic nervous system, the various skills associated with certain relatively specific tasks, and the generation of new behaviors—new ways of doing the old or doing for the first time that which is essentially new. Only for Emergents are the processes of cause-effect reasoning probably entailed.

For Emergent behaviors to be generated, the brain must have an excellent system for storing and retrieving memories, for memories are the residuals of past experience, past learning. Early assessment of great apes in constrained and unnatural laboratory tests indicated that their memory was very limited; however, we now know that their memories can be very precise and maintained over hours, days, weeks, and even years. As we have seen, Charles Menzel (1999) has shown that the chimpanzee, Panzee, has a remarkable long-term memory for specific events and uses her language skills to solve problems that otherwise would be insoluble.

Within Panzee's view, Menzel hides a favorite food of hers in the woods that surround her spacious exercise yard. At some later time of her choosing, Panzee recruits one of several friends for help. None of them knows that a trial has been prepared, much less what has been hidden or where it is. She recruits a person by quietly vocalizing while pointing to a lexigram on her keyboard, which is mounted on the wall of her cage. Generally, she will point to the lexigram that functions as a name for the object which she has seen hidden in the woods. The food might be any of two dozen or more. Once Panzee is assured that the person recruited sees the lexigram of the food that has been hidden, she then moves quickly into the tunnel that leads into her exercise yard. She gestures to the person recruited to join her out back. Her gestures appear to mean, "Come along with me. You can do it by going around the outside of the building." Once she sees her recruit on site, she then points with a finger and fixates visually on the spot where she saw the food hidden. As her helper gets closer to the spot, Panzee bobs up and down and begins to vocalize with increasing excitement.

She continues to give her helper directions until the recruit is right on the spot that holds the food. By sweeping away sticks or pine needles, the helper quickly uncovers the food, then gives it to Panzee indoors. She was successful in getting her helper to obtain the food for her on all of the first twenty-four test trials and correctly named the food to be found on all but three trials. At times she will cover her eyes with a hand to suggest that the food is "hiding," then point to the backyard to indicate the general area in which it is hiding. She will also specify at times that the food is hiding in sticks—the twigs and pine straw that cover the forest floor. Her memory is precise and specific and is indicative of episodic memory (memory of past events). Throughout, Panzee keeps her assistant coordinated with her in focused attention and action.

Clayton, Griffiths, and Dickinson (2000) have documented that birds can remember what kind of food was cached, where it is cached, and approximately when it was cached. Once food is recovered from a location, the bird rarely checks that spot again. But by important contrast to Panzee, the birds do not seem to use autonoetic consciousness: they give no evidence that they remember having placed the food in a given location, though they remember that there is, indeed, food there.

Tulving and Markowtisch (1998), argue that autonoetic consciousness requires language. That Panzee uses symbols to communicate the specific food hidden and directs her recruited helper to the specific site where it had been hidden, then, fulfills that criterion and strengthens the conclusion that her memory is, indeed, episodic.

As important as it is to learn of Panzee's remarkable memory and her effective recruitment of a helper to obtain, via specific directions, a named food, even more important for the discussion at hand is that she initiated the whole process of recruitment and directing persons to the location of hidden foods without specific training or even encouragement to do so. Across years, Panzee had learned her lexigrams and how to use them to answer questions, to name things, to ask for things, and so on. But she had had no training in recruiting a helper to obtain food that she saw hidden in the woods. Thus her effective recruitment and direction of a helper is a fine example of an Emergent. It had no specific history of reinforcement or training, and it appeared spontaneously at Panzee's initiative.

Panzee perceived the problem at hand (the food was hidden in the woods), and she needed help to get it. For the help rendered to her to be effective, there had to be symbolic communication via lexigram and gesture regarding the name of the food to be obtained and the specific site where it was hidden. Without her learning of lexigrams and mastery of them in communicative contexts in her earlier years, she would not have been able to be so creative when facing a new challenge (Beran, Savage-Rumbaugh, et al. 1998).

We end this chapter with questions pertaining to brain size and function in relation to rearing and cognitive stimulation. Several aspects of the chimpanzee Austin's brain have been examined in the context of lingering theories on the neurobiology and evolution of language and cognition in primates. In terms of morphological asymmetries, Austin (and most other chimpanzees) showed a left hemisphere asymmetry in the planum temporale (Hopkins et al. 1998) and in portions of the inferior frontal lobe, notably Brodmann's area 44 (Cantalupo and Hopkins 2001). In terms of individual differences, Austin's morphological asymmetries in these brain regions were well within the range of values observed in these samples. Notwithstanding, Austin did show a very pronounced asymmetry, indeed the largest of any ape, in a region of the precentral gyrus referred to as the knob (see Hopkins and Pilcher 2001). The knob is thought to be the region of precentral gyrus where the hand is represented, and Austin was strongly right-handed on a number of structured tests of hand use (Morris, Hopkins, and Bolser 1993). Probably the most prominent dimension of Austin's brain was its size, which was measured to be approximately 500 cubic centimeters, very large for chimpanzees (see Rilling and Insel 1999). Austin was also a fairly large ape, weighing about 240 pounds at the time of his death; however, this large size does not account entirely for his large brain. Two male chimpanzees for which magnetic resonance image (MRI) scans have been obtained, weighing about 220 and 245 pounds, had brain volumes of 311 and 388 cubic centimeters, respectively. What accounts for Austin's large brain is unclear, and simple measures of size and asymmetry are not sufficient to fully appreciate what effect, if any, his unique language-training experience had on his brain development. More detailed studies of neural connectivity, neuron distribution, and axonal density are needed to provide greater insight into the effects of differential rearing on brain processes underlying cognition and language.

16

Processes Basic to Learning and Reinforcement
A New Perspective

An organism's world consists of stimulus events that impinge upon its various senses. Not all of these stimuli can or should be responded to; to do so would lead to frantic disorganization of adaptive processes. Choices must be made. Here we explore the bases for those choices. We will discuss both how some stimuli are naturally salient and how the salience of stimuli can be profoundly altered by experience. We will examine how stimuli can become functionally equivalent through being presented together, as in sensory preconditioning. Finally, we will offer a reinterpretation of reinforcement and selected conditioning phenomena. Our purpose is to make the case that reinforcement, as traditionally defined and used, particularly in operant conditioning procedures, has its effect upon behavior not as something that strengthens an association between a stimulus and a specific response but rather as a resource that can be accessed by the organism if other considerations regarding risk and effort are in check. Reinforcers will be redefined in terms of stimulus salience, either natural or acquired, and in the imparting of their functional roles in eliciting behaviors to other stimuli. If positive or appetitive (food, water, and so

on), reinforcers will be conceived of as resources about which the subject learns, even as it learns how these reinforcers can be obtained when
they become relevant to motivation and need. If negative or aversive
(shock, pain, fear, and so on), they will be interpreted as events to escape or avoid.

A Stimulus Perspective on Salience

Some stimuli capture attention by virtue of their salience or prepo-
tency. The perceptual system appears naturally to be biased to attend
to movement, novelty, and sudden changes in intensity. These elicit involuntary shifts in attention. These environmental constraints on attention probably are part of how organisms come to perceive objects to
begin with: from birth, infants are attracted to movement, novelty, and
changes in spatial frequency that characterize edges, and these atten-
tional predispositions provide the basis upon which organisms come
to distinguish figure from background, to group features into objects,
and to transform sensations into perceptions. That is, these environmental cues provide the basis on which we come to know "what is a
stimulus," and these same perceptual learning mechanisms provide the
basis for the detection of higher-order patterns (spatial, temporal, or
causal) that characterize much of complex behavior. One assumption
that underlies the framework we are advancing is that animals (including humans) are predisposed to attend to certain environmental cues.

In textbooks on learning, the complementary topics of habituation and sensitization are often awkwardly integrated. Not seen as consistent with conditioning phenomena or higher forms of learning, habituation and sensitization nonetheless are clear examples of changes
in behavior as a result of experience. Habituation (or its complement,
dishabituation) and sensitization provide two of the sources of support
for the contention that organisms are naturally attuned to regularity or
novelty. Newborn children and other animals decline in orientation to
repeated presentations of the same stimulus (habituation) and show
renewed interest when that stimulus changes. A second assumption
that underlies the framework we are advancing is that animals (including humans) are naturally able and predisposed to detect regularities
(repetitions of patterns). These patterns can be spatial in nature, and

the gestaltists made great strides in describing the principles that govern spatial-pattern perception. But these patterns can also be temporal or even causal in nature. Stimuli that reliably occur together or in predictive sequence will be perceived as a pattern that can be recognized and responded to, perhaps as a compound stimulus or category of stimuli that provide information about a response that is required or a resource that is available.

When we say that something is salient, we mean that it is prominent, something of possible significance that merits attention. Recall Miller and Dollard's (1941) assertion that to the degree a stimulus is strong, it establishes drive; to the degree that a stimulus is clear and defined, it may function as a cue. Hence the salience of a stimulus might be attributable to its physical properties. Loud noises and marked changes in levels of illumination are salient to most organisms. Most organisms take note of something that is naturally sweet or bitter. In addition, learning experiences, as we have noted, can make relatively innocuous or neutral stimuli, such as conditional stimuli, salient; in their association with prized incentives, such stimuli can even acquire properties as reinforcers (secondary reinforcers for Hull and conditioned reinforcers for Skinner). Indeed, stimulus strength, whether natural or acquired, has been an important concept in many models of learning. For example, Hull's (1943) concept of stimulus intensity dynamism represents stimulus strength, and the Rescorla and Wagner (1972) model of conditioning assumes that the strength that might accrue to any stimulus as a conditional stimulus depends on the current strength of other stimuli established as conditional stimuli, as well as upon its contiguity with the reinforcer.

Experiential Constraints

It is an underappreciated axiom: an organism can't learn about the regularities in its experience unless the regularities are there to be perceived. With all the focus on the behaviors that are presumably controlled by stimuli by association and on the consequences of those responses, we lose sight of the fact that there are patterns in the world to be perceived, and that organisms are sensitive from birth to the detection of these patterns. Miller characterized this active pursuit for patterns to be perceived by referring to people (and computing ma-chines also) as "informavores" (Miller 1983).

However, environmental cues are not the only constraints for at-tention. Stimuli are salient not only for reasons of novelty, movement, or intensity. Salience can also be acquired. Indeed, it is reasonable to suppose that most behavior is responsive to these experience-based cues, so that what we do when faced with familiar circumstances is routinized and automatic. This is quite consistent with the tenets of the behaviorists—that is, the notion that behaviors are emitted in re-sponse to specific stimulus conditions in accordance with the results from prior responses. It is also consistent with the views of many cog-nitive psychologists (for example, Norman and Shallace 1980) who have argued that organisms normally handle multiple, competing stimuli according to contention schedules, or previously established priorities and habitual responses. According to this view, supervisory or executive attention is required only under novel circumstances or in cases where automatic responses would lead the organism away from some purpose or goal.

So how are these contention schedules established? How do events become attention demanding, and thus perceived as patterns, in the absence of changes in intensity, movement, or novelty? Does rein-forcement play the central and causal role attributed to it, rather circu-larly, by behaviorists?

There are two procedural constants in every successful instance of operant conditioning: a reliable stimulus-response pattern that can be perceived, and a reinforcer that informs the organism of some avail-able resource. The behaviorist claims that an association between a re-sponse and the stimuli that preceded it is strengthened by the conse-quences of the behavior—that is, that behavior comes under stimulus control as a function of the reinforcer. The reinforcer is then defined as any event that serves to strengthen the association between stimulus and response. In decades of research, this practical principle has re-peatedly been confirmed. Clearly, one can alter the probability of a be-havior by altering its consequence. This research has not, however, produced a satisfactory and noncircular definition of a reinforcer, or a way to predict whether a stimulus will serve as a reinforcer.

We argue that the reason for this is that the reinforcer does not provide the causal force in learning. Humans and nonhuman animals do indeed acquire habits and other operants by means of the conditioning procedure, but the reinforcer is not the reason for this learning. The stimulus is not in control of responding. The stimulus and response don't get hammered in as some simple association. Rather, "the reinforcer" might more properly be termed "the motivator." That is, there are predictable relations in the experience of the organism to be learned (the sound of the bell reliably precedes the presentation of food, studying for an exam results in a variety of pleasant long-term consequences, the layout of the roads that constitute a trip to a shopping mall suggests that a more direct shortcut might exist between the two points, and so forth). But why should the organism care about these relations? Why should the pigeon attend to the consequences of pecking the disk, let alone the differential consequences of disk pecking as a function of whether the light is illuminated? Why should the rat care about the layout of the maze? Why should a monkey care that the numeral 8 represents more of something than the numeral 7? Of course, they shouldn't—and they won't—unless they are given some reason to care, to attend, to learn. Reinforcers are payment for work performed, nothing more. They inform the animal of some valued resource that can be earned. Reinforcers (or rewards, as they are more properly considered) do not cause the animal to learn. They cause the animal, if anything, to act, and by this action the animal becomes exposed to regularities that can be learned. Thus reinforcement is to learning as stress is to catching fish. Stress (or the relief of stress) may be what motivates us to be fishing. But we don't catch fish because we're stressed; we catch fish because we're fishing and there are fish to be caught. Stress is neither necessary nor sufficient for catching fish; but being stressed can undeniably alter the probability that one will catch a fish.

As decades of research have shown, reinforcement is neither necessary nor sufficient to produce learning. This same corpus of research also makes clear, however, that reinforcement (or reward, or relief, penalty, punishment, or any resource that is or is not available) will alter the probability that learning will occur.

Salience and Novelty

Salience and novelty are related, but they are not the same thing. Novel stimuli frequently are salient and stimulate exploration, but even familiar stimuli can be highly salient. Novel stimuli are, by definition, ones never before seen by an organism. Although novel stimuli are generally salient because they are new and offer something for the subject to explore or to withdraw from, we must know that never before have the stimuli been encountered by the organism that one is studying for them to be properly termed novel. Furthermore, weak novel stimuli may not have sufficiently high salience to draw attention.

Our point of departure is the basic proposition that organisms give special attention to and learn about things and events that are reliably associated in time. Sensory preconditioning is established simply by presenting two stimuli always as a pair. Given that each of two stimuli is sufficiently salient to attract at least passing attention, it is in their association as a pair that they accrue a unique and substantial degree of salience. This dimension allows for the associated components to acquire a functional equivalence with one another. Because all procedures in the conditioning of responses entail the alteration of functions of stimuli (for example, the conditional stimulus and the discriminative stimuli, S^D and S^Δ), this most basic of all conditioning procedures, sensory preconditioning, merits closer consideration than it has been given in the literature. Let us review the basic procedure for its study.

After repeated presentations as a pair, one stimulus, S_1, is then used as a conditional stimulus (Papini 2002, 497). After it becomes an effective conditional stimulus for eliciting a response, then the second stimulus, S_2, is tested for its effectiveness as a conditional stimulus, even though it has never been used as such in conditioning procedures. If it is an effective conditional stimulus, sensory preconditioning is said to have occurred: S_2 has accrued both enhanced salience and a functional equivalence with S_1. Its enhanced salience is confirmed in that it is reliably attended across the course of test trials. Its functional equivalence with S_1 is confirmed in that it is now perceived and responded to by the organism as a conditional stimulus—not because it has served in the role, but simply because of its prior pairing with S_1. The stimulus components have become functional equivalents because of their unique association with each other, an association that sets them distinctly apart from other randomly occurring events. It is in their association that they have accrued additional and highly significant salience. Thus we propose that it is through the pairing of stimulus events, even in classical and instrumental conditioning procedures, (1) that the salience of stimuli is modified, (2) that basic processes of learning can be accessed, and (3) that the nature of what historically has been called reinforcement is subject to explanation and redefinition.

We contend that in sensory preconditioning we find, then, a process that is fundamental to the conditioning of both respondent and operant behaviors. Indeed, the protocols for conditioning are designed to ensure that some stimulus (for example, the conditional stimulus in classical conditioning or the discriminative stimulus in operant conditioning) is rather closely paired in time with another stimulus (the unconditional stimulus or the reinforcer). In both respondent and operant conditioning procedures, some naturally salient stimulus event ensues (the unconditional stimulus in classical conditioning or the reward or reinforcer in operant conditioning) very shortly after the presentation of the conditioned stimulus or the discriminative stimulus. Both the conditional stimulus and the discriminative stimulus are relatively subtle, compared to the natural salience of the unconditional stimulus and the reward. They are termed subtle because they don't elicit strong responses, certainly not the response to be conditioned. Nonetheless, because they are presented in rather tight temporal patterns with other highly salient stimulus events (the unconditional stimulus in respondent conditioning and the reinforcer in operant conditioning), we believe that, just as in the processes of sensory preconditioning, the conditional stimulus and the discriminative stimulus acquire functional properties that inhere in the unconditional stimulus or the reinforcer, respectively.

Instincts and Conditioning in Terms of Salience and the Functional Equivalence of Stimuli
Instincts

From an ethological perspective, sign-stimuli (that is, releasers) are perfect examples of salience defined (1) by genetics, (2) by their appearances, and (3) by the behavior that they elicit. Sign-stimuli and releasers are markers of their species, and generally those markers can be detected readily. They are highly salient and effective to members of the same species. The behaviors that they elicit are predictable across individuals within a species. They are both, in effect, strong stimuli in that they reliably induce activity that is well-defined or directed. Yet what assuredly will be salient and attractive to a male baboon as he spots the sexual swelling on the rump of a female baboon most assuredly will be salient but aversive to many visitors who, while visiting zoos, catch their first view of such a baboon. The red dot on a gull's bill that will attract the attention and elicit the pecking of young gulls to obtain food from the parent's gullet might not even be noticed by other birds and mammals.

If one exaggerates the salient attributes of sign-stimuli, one can expect generally an amplification of responses to them. Gulls will work with extraordinary effort to retrieve very large "eggs"—supernormal sign-stimuli—placed by an experimenter near their nest, for example. The bird will reach out with an extending neck, then try to rake the "egg" into the nest with its bill. Supernormal sign-stimuli can result in extraordinary effort that is much greater than that elicited by normal stimuli, a result that reflects an increased orienting response as defined by Denny and Ratner (1970, 208). Another striking example of this principle is that increasing the coloration and size of the abdomen of models of female stickleback fish to make them seem swollen with mature eggs enhances their attractiveness to males prepared to fertilize real eggs. The males' attention to the model is clear in that they initiate courtship behavior and attempt to get the model to swim through a tunneled nest that they have built (Tinbergen 1951).

Salience, then, not only inheres in sign-stimuli, it can be amplified with reasonably commensurate effect. Thus even though genetics can determine whether at least some basic stimuli are salient, enhancement of their salience can have marked effects on the behavior.

Classical Conditioning: Salience and the Acquired Equivalence of Stimuli

Unconditional stimuli are inherently salient. In general, though not without limit, the stronger the unconditional stimulus, the stronger the unconditional response and the stronger the conditional response.

As with sign-stimuli, unconditional stimuli by their very nature have cue properties. Each unconditional stimulus elicits a unique and relatively well-defined response from the nervous system. Hence the properties of the unconditional stimulus support the view that it has salience that both generates and directs behavior.

As conditioning progresses, the conditional stimulus acquires cue properties and elicits behavior as though it were, at least in part, the unconditional stimulus. (However, the response elicited by the conditional stimulus is rarely, if ever, identical in pattern, strength, and promptness to the response elicited by the unconditional stimulus.) As conditioning progresses and the effectiveness of the conditional stimulus increases, one might also say the stimulus has accrued strength and attendant drive-inducing properties, and also that it has acquired newly relevant cue properties. Its salience is acquired and is derived from its reliable temporal relationship with the unconditional stimulus. Conventionally, deletion of unconditional stimuli or rewards is said to induce experimental extinction. Here we will hold that the conditional stimulus derives its salience from a temporal relationship with another event (the unconditional stimulus) and, accordingly, loses its salience because of deletion of that event. Even more pointedly, we offer the interpretation that this is the case because of the functional equivalence of roles that has been established by the close temporal pairing of the conditional stimulus and unconditional stimulus. Salience can be a basic result of perceiving reliable associations between the occurrences of events in time, either concurrently or sequentially, as is the basic procedure for instating sensory preconditioning.

Whereas the acquired functional effectiveness of the conditional stimulus is apparent, the acquired functional equivalence of the unconditional stimulus for the conditional stimulus is generally not noted. Perhaps the reason that it is not generally noted, if even extant, is that the experimenter selects for use as a conditional stimulus one that is quite neutral in that it elicits no strong response, at least none as strong as that of the unconditional stimulus. Indeed, from the perspective here presented, what we term a conditioned response is nothing other than a manifestation of the functional equivalence, within measure, of the conditional stimulus for the unconditional stimulus. It might be fruitful to conduct research in which the conditional stimulus does, in fact, elicit a significant response of its own (as a relative weak unconditional stimulus might) and determine whether the unconditional stimulus acquires the functional equivalence of eliciting it along with its own response on test trials on which, after conditioning has been established, the unconditional stimulus alone would be presented.

But why is Pavlovian conditioning greatly facilitated by having the conditional stimulus precede the unconditional stimulus by a brief interval (for example, one-half second)? We propose that this sequence is necessary because the conditional stimulus inherently is not a very salient stimulus. What salience inheres to it is lost in the salience of the unconditional stimulus as it occurs and elicits a strong response from the organism. It is for this reason as well that having the conditional stimulus follow the unconditional stimulus (backward conditioning) rarely is effective in establishing a conditioned response to it. When it is effective, it is the consequence of introducing it with some element of surprise to the subject (Wagner and Terry 1975). Animals typically learn the regular and predictive relations that govern the availability of food, water, pleasure, relief from discomfort—or the stimuli that are reliably associated with those states.

Operant Conditioning from the Perspective of Salience

In operant or instrumental conditioning, we have nothing like a sign-stimulus or a conditional stimulus involved as in respondent or classical conditioning. What we do have is an organism surveying its environment. The motivational states of an organism will determine in large measure what it attends to and examines. Given hunger, any number of materials will afford odors that will attract attention. A hungry rat will, of course, attend to food. The food is salient because of the rat's motivational state. If it is a relatively simple situation, such as in a box with a lever, the pressing of the bar is not likely to be salient on the first few occasions; however, given that bar pressing is followed by a very salient event—the delivery of food—it derives salience. More specifically, all of the contextual cues and the response-produced cues of pressing the bar acquire salience and strength. Here we attempt explanation of the traditional reinforcers not because they "work," but because the food (the reinforcer) is salient, relevant to motivational states, and imparts its strength and salience to those stimuli associated closely in time with its becoming available as a resource to the subject.

Across time, the stimuli produced by bar pressing become both more distinctive and stronger, and bar pressing becomes highly proficient. These stimuli are assumed to acquire the properties of conditioned or secondary reinforcers, hence potentially capable of making even more remote stimuli (for example, those associated with being put in the lever box) both stronger and salient as conditional or discriminative stimuli. This perspective is reminiscent of Hull's (1943) gradient of reinforcement, used to account for the elimination of maze-running errors backward from the goal box. It also is compatible with Denny and Ratner's (1970) consideration that in this kind of learning situation the animal generates its own discriminative stimuli from among those associated with pressing the bar. It is by the close attention to all stimuli in the context that the learner sorts out those that are reliably associated in time and that predict increasingly salient events. In other words, the learner must differentiate cues and events according to their sequence in an orderly progression across time so as to be able to respond in a manner that results in obtaining the food pellet. This kind of close attention is not unlike the attention and decision making used by rats as they try to learn which way to turn at a choice point in a maze so as to get to the goal box, called Vicarious Trial and Error, first by Muenzinger (1938) and then by Tolman (1948). The probability of hesitation at choice points in complex mazes increases as the probability of eliminating errors (learning) increases. Both Muenzinger and Tolman viewed Vicarious Trial and Error as behavior that reflected decision making by the rat. One can see that Tolman's "expectancy" might form as the subject begins to track stimuli and responses across time until a goal or reward is obtained. Given close temporal association between the initial occasion of pressing the bar (versus doing nothing) and the delivery of a food pellet, this kind of learning is highly probable.

But what are the underlying processes of what has been called operant conditioning? Is it necessarily a reflection of reinforcement, as advocated so vigorously by Skinner? Might there be an alternative explanation?

In measure, we can see the basic phenomenon of sensory preconditioning operating in operant conditioning. Let us examine a situation that entails a discriminative stimulus such as a light, that serves to
signal a bird, for instance, that pecking at a target will result in grain—
reinforcement. With the discriminative stimulus closely coupled with
the access to the stimulus afforded by the grain, we have the basic
condition prevailing for these two stimuli to become functionally
equivalent in their response-eliciting roles. What is the evidence for
that happening?

In the first instance we have the very interesting fact that the bird
pecks the target key as though it is pecking grain. By contrast, if water
is used as the reinforcer for a thirsty pigeon, it pecks the key as though
it is drinking water (Jenkins and Moore 1973). Thus the stimulus of the
light has accrued, in measure, the functional equivalence of grain or
water. The operant formed is not arbitrary in its form but rather bears
the signature of the consummatory behavior relevant to the resource
that ensues.

In the second instance of support for our thesis, let us examine
the phenomenon of auto-shaping (or sign-tracking as discussed by
Domjan 1999, 58). Instead of the experimenter adroitly shaping a pigeon to peck an illuminated target that triggers a grain-access mechanism, auto-shaping entails simply the presentation of a lighted target
followed by access to grain. The bird is not required to peck the target
to get the grain. Nonetheless, across trials the bird spontaneously starts
to peck at the target, particularly as it becomes lit before the grain hop-
per is made available. Thus "shaping" of the intended operant to be
conditioned is achieved without formal training. Why does this happen? Once again, our consideration of sensory preconditioning im-
plied that, with the paired presentations of the lighted target key and
access to grain, those two stimuli will become functionally equivalent
in their roles—and they do. Again, the bird not only begins to peck at
the target key, it pecks at it firmly as though it were grain. If the reinforcer is water, the bird pecks at the target key with an open beak, as
though it were scooping water to drink. In a similar vein, rats are more
likely to mouth and bite the lever with which they work to get food
and are more likely to lick the lever when they work for water (Davey
and Cleland 1982).

Instinctive drift was the explanation introduced by Breland and Breland (1961) to account for why pigs initially carried wooden "nickels" to a model bank and deposited them for food reinforcers but later rooted at the nickels and chewed on them as though they were food. Similar kinds of interfering behaviors emerged in a variety of farm animals carrying out instrumental tasks, and the Brelands used instinctive drift to account for the interference. Our approach, from the model provided by sensory preconditioning, is that as the nickel and the food were paired in time, they became functionally equivalent. Thus the pigs came to respond to the nickels as though they were food. No special change in the pigs' response to their food reinforcers was reported, but we would offer that there might have been changes there as well, such as holding and biting the food as though it were a wooden nickel. There is also an implication that if the delivery of food were delayed for some time after the pig deposited the wooden nickel in its "piggy bank," the pig would not be so likely to come to treat it as food.

A Perspective of Reinforcement

Reinforcement is probably the most frequently used procedural term in psychology. Reinforcement must be a salient event; otherwise the organism would not even attend to it. Let us consider it in somewhat closer detail.

The concept of reinforcement has been used broadly in the history of learning theory and research to account for what is and is not learned. Most theoreticians have argued about what constitutes reinforcement, though generally they agree that it plays some role in learning. Even Tolman (1932, 1948), who eschewed the stimulus-response-reinforcement model, held that the learning of associations between stimuli (stimulus-stimulus associative learning) was enhanced by the consequences of goal achievement.

One reason for our reexamination is that, as noted earlier, no one has succeeded in defining comprehensively and noncircularly the attributes of things and events in general that have been called reinforcers or rewards. What are the mechanisms of reinforcement? To define them only as things or events that increase the probability that foregoing behaviors will recur is satisfactory from the perspective of pragmatics and the operational definition of the term. To define a reinforcer as the more probable of two responses (for example, because eating is more probable than lever pressing, eating can reinforce lever pressing; Premack 1963, 1965) is insightful and pragmatic, but it does not address the underlying mechanism of reinforcement. That said, such a definition is irrefutably circular and, consequently, an admission that we have little scientific understanding of how or why reinforcers work. Of course, the success of our venture here will similarly depend on the degree to which we can eliminate the circularity that might otherwise plague the definition of salience.

Early on, Hull (1943; Sterritt and Smith 1965) emphasized biological-need reduction as the basic mechanism for reinforcement. Tissue needs would include requirements for nutrition and hydration. They also might entail the need for more or less heat or the alleviation of pain, for example—the escape from or the avoidance of noxious or painful stimuli. Apart from tissue-need reduction, stimulus events could become secondary reinforcers only if they had some well-defined past association with a primary (tissue-need) reinforcer (Perkins 1968).

But then there were reports that appeared to be incompatible with an explanation in terms of tissue-need reduction. For example, saccharin is nonnutritive. Its sweetness might be considered a secondary or learned reinforcer because sweetness is a reliable associate of eating sugars. But saccharin never lost its reinforcement value, as long as nutrition was otherwise availed to the subject (Sheffield and Roby 1950). Captive elephants were shown to spend more calories to obtain a pellet of food than the food returned to the nutritional needs of the elephant. With the discovery of the pleasure center in the brain, the tissue-need mechanism of reinforcement was further challenged. Rats would work to stimulate their brains with electric current in preference to earning food, the consequence of which could be starvation. Though one might argue that the state brought about by such stimulation was reinforcing in that it perpetuated bar pressing, it clearly was not a reinforcer in the sense that something was delivered or given to the rat that would serve adaptation. On the other hand, the state induced by stimulation of the rat's pleasure center was not lacking in its effectiveness. Whether or not its effectiveness rests in salience is a moot point, for such stimulation bypasses conventional sensory and perceptual systems. Attempts to avoid circularity by defining reinforcement as a reduction in tissue needs have generally been unsuccessful. Such explanations appear to be contradicted by the effectiveness of reinforcers like saccharin and brain stimulation. Yet if one examines the consequences of pleasure center stimulation in the rat, there is evidence that seminal fluid is produced (Herberg 1963)—the process of which might well be highly salient to the rats.

The protracted controversy in the latent-learning literature was never resolved to the complete satisfaction of those holding divergent perspectives regarding one important question: Can learning occur in the absence of reinforcement relevant to a drive state (food for hunger, water for thirst, and so on) and be activated so as to direct behavior at a later time when the drive state becomes relevant? In balance, tissue-need or drive-reduction theory simply couldn't account satisfactorily for why the locations of nutrients and water were learned without ingestion of them during the course of training trials. Accordingly, the drive-reduction theorists revised their perspectives and suggested that contiguity between stimuli and responses was, in fact, sufficient for learning. What had been viewed as reinforcement by Spence (1956) became an incentive. Motivations for incentives are in total keeping with the perspective that we work to develop in this book; incentives are salient to the degree that they relate to extant or anticipated needs of organisms (for example, food and water for hunger and thirst) or have accrued salience through past learning (money and certificates of recognition).

We need a better perspective regarding what have been termed reinforcers and reinforcements and the conditions that support learning, both simple and complex.

A Revised Perspective on Reinforcement

We have proposed that the basic process that provides for Pavlov's respondent conditioning and for Skinner's operant conditioning, as well as for instrumental conditioning more generally, is the same process that provides for sensory preconditioning. In sensory preconditioning procedures there is no reinforcement, no reward. Accordingly, we propose that what traditionally has been called the reinforcer essentially is but a salient stimulus that imparts its function in eliciting behavior to other salient stimuli in the context, including the conditional stimulus, the discriminative stimulus, and the conditioned reinforcers or secondary reinforcers. What appears to be a one-way sharing or imparting of impact from the reinforcer to these other stimuli is probably more suggestive or specious than real, in that those stimuli are inherently not of the kind that elicit strong responses. Whatever the impact of the conditional stimulus and the discriminative stimulus might be upon the reinforcer or upon the unconditional stimulus or the reinforcer surely is subtle. Even so, it should be subject to measurement.

What, then, are "reinforcers" and their functional role? Their role is not that of strengthening specific responses to specific stimuli, as held by the stimulus-response-reinforcement model, but rather to inform organisms about contextual resources and how they can be accessed by certain kinds of behavior. Organisms learn how to harvest the resources of their environment, depending upon their motivational states now or in the future. Thus the organisms learn via traditional reinforcement methods about resources and behaviors that access them. But they are not locked into a specific behavior or response, unless the one who controls the "reinforcer" resource demands specific responses of the organism if it is to get available resources. For example, once rats have learned to run a complex maze, they can swim it and otherwise negotiate it. The learning is about the situation, the task, and secondarily about specific responses that access them.

Salience and Other Phenomena of Conditioning

Let us now consider some basic phenomena of conditioning and see how they can be accounted for in terms of salience.

Salience decreases with repeated presentations of stimuli (other than the very noxious or painful ones) until they are no longer attended to, provided that the stimulus is not followed by a more salient stimulus, as in classical and operant conditioning procedures. Stimuli that have little or no consequence lose essentially all of their initial salience when they are first encountered. On the other hand, any marked change in the strength of a stimulus may reinstate attention to it. By contrast, an organism becomes increasingly sensitive even to a very weak stimulus that portends something really important. Thus a mother awakens to altered breathing patterns of her sleeping infant. The sound of a doorknob being tried in the middle of the night can awaken almost anyone from a deep sleep. These stimuli have accrued meaning and have become highly salient, though as physical events they are quite weak.

Extinction of responses, once conditioned, is accomplished by deletion of the unconditional stimulus in Pavlov's conditioning protocol and by deletion of the reward or reinforcer in instrumental or operant conditioning. How can extinction be interpreted within the context of salience and the functional role equivalence of stimuli?

In Pavlovian conditioning, the effective stimulus strength of the conditional stimulus accrues salience and, in part, the functional role equivalence of the unconditional stimulus during training when, upon its presentation, the unconditional stimulus follows shortly. In extinction procedures, the stimulus strength of the conditional stimulus (its salience) and its effectiveness in eliciting behavior diminish when it is no longer associated with the unconditional stimulus from which its acquired salience and altered functional effectiveness were derived. In Skinner's operant conditioning, we would offer that the deletion of the reinforcer diminishes the salience of all stimuli emanating from the performance of the operant (for example, bar pressing). Stimuli associated with the dominant motivational strength of the subject (for example, hunger, thirst) continue unabated; given the opportunity, the subject would move on in its search of nutrients. In Skinner boxes, this generally is not provided for; consequently, the subject just quits responding, thereby conserving its waning energies. Nonreward might be viewed as a source of frustration, for, as we have seen, it is not uncommon for the operant rate to increase at least for a short time once nonreward or extinction is begun (Wagner 1961, 1969).

By our definition, both the onset and termination of electric shock, extremely loud noises, very bright lights, noxious odors, and so on are strong and salient stimuli. But their onsets are not appetitive resources, like food and water, which organisms work to obtain. These kinds of stimuli cause discomfort and are to be avoided lest tissue damage be incurred. If encounter with them is unavoidable, then they are to be escaped from as expeditiously as possible. The avoidance or termination of such noxious stimuli is the goal that motivates learning relevant to these kinds of events. Escape and avoidance learning can diminish discomfort or pain, so the diminution or curtailment of aversive stimulation becomes the appetitive state.

Do the principles of salience apply to other conditioning phenomena, such as blocking, shadowing, spontaneous recovery, and stimulus generalization, in addition to the instance of sensory preconditioning discussed earlier in this chapter?

Blocking refers to the phenomenon whereby the conditioning of a response to one stimulus can preclude another stimulus's becoming an effective conditional stimulus for that response, even though the second stimulus presentation is paired with the effective conditional stimulus. The interpretation generally given for this phenomenon is that the second stimulus adds no new information, is redundant, and hence is not learned (Roitblat 1987). Here we suggest that it is the acquired salience and functional role equivalence of the first conditional stimulus with the unconditional stimulus that dominates the context, to the exclusion of another stimulus, even if new. Thus the second stimulus is precluded from becoming effective as a conditional stimulus. As noted earlier, blocking can be eliminated if the subject is surprised with a new or markedly changed unconditional stimulus.

Overshadowing can be illustrated when a compound conditional stimulus consists of two or more stimuli that are used together in temporal association with the unconditional stimulus (Reiley and Roitblat 1978). The stronger, more dominant stimulus frequently becomes the only effective part of the compound conditional stimulus and hence overshadows (Pavlov 1927) the other parts. The salience framework would suggest that the stronger stimulus is perhaps singularly effective as a conditional stimulus because it is the stimulus that first captured the attention of the subject. The attention of the subject has been caught, of course, in relation to the reliable pairing of this stronger stimulus with the unconditional stimulus in time. What is not attended to (the weaker stimulus) is not learned.

In stimulus generalization, responses tend to weaken as a test stimulus varies in frequency or strength from the one used as the conditional stimulus. The salience framework suggests that the test conditional stimuli simply are not as salient as the original conditional stimulus, the stimulus that had accrued salience and functional effectiveness in its temporal association with a stronger, more salient stimulus—the unconditional stimulus. The result with the test conditional stimulus is a lessening of response probability and strength.

Disinhibition is said to have occurred if, subsequent to extinction of a response to a conditional stimulus, the conditioned response reappears with the intrusive presence of a novel stimulus. Thus the presentation of a sound or light or any other kind of stimulus that distracts the subject even momentarily might lead to the reinstatement of conditioned responding. The salience framework would attribute this return of the conditional response to the probability that the introduction of a new stimulus distracts the subject from the extinction procedures. The novelty makes the representation of the conditional stimulus a somewhat more salient stimulus and it becomes effective, for at least a few presentations, in eliciting the conditional response.

Spontaneous recovery of an extinguished response is said to have occurred when, after a rest, the conditional response appears subsequent to the presentation of the conditional stimulus. The lapse of time would have made the conditional stimulus somewhat more novel, hence salient in its representation, thus at least fractionally effective in eliciting the conditional response.

Do the principles of salience apply to responses to novel events, curiosity, and inventiveness? Any stimulus or context that is new or relatively new will attract attention and probably responsiveness. Such is the case as well with the dynamics of social play. Play bouts are, by definition, changing and dynamic. They not only are marked by change but also can be highly salient if play is active. Play affords a stream of salient stimulus events that elicit attention and response and that can be learned in their temporal relationships in play and its outcome. Encounters with strangers or reencounters with others of the same species after a time of separation are events of high salience and provide a plethora of opportunities to learn about their co-occurrence and sequels. These kinds of experiences can equip the participants with a rich body of knowledge regarding social events. Thus the avid play behavior of lion cubs and wolf pups probably helps to prepare them for successful hunting.

The salience of stimuli in social events inherent to new or relatively new encounters between individuals can engender grooming, breeding, physical exploration, and fighting. All such situations afford an array of opportunities for the subjects, be they participants or observers, to learn about the logic-structure and rules of many dynamics of behavior.

Salience as a Facilitator of Attending to What Is to Be Learned

That events that might be obvious to us may not be obvious to monkeys was made clear in an initial effort to establish learning sets in two squirrel monkeys (Rumbaugh and McQueeney 1963). Our first two simian subjects were given a seemingly endless series of two-choice visual discrimination problems, each for six trials, much as had been done by Harlow (1949). Yet after administering five hundred such problems, each for six trials, absolutely no learning set had developed. We reevaluated our apparatus and concluded that perhaps the tethering of the objects, about one inch behind the leading edge of the panel on which choices were made manually, made it difficult for the squirrel monkeys to learn to attend to the objects to be discriminated, one being food rewarded if selected and the other one not. We decided to ensure that each monkey learned about each of the next problems before going on to the next. Accordingly, training continued on a series of problems until the criterion of twenty correct responses within a span of twenty-five trials was achieved per problem on ten of eleven consecutive problems. The result was that the problems were learned more and more rapidly, and when we next returned them to a series of six-trial problems, the monkeys' learning set was robust and continued to develop. Although the objects to be discriminated were salient to our eyes, they obviously were not to our monkeys. Yet with a bit of help, they came to attend to them rather than to whatever else had been their point of focus.

The role of salience in discrimination learning is also exemplified in research that was designed to explore the roles of illumination and color in the learning of geometric patterns by individuals with mental retardation. The stimuli to be learned were arbitrary geometric patterns of the kind used as words with children and adults who are language challenged. They also were like the patterns used as lexigrams in studies of apes' language skills.

In the first studies, the patterns used as discrimination problems were embossed on translucent boxes. The boxes were four-inch cubes weighing but a few ounces. They were easy for the subjects to lift so as to indicate choice on a given trial. They contained small battery-powered systems so that they could be illuminated from their interiors whenever they were picked up. In one condition, the patterns themselves illuminated if the subject made a correct choice. The backgrounds were black and opaque, hence were not illuminated. In a second condition, the patterns were opaque and surrounded by translucent backgrounds. These two main conditions were compared with control conditions that were in every way similar except for the fact that no lighting of the boxes was employed.

From the perspective of salience, both treatment conditions were highly salient in that they entailed illumination of patterns selected whenever the selections were correct. Yet the results indicated enhanced learning with illumination only when the patterns themselves, and not their backgrounds, were illuminated. It is probable that the illumination of the patterns' backgrounds distracted the subject from the relevant cues of the patterns to be discriminated and, by the same token, that direct illumination of the patterns directed the learning to them (Meador et al. 1984).

In another experiment, performed by Meador (1984), the role of color in the learning of patterns was explored. If patterns were black but with different background colors, the subjects learned nothing at all about the patterns. They learned only "which color" to choose. On the other hand, if the lexigrams themselves were randomly colored across the course of trials with a given pair of the series to be learned, the patterns were learned substantially more quickly than if they were not colored. When color was removed from the patterns for test trials, it was clear that the individuals had, indeed, learned to differentiate correct from incorrect patterns. Color had facilitated learning, but the learning was not specific to the colors. In still another experiment, color was randomly assigned across trials, but only to the features that distinguished one pattern from another. Features in common were black; unique features were randomly colored across trials. This condition produced the most rapid learning and most successful transfer to test trials where the lexigrams were, as above, simply black with white backgrounds.

These studies indicate that salience as such does not ensure learning, but salience can facilitate learning when it is directly associated with the specifics of the stimuli to be learned. It is of great significance as well that the facilitation of salience, if specific and directional, engendered learning that could be transferred to new situations where salience, as used to learn, was absent. Clearly, such could not possibly be the case if salience were one and the same with what traditionally has been called reinforcement.

The Ascending Intensity of Salience Within Basic Units of Conditioning

Whenever some attribute defines or follows a basic pattern in diverse situations, one wonders whether it is of consequence. With the events of each trial of classical and operant or instrumental conditioning, salience as defined by the events that occur escalates. We suggest that this growth of salience, culminating in the unconditional stimulus or the reward, might be fundamental to organization of what is learned. Early on, Muenzinger wrote of the Start-to-End Phase analysis of behavior and attendant learning, though he offered no set criterion as to what defined the endpoint. We suggest that the culmination of increasing salience, defined by the reward or goal being achieved, declares an endpoint in time to a unit of behavior. In experiments, these are called trials; in real life they are called experiences.

The patterns of learning that take shape, be they simple or complex, can be termed Gestalts with good form and proven value in adaptation. We suggest that it is the final component of each pattern—be it the outcome produced by responding to a sign-stimulus (for example, pecking a red dot and then being fed by the parent) or by unconditional stimuli or by rewards and reinforcers—that in some manner topically labels the subject material of each Gestalt. These final components may have this function because they are, indeed, the ones with the greatest levels of salience in each pattern.

Within each pattern there generally is an ascending order of salience that culminates with the final component. Each pattern might begin with a relatively innocuous stimulus, or with a response-produced stimulus, as in the first instance of instinctive behavior, such as pecking of the dot on the mother gull's beak by very young gulls. That response leads to a rather remarkable and surely salient stimulus event, as the mother gull regurgitates food into each chick's beak. In the case of classical conditioning, the first component of the pattern to be formed is a rather neutral conditional stimulus. The conditional stimulus rapidly gains salience, however, as it derives it from its being followed closely in time by the unconditional stimulus, which undoubtedly is profoundly salient as a stimulus that elicits a strong and distinctive response to be conditioned. Operant conditioning patterns begin within a context, such as a Skinner box with a bar protruding through a side. Initially, the chance pressing of the bar, produced as the rat explores the chamber, is relatively nonsalient; however, when it is followed by a reinforcer relevant to a rat's dominant motivational state, it rapidly derives salience. Thus in each of these kinds of behavior, the initial step is one that is a relatively innocuous response or neutral stimulus, followed rather assuredly by a rather strong component, receipt of food. This ascending order of salience is nearly universal and might ensure that organisms benefit from the announcement afforded by relatively subtle events that one or more major events are imminent. The ascending salience gives an opportunity for adjustment, for adaptation. Were the pattern generally reversed, it would only signal that the event was over.

A real-life encounter might entail, for instance, the innocuous stimulation associated with looking at and reaching for what might appear to be a perfectly safe item, such as an outdoor mailbox. If, however, a snake then drops from a tree onto the extended wrist, the salience of that event instates new learning, learning that is likely to dominate whatever news might be in that day's mail delivery. Such learning is highly resistant to counterconditioning or forgetting, as can be verified by Rumbaugh, who experienced this incident. One such experience sets a memory that transcends years, only slightly diminished by time.

Further evidence in support of the crescendo pattern of the components' relative salience is nested within the well-established corpus of data that indicates (1) that the stronger the conditional stimulus and unconditional stimulus, within limits, the more rapid is the course of Pavlovian conditioning and (2) that highly preferred rewards can be more effective than those less preferred in learning and execution of instrumental or operant responses. As the levels of salience build within each pattern, note that it is the final component, the strongest of all, that defines the topic or categorical theme of the Gestalt—some for feeding, others for socializing, sleeping, feeding, drinking, fleeing, fighting, and so on.

Gestalts—their organization of individual components and their overall structure—become committed to long-term memory. Just how this takes place is only marginally understood, but their assignment is not random. Rather, there is logic to the process that encodes or relegates each learned pattern or Gestalt to one or more of the systems that structure memory. If it were not so, it would not be possible to harvest the benefits of learning. Patterns learned must be remembered systematically if they are later to be recalled selectively and appropriately. They must, of course, be encoded for their value in adaptation in the relatively specific contexts in which they formed, with allowance for the certainty that the details are subject to change across time. Their value can be profoundly increased, however, if they are stored in files or systems that logically relate patterns to one another.

Neuroscience has much to learn about how a memory is stored and appropriately recalled, then used or integrated with other memories. One model holds that declarative memories are stored by a two-stage process. The learned information in the waking brain is transiently stored in the hippocampus and played back in a compressed manner to the neocortex during sleep. The compression of neuronal sequences allows that events experienced far apart in time are brought together at a temporal scale relevant for plasticity (Buzsaki 1989; Harris et al. 2002).

The Relation of Salience to Traditional Views

Our perspective is consistent with Tolman's psychology. Animals learn the lay of the land, or form field maps, as a result of the regularity that is in the environment to be perceived. This spatial metaphor applies with equal accuracy and facility to the temporal "lay of the land" (the salience of stimuli or events as they co-occur in time, simultaneously or sequentially). In the formation of these cognitive maps, reinforcement and rewards play important roles as a function of their salience and, consequently, become major landmarks. In our perspective, however, it is best not to assign them their traditional roles of strengthening responses to stimuli.

Our perspective is not inconsistent with Guthrie's (1952, 1959; Guthrie and Horton 1946), who viewed conditioning as a consequence of the contiguity between movement and stimulus elements. For Guthrie, learning resulted whenever something changed the stimulus situation and thus protected the last association made. Just as contiguity was all important for Guthrie in establishing relations between stimuli, so, too, is contiguity basic to the framework here developed. In addition, however, we have emphasized that such associations (1) are inherently salient, (2) result spontaneously in the sharing of functional roles or effectiveness of stimuli, and (3) are in turn prime movers in the dynamics of conditioning and learning. Thus the conditional stimulus comes to function as the unconditional stimulus in classical conditioning and the conditional response can carry the signature of the consummatory responses to the reinforcer both in operant conditioning and in the Brelands' misbehavior of organisms.

From whatever sources, stimuli that occur together either concurrently or in close temporal relation acquire additional salience in being coupled. Lightning and thunder in that order can become relatively trivial events because they no longer elicit fear. Notwithstanding, when one perceives a flash of bright light, it is common to listen for the sound of thunder. These associations, once formed, might remain latent for relatively long periods of time, yet they become available for recall on some future occasion.

Our perspective also is consistent with that of those who emphasize the role of some form of reinforcement in the learning process—Thorndike's satisfying state of affairs; Hull's initial emphasis on drive reduction via the satisfaction of tissue needs; and Skinner's definition of reinforcers as those events that support recurrence of an operant in a situation, to name a few. In our framework, however, what they call reinforcement remains important because reinforcements are unquestionably salient events that impart their functional roles in behavior to other temporally contiguous stimuli. The salience of reinforcers is predictably and logically clear when, as with Hull, an event reduces strong levels of drive or intense tissue needs. We differ with these theorists in that we do not hold that reinforcement strengthens associations between specific stimulus events and specific responses. Rather, they alter the functional roles of other stimuli with which they are associated. Throughout this book we emphasize that learning tends to be much more comprehensive than suggested by the traditional stimulus-response framework.

Our perspective is compatible with Rescorla's (1988) framework. Again, with reference to sensory preconditioning, neither the sound of a bell nor a flash of light may naturally produce an eyeblink. If the bell and the light are repeatedly paired, and then the bell is paired temporally with a puff of air to the eye (which does produce an eyeblink), the result will be that both the bell and the flash of light will produce an eyeblink (even in the absence of the puff of air). How does this happen? Clearly the preconditioning cannot depend on reinforcement in the traditional sense, because the eyeblink has never occurred in the presence of the flash of light, and thus has never been reinforced. Similarly, there can be no direct informational relation between the stimuli. The animal might indeed learn, as Rescorla suggested, that the bell provides information about the imminent and predictable appearance of the air-puff stimulus, and thus that the bell produces an eyeblink because it reliably signals the unconditional stimulus, not because it substitutes for the unconditional stimulus. But the flash of light has not been used to signal the imminence of the puff of air. Its utility as a conditional stimulus depends on the fact that the flash of light and the bell have come to be recognized as a compound stimulus (or perhaps as a category of stimuli) as a result of the temporal pattern previously established.

Recall and Generativity: How Is Learning Stored? How Is Memory Accessed?

The questions of how learning is stored and how memory is accessed await answers from neuroscience. That said, it is clear that by virtue of some processes, appropriate behavior is subject to recall. When there is no appropriate behavior to be specially recalled, then the generative processes serve to structure new options. Emergent abilities or emergent behaviors take form. And though this would be accomplished by totally natural operations and systems of the brain, we propose that how it is generated is an elemental form of reasoning, of rationality. Such is basic to the framework of Rational Behaviorism.

We propose that it is via emergent organizations that new modes of response or behavior are generated to serve the interests of survival and adaptation. Outcomes, whether they are sequels of stimuli being temporally associated (as in sensory preconditioning) or of behavior compelled by genetics to sign-stimuli or releasers, or whether they be unconditional stimulus or rewards or reinforcers as traditionally used to "strengthen responses" in conditioning procedures, are important because they define for the organism resources and the conditions under which they might become available. But it is in the enhancement of the salience of initially subtle cues (the conditional stimulus and the context of operant conditioning, including the discriminative stimulus) that they become the functional equivalents of other and more salient stimuli (the unconditional stimulus and the reinforcer or reward) that bring forth learning.

The totality of what is learned is likely a Gestalt that relates the components learned and experienced into patterns. And when new responses are needed with which to address heretofore unfamiliar challenges in the environment, the generative processes of the brain formulate new options that draw upon the functional relations and equivalencies that have been learned. In its most advanced and complex forms, we have the ubiquitous students, artists, musicians, philosophers, mathematicians, engineers, theologians, and scientists attempting to map the unknown.

In the area of primate behavioral development, Mason (2002) sees emergence as a concept that is fundamental to the understanding of behavioral development and that requires new descriptive categories and measurement. Just how new phenomena are generated in the course of development and learning is imperfectly understood. When asked how they are formed, one eminent neuroscientist replied, "God only knows." To come to understand the parameters of Emergents at any level will take decades of research at all levels, but to understand them better along the way will be reward sufficient to the task.

Areas for Research

We anticipate that renewed research on the parameters of sensory preconditioning should be highly informative regarding the consequences of selecting stimuli for pairing from the same natural class (photos of two fruits, vegetables, beverages, persons, locations, and so on) or from different natural classes (for example, a photo of a fruit paired with one of a location). Variations in relative size and brightness of the stimuli to be paired might reveal that the impact of pairing is some positive function of the strength of the individual stimulus members—stronger stimuli (larger and brighter ones) should more readily impart their subsequent roles to the smaller, dimmer ones, for example. Relations between the stimulus members paired and the reward to be given in conditioning paradigms, where one member is used as a conditional stimulus, might tell us of the role of relatedness between stimuli and their role-sharing potential in relation to or synergized by the reward to be obtained in learning situations. Will the sensory preconditioning of stimuli result in quite altered findings in studies of blocking, overshadowing, disinhibition, and so on, contexts in which a stimulus is added after a procedure has been implemented? Will a stimulus that has been sensorily preconditioned with another disinhibit extinction established where the other stimulus had served as the conditional stimulus in learning?

Our frame of reference serves to unify behaviors at several levels and suggests many lines of empirical research that will help to assess the validity of the ideas and hypotheses here advanced. Data are always the best way to assess ideas and theories. With that we are in full accord. That said, we know of no area that cannot be embraced by the theory advanced here. We remain convinced that studies of the temporal associations of stimuli will in the future tell us a great deal about basic learning processes from sign-stimuli through mediational learning and creativity.

17

Harlow's Bridge to Rational Behaviors

Let us now examine a phenomenon that was pivotal to the design of the San Diego Zoo research program, to the formulation of Emergent behaviors, and to the measurement of basic parameters of primate intelligence. The phenomenon is learning set—learning how to learn—defined by Harlow in his classic article of 1949 (Harlow 1949; Rumbaugh 1997). Although we have already discussed learning set with respect to the comparative assessment of intelligence, our current examination of learning set will be from the perspective of the bridge afforded between radical behaviorism and what we call Rational Behaviorism.

Harry F. Harlow is still well known for his discovery of learning-set phenomena, as well as for his studies of social and cognitive development of rhesus monkeys. Although Harlow was not burdened with undue humility, he probably failed to recognize fully the significance of his definition of the conditions under which learning sets form.

A Revolution Within Traditional Behaviorism

Harlow seems to have been more than happy to rebel against the strictures of traditional behavioral theories, which held that learning entailed the establishment of associations, bonds, or habits between stimuli and responses (S-R) or even between stimulus and stimulus (S-S). Anyone who doubts that psychologists, even those focusing on animal behavior, are now on a serious quest for a scientific understanding of rational processes wherever they occur should review the work of Murray Sidman (1994). Sidman advocates the radical behaviorism of B. F. Skinner and eschews any tolerance for cognition. Yet even in his quest as a radical behaviorist for an experimental analysis of the class of phenomena termed stimulus relations, Sidman allowed for emergent relations among stimuli, among responses, among reinforcers, and among all possible combinations thereof. For Sidman, the emergence of stimulus relations is held to be the natural process of reinforcement. By contrast, we hold that it is more reasonable that they reflect the natural operations of a relative complex brain—brain business. Sidman likened his challenge of accounting for equivalence relations and word meaning to that of accounting for induction. We agree. That said, we emphasize that for Sidman, accounting for the processes of induction is a behavior, not a logical process (Sidman 1994, 16, 553).

Stimulus relations and emergent relations are ones never specifically reinforced, never part of the A-B and B-C associative training sessions. In those sessions, where a choice between two objects or patterns is to be made, one learns to select stimulus B in the presence of stimulus A and to select stimulus C as the correct choice when paired with stimulus B, and so on. Notwithstanding the limited and highly structured nature of that training, subsequent tests reveal that untrained relations have emerged. When presented B, the subject selects A rather than another stimulus and also selects A rather than its paired member when C is presented. There are, then, emergent associations between B-A and C-A and even the A-C and C-A equivalence relations that transcend experience with stimulus B. However, Sidman argued that his approach and interpretation were in keeping with Skinner's radical behaviorism and were not the operations that entailed the "C" word—Cognition. Others, including the present authors, would find the phenomenon of stimulus equivalence to be quite consistent with cognitive perspectives on learning and categorization (see Rumbaugh 1995 for a review and further details on this debate).

Harlow was not looking for rationalism in his rhesus macaques during the 1940s. It was a serendipitous finding that literally was made as he pored over his data and reflected upon their meaning. Harlow was attentive both to behavior real-time and to data. His attentiveness led to his several discoveries. The finding was that his monkeys were inexplicably getting better and better in each of a series of studies in which they participated. They were accumulating some kind of positive benefit across time and across studies. Before we explain further just what his discovery amounted to, let us learn a bit about Harlow and the conditions that led to his discovery of what he termed learning set.

A Brief Biography

Harlow got his first faculty position at the University of Wisconsin in 1930. He was hired as a comparative psychologist, but on his arrival he found that Wisconsin's animal laboratory had been recently destroyed. One account holds that in 1932 he converted a house into a primate laboratory. Another account is that without permission he had the lab put up on university property, an action that almost cost him his job. Later, in 1953 and with the endorsement of his university, Harlow converted an old cheese factory into a primate laboratory. That laboratory became the Mecca of primate learning and development. It still stands to this day, and it bears Harlow's name.

Science was not well supported in those years, and Harlow had few financial resources to support his research. At times, his best efforts were beset with disaster. One of his colonies of monkeys was wiped out by tuberculosis. But Harlow was tenacious and refused to quit.

Because of severe financial constraints due to the depression of the 1930s, Harlow had only a few monkeys. As a consequence he used them over and over in a variety of learning studies. It was at this point, when giving close attention to data across the course of the monkeys' service in experiments, that he noted that their learning improved with each experiment. A generalized improvement in their abilities led to more and more facility in learning. Harlow found no reason to attribute their enhanced learning skills to procedures used in experiments.

Insight

Although not a formal student of Harry Harlow's, I (Rumbaugh) was impressed with his work and was totally taken with his definition of learning-set formation. Over a late-afternoon refreshment, while I was visiting his laboratory in the 1960s, he confided that he had written an article in which he had argued that his monkeys had insight capabilities—not unlike those of Köhler's (1925) chimpanzees. At that time, insightful learning was viewed as an epiphanic capability that Köhler's and Yerkes's (1943) chimpanzees brought to their problem-solving proficiencies.

Insight learning was a contribution of Gestalt psychology. Insight was viewed as a process brought about by perceptual reorganization of a variety of experiences across time. That kind of reorganization was antithetical, obviously, to the S-R bonding advanced earlier by Thorndike, then by Harlow's contemporary Hull in the 1960s as habit strength, and by others as well. Insight learning was thought to be limited among animals to the great apes. Had Harlow published his paper advancing the argument that rhesus, along with apes, have the capacity for insight, the role played by past experience in diverse experiments to the rhesus monkeys' learning might have been lost.

One-Trial Learning

But the article fortunately was never published! Harlow came to see that his monkeys' insightfulness in learning was a cumulative product of their long-term experience in discrimination-learning experiments. Their insight was a primary function of their experience and not of their primate heritage. By implication, Köhler's (1925) and Yerkes's (1943) apes had come to be insightful by virtue of their previous experiences of various kinds.

The hypothesis was that the brain of the rhesus, as well as of the chimpanzee, could benefit generally, and not just specifically, from long-term experiences in learning. An interaction between complexities of their brains (nature) and experiences (nurture) across time might serve to enhance generally not only how adept they might be at learning but also how intelligent they might become.

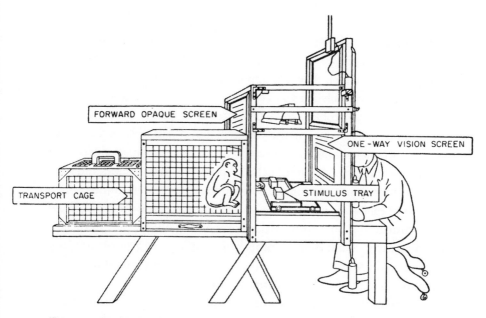

Figure 26. Harlow's Wisconsin General Testing Apparatus (WGTA; Harlow 1949).

The implication was clear enough. A fine brain, stimulated long-term by varied experiences, just might change the nature of the learning process from S-R or S-S associative learning to insightfulness, broaching on rationality held to be unique to humans due to the chasm of language then held to separate humans from other animals. The biomechanical perspective of animals as only Cartesian beast machines (Kennedy 1992) was about to take a body blow. (See Rumbaugh 1994 and Savage-Rumbaugh and Lewin 1994 for a critique of Kennedy's mechanistic view of animals and their behaviors.)

The vehicle that was to move behaviorism into a more rational domain was the Wisconsin General Test Apparatus (WGTA; Harlow 1949; fig. 26). The design characteristics of the WGTA included a simple tray with two food wells located near the front edge. The experimenter viewed the monkey's choices through a one-way vision mirror. An opaque screen on the monkey's cage was positioned so that the monkey could not watch the baiting of the food tray.

Harlow purchased new rhesus monkeys for the study about to

begin. Their brains were pure, clean, and unblemished by learning experiences of any significance. The learning-set protocol that he designed was to give his primate novitiates a programmed learning history—one in which they had opportunity to work on, but not necessarily to master, each of a series of hundreds of discrimination-learning problems. Each problem to be presented to the monkeys consisted of randomly paired stereometric (three-dimensional) objects for ease of perception. The items were small items that could be obtained from kitchens and office drawers, such as aspirin tins, bits of shoes and toys, plastic forms, and random cuts of wood. Chance determined which object of each pair was "correct." If the monkey chose the correct item and displaced it on a given trial, a bit of food would appear in the underlying well. Choice of the other object, in a given pair or problem, was not so rewarded. Kernels of corn were frequently used in the experiments as reinforcers for correct choices.

Each problem was presented for just a few trials, nominally six per problem. (The first few problems were given for more than six trials, possibly resulting in mastery of some of them. That possibility, however, is irrelevant to the point of the experiment and the present discussion.) Despite the insufficient opportunity to learn each problem, Harlow's monkeys showed gradual improvement or facility in learning. Initially, the improvement on trials 1–6 was gradual and had the suggestion of an S-shaped function, characteristic of a simple learning curve.

Gradually, the monkeys' intraproblem improvement became rapid. By the end of the study, the rhesus were correct on more than 90 percent of all trials of any new problem, with the first trial deleted from the calculation because the rhesus could have no clue which object was correct.

The learning curve by groups of discrimination problems changed from one that was gradual and suggestive of trial-and-error learning to one that indicated one-trial learning. One-trial learning was one of the usual criteria for concluding insightfulness. Hence it was argued that the rhesus shifted from apparent trial-and-error learning to insightful learning. Harlow exulted that the monkeys became liberated from Thorndikean bondage where specific responses were associated with specific stimuli. Had Thorndike's principles of learning been operative

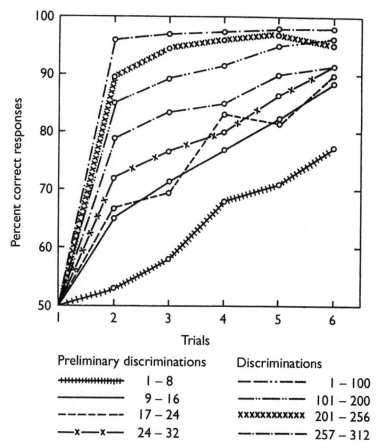

Figure 27. The formation of learning set as revealed in percentage responses correct as a function of successive blocks of training problems. Although performance improved only gradually across trials 2–6 of the first (lowest curve) block of problems, it became nearly perfect on even the second trial of each problem after extended training. By a well-defined course of training, the monkeys' mode of learning changed from one that suggests trial and error to one that is reminiscent of insight. Insightful learning is facilitated by a large brain, but the brain must have knowledge and experience relevant to any new task (Harlow 1949).

in Harlow's study there would have been no interproblem improvement, let alone the eventuality of learning problems in a single trial. The curves that described intraproblem learning had changed from continuous and gradual growth to ones that were discontinuous, after the first trial on each new discrimination problem (fig. 27).

Thinking

With the certainty of any dreadnaught, the monkeys escaped, metaphorically, from the strictures of Thorndikean S-R bondage and entered the domains of reason. Many psychologists of that day were fear-
ful to allow monkeys to so venture—and weren't all that happy even to
allow that we humans reason. But for the first time, there were data to
argue that Harlow's monkeys had come to think. That conclusion
would have been *un*thinkable were it not for Harlow's having carefully
formulated the procedures by which they became seemingly rational in
their learning processes. Harlow's training procedures for the monkeys
operationalized the emergence of insightful learning. The attention of
researchers changed direction to understand how the brain benefits
from experience in the cultivation of its learning and performance capabilities.

Models were developed to account for the rhesus monkeys' facility for learning. The models advanced rules or principles, such as the
strategy of "win-stay, lose-shift": if choice of an object wins a reward,
stay with it, but if a choice loses, shift to the other object on following
trials. But whence did such a strategy arise? Though it served as a
model for science to account for the emergence of learning, was it also
the model whereby the monkeys could be freed of their historic shack-
les of having their responses indentured to stimuli?

Hull (1943) had argued that the basis for learning was primary reinforcement, or the reduction of tissue needs in the body as associated
with the ingestion of food when hungry or water when thirsty. There
also could be secondary reinforcement, or the presentation of something reliably associated with food or water in the past. Secondary reinforcers acquired their effectiveness as rewards in their association
with items that actually did reduce tissue needs. (Cowles 1937 had
chimpanzees work for tokens used to "buy" food.)

Just what served as the reinforcer for correct responses in Harlow's learning-set research is of no trivial interest. Recall that the monkeys received bits of food for correct choices. But Harlow observed that
the monkeys would stuff their reinforcers, kernels of corn, into their
cheek pouches—only to punch them out with a hand so as to continue
to eat them even as they made errors on subsequent trials! What were

the boundaries of reward? And what was to be done when Harlow's students learned that just the opportunity to manipulate puzzles and objects was sufficient to support learning and that the introduction of food rewards for so doing served only to disrupt the manifest curiosity—or salience (see Butler 1965).

Rationality

Just where was psychology going? Indeed, the monkeys and psychology seemed to have been spared the fate of "going to Hull." And they have not. Studies of animals and their learning and behavior have become increasingly rational from every vantage point since Harlow's report of learning set. Facility of learning by animals was possible, but it was not the dictate of genes alone. Rather, it requires maturation and development through generalized, yet relevant, experiences.

Harlow's report of learning-set formation had a great impact in that the frequency of maze studies diminished as WGTAs were designed and built to enable research with a variety of animals. Primate programs of research and study were spawned in universities across the land. Psychologists were apparently aware of the profundity of learning-set phenomena as presented by Harlow in his 1949 presidential address to the Mid-Western Psychological Association. Everyone was extraordinarily quiet. Even the clinking of ice in glasses was silenced, and conversations were hushed as Harlow made his revolutionary presentation on learning sets. For those of use who knew Harlow but did not hear his address, it is not difficult to imagine his stentorian voice, clear as a trumpet and crisp with the thrill of the moment, articulating the methods whereby insightful learning could be instated in brains of otherwise naive primates. The implications for the development and understanding of even human intelligence were manifest. A revolution had been started that would move us from radical to Rational Behaviorism.

Harlow's selection of macaque monkeys was a requisite to the success of the study. The species probably was selected because they were being imported in large numbers for polio research, and consequently were available. Had Harlow used any of the prosimian primates, or some other small-bodied monkey, such as the pygmy marmoset or lemur (see Napier and Napier 1994), he probably would not have lived long enough, or persevered long enough, to observe dramatic improvement in their learning facilities across experiments. Macaques probably have the best learning facility of all the monkeys, both New and Old World. Their brains, large and complex, serve well the operations of complex learning.

Children, several primates, a variety of other mammals (cats, rats, squirrels, and horses), and even chickens were assigned to learning-set research (see Fobes and King 1982). Gradually it became clear that, as suggested by Harlow, brain evolution and its cortical elaborations were important to the formation of learning sets. Training did not have equivalent effects on all species. Contingencies of reinforcement could select responses, but they could not instate the strategies, the hypotheses, the insights necessary to the formation of learning sets.

New studies of brain structure and function were undertaken. Macaque brains were lesioned to determine where the loci of learning sets were. The critical importance of the cortex generally and particularly the frontal region became apparent. Recall that elsewhere we have discussed improved methods based in learning-set methodology, and that it is with the absolute amount of extra brain tissue afforded by the processes of encephalization that learning-set formation is enhanced for the larger primates (Rumbaugh, Savage-Rumbaugh, and Washburn 1996).

A Concept Whose Time Had Come

Why had Köhler and Yerkes not developed the concept of learning sets? Both had a basic sense of its operations. Robert Yerkes used the phrase "learning to learn" in one of his books (Yerkes 1943, 130), as he considered the general contribution that experience offered to learning and problem solving by the apes. He even recounted that chimpanzees' initial learning of discrimination problems is specific and limited to the objects of a given problem. With protracted experience, however, learning become "extended, generalized," or "relative." "I have long suspected that in many of our experimental studies of habit formation our chimpanzees really do not perceive the essential aspect or aspects of the problem for a long time, and that they may not rightly be said to have begun to profit by experience until this perceptual process occurs" (Yerkes 1943, 130). And Köhler (1925) had reported that if the difficulty of problems for the chimpanzee became too hard too quickly, it deterred the cultivation of their insightful problem solving. Indeed, Schiller (1952, 1957; Schurcliff, Brown, and Stollnitz 1971) learned that only if a chimpanzee is thoroughly familiar with sticks is it likely to use them innovatively as tools to solve problems. Every researcher with apes has learned that they will balk and simply stop working if problems encountered are in any manner beyond them.

All we can suggest is that the concept of learning set had not reached its time. Neither psychology nor the public was ready to receive and understand it. Then, too, the charisma of Harlow's personality and speaking are not to be discounted. He worked hard and well at advancing his ideas and findings.

Much of the opposition to the use of primates in research probably stemmed from the combination of Harlow's learning-set data with rhesus and his subsequent studies with rhesus infants to determine the effects of social isolation upon development. He wanted to discern how total social isolation affected the infants' long-term learning, social, breeding, and parental competence (Harlow and Harlow 1962). It was at this point that voices in the classrooms started to change from exuberance about learning-set formation to protest as infant monkeys were put into "pits of despair," as Harlow called them. The students seemed to object to putting any creature so bright as the rhesus had proved to be in learning and cognition into aberrant rearing conditions. So as an unintended consequence of Harlow's work, the animal rights movement has gained great impetus (see Blum 1994). Because monkeys have marvelous learning potential, they must have good familial rearing—rearing that affords both good parenting and playmates.

Harry F. Harlow started a revolution of thought and value regarding animals. The idea inherent in Harlow's learning-set research is that animals can indeed think (Harlow and Harlow 1949). To many psychologists, this has been a revolting conclusion. To others it lit a slow-burning fuse that has inspired rethinking of how animal learning and intelligence should be researched and conceptualized. At the same time, the continuity of complex learning processes between monkeys, apes, and humans had been further affirmed. That animals can think does not disturb most laypeople, especially pet owners. Philosophers and staid psychologists of yesteryear are more likely to resist that notion.

Learning set is an emergent change in the learning process. Harlow's contributions were to underscore the significance of learning set and, as important, to provide the definition of the procedures whereby it can be expected to emerge. His contribution to our concept of Emergents, as a category of behavior and learning coupled with Respondents and Operants, is both exemplary and basic. Just as Harlow documented the shift from trial-and-error learning to one-trial insightful learning, a major challenge has been to document similar shifts as a bonobo, for example, comes to comprehend novel sentences of request and to engage in novel forms of complex communication.

18

Rational Behaviorism

Now the tradition in psychology has long been a search for the property of the stimulus which by itself determines the ensuing response, at any given stage in learning. This approach . . . is no longer satisfactory as theory.

Hebb (1949, 4)

Research reviewed in this book, along with the vast body accumulated during the course of the twentieth century, supports the conclusion that animals, and notably the primates, are intelligent (Heyes and Huber 2000; de Waal 2001; Gallistel 1992). They have mastered problem-solving, cognitive, and social skills that require high-level symbolic operations thought impossible of them even twenty-five years ago. Neither their complex skills nor ours are to be accounted for satisfactorily in terms of basic associative conditioning. The complex processes of learning-set formation; speech comprehension by apes; the creative use by apes of flint for knapping sharp chips for use as cutting tools; and primates' planning, prediction, and symbolic skills for language and counting are but a few of the complex phenomena that entail the syntheses of knowledge and experience by complex brains.

The conditioning of responses and the detailing of behavioral patterns, whether in the laboratory or in the field, remain important, but it is now acknowledged that behavior may be well beyond specific responses conditioned. And the experiences of everyday life even during infancy can have major effects upon how learning takes place and how learned information is or can be used.

The quality of rearing conditions, contexts, and methods can have life-long influence on learning ability, intelligence, social behaviors, and all facets of reproduction, including breeding and infant care. Adult competencies of adult primates rest in large measure upon their early environmental rearing, learning, and experiences. It is not an overstatement to assert that their abilities for the really complex dimensions of learning, comprehension, problem solving, inference, tool making and use, and creativity is born in the interactions of nature and nurture from birth onward to adulthood. Although rewards and goal achievement are important to behavior and learning, by themselves they do not generate the intellectual structures and systems that will enhance the animal's generalized cleverness in a broad field of novel challenge. And here it should be noted that the rearing of captive primates for exhibit and for biomedical research generally does not afford optimal conditions for extraordinary intellectual and social competence in adulthood. Thus any one small group of chimpanzees in captivity is what it is, but it certainly is not a standard, typical, or normal group from which one can make statements about chimpanzees wherever they are found. Their strains of intellect and social complexity vary widely with the contexts and laboratories within which they are bred and reared. Hence discrepancies regarding reports of what apes can and cannot do can be specious in that they are reflections of artifactual differences in their rearing and maintenance.

Tolman's Impact Upon Rational Behaviorism

As we have seen, traditional behaviorism, from the early 1900s to the present day, has focused upon learning processes basic to classical conditioning, operant and instrumental conditioning, and discrimination learning to the end of accounting for the establishment of connections between stimuli and responses (S-R) and between stimuli and stimuli (S-S). The emphasis was upon understanding basic learning processes in the anticipation that, once they were well understood, we would understand even the most complex learning and behaviors of humans. One notable exception was Tolman's work (1948).

Tolman was heavily influenced by Gestalt psychology, yet he viewed himself as a traditional behaviorist: he believed, along with Hull and others, that if an understanding could be achieved of a rat's behavior at choice points in mazes, the majority of even human behaviors would then also be understood quite quickly. His concept of a cognitive map approximates something of an understanding that an organism might achieve as a function of exploration and learning in complex situations, such as in the organization of house, office building, or city. He argued that animals could learn to relate behaviors and goals and, as a consequence, be clever when faced with a novel challenge, such as having one or more routes to the goal box blocked. He also argued that rats formed hypotheses about how to execute choices in complex situations, such as in mazes, and that they formed expectancies about what they would encounter or obtain by certain behaviors. Their behavior was not random but rather organized and patterned—strategic, if you will. If their expectations were exceeded, as with a special bit or amount of food at the end of a complex maze, their behavior markedly improved. On the other hand, if their expectations based on past experience were not met, their performance deteriorated in speed and accuracy. Tolman's psychology is very much alive, and the framework here advanced is compatible with his school of thought.

We should note at this point that the connectionism of today, however, portrays quite a different picture of learning and adaptation when contrasted with traditional behaviorism of yesteryear. With the advent of computers and neural-net or parallel-distributed models, learning and behavior across time and experience are simulated and modeled. The simplistic associationism of the past is supplemented in contemporary connectionism by the rulelike patterns of activation that emerge (in exactly the sense that we're describing in this book) in the hidden layers of the network. Relational learning (acquisition of the *exclusive or* rule, XOR) can be recognized in the general symphony of activity of the nodes that individually are responsive only in associative ways.

The point, however, is that traditional behaviorism did not really attend to the emergence of complex behaviors and skills of animals. Tolman did; modern connectionism can. Though Köhler's and Yerkes's studies of insight learning were of interest even to the behaviorists, they were viewed as something to be understood as forms of learning in conditioning, maze learning, and discrimination learning, for example. Neither K. W. Spence (in his research at the original Yerkes Laboratory in Orange Park, Florida, and arguably Hull's prime student) nor Vatsuro (*The Study of Higher Nervous Activity in Anthropids,*

1948, available only in Russian) found anything in apes other than basic conditioned skills. In no measure were their findings of such a nature because of the training given to their chimpanzee subjects in highly constrained situations. The Russian colleagues of Vatsuro, one of whom was Pavlov, agree that the ape's special intelligence was wholly a reflection of more labile conditioning and in no manner included the insightful problem solving reported earlier by Köhler. The Russians attributed the "idealess" behaviors of their chimpanzee to its lack of true language. We, of course, judge the negative findings and conclusions of these notable scientists of yesterday in contrast to the programmatic research findings reported in this book that serve to document substantial verbal-skill accomplishments by apes and to illustrate how modern computer-based methods serve to facilitate both language learning by apes and remarkable problem solving by them and rhesus monkeys.

Rational Behaviorism allows for the emergence of new behaviors generated by cognitive operations of the brain. In addition to recognizing behaviors formed by respondent (Pavlovian) and operant (Skinnerian) conditioning procedures (see Domjan 1998), it incorporates a new category of acquired behavior—Emergents (Rumbaugh, Washburn, and Hillix 1996). As with both respondents and operants, Emergents have their defined antecedents and consequences, although these antecedents and consequences are quite different from the ones corresponding to respondent and operant conditioning. As we shall see, the antecedents of Emergents are not so clearly behavioral functions of single independent variables and training as are the antecedents of respondents and operants.

Emergents, then, embrace all forms of animal cognition—the abilities to acquire concepts, to learn insightfully, to learn complex skills and behaviors via observation, to make and use tools, to learn the basic dimensions of language, and in many other ways to manifest advanced intelligence. Rational Behaviorism is advanced within a comparative behavioral framework, one that rests on the Darwinian principle of continuity, both psychological and biological, particularly from apes to humans (Andrews and Martin 1987; Sibley and Ahlquist 1987; Bates, Thal, and Marchman 1991; Beran, Gibson, and Rumbaugh 1999; Le Gros Clark 1959; Tuttle 1986). The term *rational* reflects the inclusion of all forms of Emergents generated by learning and cognition; the term *behaviorism* acknowledges the fact that the only data available to our science are behavior. In that light, all psychologists fundamentally are behaviorists. What many psychologists, ourselves included, do not subscribe to is the assertion that traditional behaviorism is a reasonable way to account even for animal learning and behavior, let alone human learning and behavior.

A Three-Part Framework

Rational Behaviorism acknowledges and embraces, then, all behaviors—respondent, operant, and emergent—including those that are usually classified as instinctual. Though there are basic mechanisms and processes of learning and behavior that are not necessarily rational, instinctive behavior being the clearest instance, we hold that the rational operations of the brain have their roots in the basic processes whereby behavior is changed by a widespread set of operations, including those of respondent and operant conditioning and even those attendant to instinctive behaviors. For example, homing pigeons learn to home, in large measure, because homing has been genetically selected. Experience is necessary, however, for their homing to become proficient and effective under a variety of extreme conditions. Does the birds' improved performance across time reflect the formation of cognitive maps, of sets of variables that would enhance their homing competence if moved to new terrains and quarters? How have their learning and homing skills been improved as a result of homing under a variety of conditions while maturing?

We propose that particularly with our own species we have a great deal to learn before we can comprehend how powerful unlearned tendencies and instincts are to our individual and social lives. Are our perceptions of and decisions about other individuals and nations influenced more than we comfortably are ready to acknowledge because of unlearned inclinations to fear difference and to deal harshly with it?

Manifestations of Emergents

Emergents can be manifested in at least two distinct forms. First, they can be manifest as new behavior patterns that are noted for being syn-

ergistic, integrative, and clever. Second, Emergents also can be manifested as new capabilities, such as speech comprehension and flint
knapping, that are not to be accounted for satisfactorily as simple conditioned responses or behaviors, established by conventional conditioning procedures.

But our framework proposes that learning instated via basic respondent and operant conditioning affords elements essential to the
formation of emergent behaviors and capabilities. They do so because
they afford opportunities to learn of predictive relations and patterns
between events and behaviors. Once learned, those predictive relations
can be subject to the integrative processes of complex brains. In sum—
though at the risk of oversimplification—conditioned behaviors are
responses based on glands and muscles in relation to antecedent and
consequent events; Emergents are new behavior patterns based on
principles or new capabilities generated by the natural integrative
processes of brains. Emergents reflect what we assume to be the natural
operations of the brain in functions of detecting patterns, defining categories of perceptions and experiences and the relations between those
categories.

The Logic of Memory Systems

Some of the most compelling data in support of this point regarding
Emergents come from the several studies with Sherman and Austin
(Savage-Rumbaugh 1986). Sherman and Austin were remarkable in
that they classified their several word-lexigrams very accurately into
two categories, foods and tools, that were designated by their own
word-lexigrams. They also were precise at categorizing items for which
they had no word-lexigrams into those categories. In cross-modal testing, when shown only word-lexigrams, they nonetheless were able to
select by touch alone an exemplar for it (Savage-Rumbaugh, Sevcik,
and Hopkins 1988).

Moreover, whenever Sherman and Austin learned the name of an
item, their conceptual skills for similar ones spontaneously and accurately were applied to the new name and examples of it. If they learned
the name for a new food, all their skills with food word-lexigrams
transferred spontaneously to that name; if the word they had just

learned was a tool, all of the conceptual skills that they had mastered in relation to a set of tools applied spontaneously to that name as well. Their conceptual systems seemingly embraced new entries, sorted them into the appropriate category for memory, and applied to them skills mastered for materials and events related to other members of that category. This, in turn, suggests how the processes of redintegration work to call forth from one small cue, or a fragment of a memory, other information that fleshes it out. It also suggests how, when the subjects are confronted with a new challenge, that relevant information and memories are recalled on some kind of priority basis. Thus chimpanzees who know about boxes will be likely to stack them for use to obtain overhead incentives, such as bananas; however, if they know nothing of boxes, they will be unlikely to stack them for novel use. Although a chimpanzee might use a stick to knock down a banana tethered overhead, it must know about sticks and how otherwise to use them to do so. If a chimpanzee, as in a zoo setting, knows nothing of sticks, it will probably be afraid of the stick initially and will spend a great deal of time learning of the stick's properties and trying out its use in various ways.

We assume, then, that the brain is, by virtue of its evolutionary history, a natural system of detection and synthesizing systems. The patterns detected include those obtained from classical and instrumental conditioning. Our position is compatible with Roitblat's (1982) view that all learning entails some form of representation; both stimulus-response conditioning and learning as well as cognition reflect representations. In addition, the patterns detected include recurring experiences and observations obtained through the course of everyday life. Whether the patterns to be detected are provided by conventional conditioning paradigms or through observations of daily events, it is the reliability of their individual logic structures that affords information to the organism from which Emergents might be generated. The brain might be thought of as coming to differentiate the predictable from noise, to define the salient apart from the trivial of the world. As we have seen, salient events may be inherently captivating by reason of genetic declarations (sign-stimuli and releasers of instinctive behaviors) or of their natural energies (thunder, for example) or by reason of experience with them (for example, conditioned stimuli).

Characteristics of Emergents

Although Emergents probably incorporate a broad spectrum of the animal's respondent and operant conditioning history, several significant points clearly differentiate Emergents from respondents and operants (see Rumbaugh, Washburn, and Hillix 1996). Some of the main points of contrast are that

- Emergents' initial appearances come as unanticipated "surprises" to the researcher;
- Emergents provide novel response patterns and solutions to problems;
- Emergents form covertly, hence unobtrusively or silently;
- Emergents generally cannot be charted (learning set is a notable exception);
- Emergents afford new behaviors that have no specific reinforcement history;
- Emergents emphasize a class of experiences;
- Emergents entail the syntheses of individually acquired responses and experiences;
- Emergents are not subject to specific stimulus control, as are respondents and operants;
- Emergents frequently reflect rearing conditions or early experience;
- Emergents tend to be positively associated with brain complexity (per species and maturation).

Areas of research of the kind that are known to generate Emergents appear in table 1. The list is not exhaustive, but rather illustrative.

Assumptions

Every scientific frame of reference entails working assumptions that, over the course of time, might or might not prove reasonable. Nonetheless, assumptions can have heuristic value that can be considerable at least for the foreseeable future. Despite the great progress that has

Table 1. Research Areas That Produce Emergents

Emergent	Investigators	Characteristics
Learning set	Harlow 1949; see Schrier, Harlow, and Stollnitz 1965 for a review; Treichler and van Tilburg 1996	Primates' and childrens' learning changed from trial and error to one-trial learning as a function of number of problems. Lists of learned discriminations were integrated through simple training with the first and last members of those lists.
Transfer index	Rumbaugh and Pate 1984; Rumbaugh, Savage-Rumbaugh, and Washburn 1996	As an interaction between increased brain complexity across taxa and increased learning prior to test, primates' transfer of learning changed from negative to positive (see fig. 4).
Mediational learning	Rumbaugh and Pate 1984; Rumbaugh, Savage-Rumbaugh, and Washburn 1996	In association with increased brain complexity across taxa, learning shifted from associative to mediational or relational.
Ape-language research	Savage-Rumbaugh 1986; Savage-Rumbaugh and Lewin 1994; Savage-Rumbaugh et al. 1993	Chimpanzees learned to use arbitrary symbols to represent items, to categorize them symbolically, and to communicate about them in their absence. Also, they learned symbols by observation and came to comprehend syntax of human speech (see fig. 1).
Stimulus equivalence	Sidman 1994	Reinforced choices of specific stimuli in discrimination learning generated many other relations between stimuli.
Latent learning	Blodgett 1929; Tolman 1948	Rats learned about mazes by exploring them, and were able to choose a food location when hungry and a water location when thirsty.
Mapping	Menzel 1973	Chimpanzees, carried and shown lo-

(continued)

Table 1. (continued)

Emergent	Investigators	Characteristics
		cations of foods in an open field, subsequently obtained them by traveling a route that required minimal effort.
Recognition of self in mirror	Gallup 1987	Chimpanzees, if reared in social groups, came to recognize their images in mirrors, but did not do so if reared alone.
Counting by a chimpanzee	Beran and Rumbaugh 2001; Rumbaugh et al. 1989	Lana, chimpanzee, learned to count in that she could remove one or more boxes from a video screen in accordance with the value of each trial's target number, ranging from 1–7, with only her memory of intratrial events to guide her choice.
Ordinal judgments of numerals by macaques	Washburn and Rumbaugh 1991	In transfer tests, rhesus monkeys were able to choose the larger of two numerals, never before paired, as a consequence of learning the relative pellet-values of experience with other pairs of numerals 0–9, during training. They had acquired a matrix of relations between all numerals.
Integration of temporally separated explorations of maze segments	Ellen, Soteres, and Wages 1984	Rats learned a three-table "reasoning-type" problem via unreinforced exploration of separate segments on separate days.

Source: Reprinted by Psi Chi, The National Honor Society in Psychology. © 2002. All rights reserved. Reference: Rumbaugh, D.M. (2002, Winter). Emergents and rational behaviorism. *Eye on Psi Chi, 6,* 8–14.

been made in brain research, we still know remarkably little about how the brain does its business. How does it store learning, memories, and knowledge, and how does it afford selective retrieval of information relevant to the moment? One thing is certain, the brain is not an organ to be conditioned in any simple manner. It is a highly sophisticated system that is bent on making sense out of the storms of stimuli that buffet it. It has an active role to play in challenges of survival, and it appears always to be on line (even during sleep) and to function synergistically to that end.

Here we assume that through the course of development and attendant general exploration and experience in the environment, the organism (especially if a primate) will learn both specifically and comprehensively about that environment. The organism might well learn, predicated by its genetic preparedness by way of instincts and readiness to attend, that the environment affords

- events, some of which are controllable, in that their causes can be identified and manipulated, some of which are not;
- resources, some of which prove useful and beneficial, some of which are useless or irrelevant;
- risks, the unknown, dangers, or painful events, all of which generally are to be avoided.

We further assume that the organism will learn of

- costs: all activity, all behavior entails metabolic costs and, in the extreme, discomfort and pain. Every opportunity entails risks and costs.

Accordingly, the animal might well learn by exploratory behavior and observation of others how some events and resources can be managed or controlled. Things learned might include how to find and prepare foods for eating and how responses to available items can lay the foundation for creative problem solving (Birch 1945; Hall 1963; Schiller 1957). These kinds of daily events generate emergent behaviors that might be more efficient and more interesting ways of obtaining or using resources than those prescribed by convention (Rumbaugh, Riesen, and Wright 1972). Rational Behaviorism posits, just as did Tolman, that the organism will come to attend to the consequences of its behavior. As the organism learns to do so, it will be observed to monitor the environment and to monitor the consequences both of its own and others' behavior. The organism will monitor its behavior to the physical and social environs as though it is alert to the detection of possible cause-effect relations.

In sum, even in its elementary expressions, behavior and its governing parameters have been selected via genetics, brain evolution, perception, and learning to be oriented insofar as possible to controlling events in the service of sustaining life, and to maintaining states that are not aversive but rather afford relative comfort. Behavior makes it possible for organisms to strive for control over their environments and themselves. The achievement of control becomes more noticeable in complex organisms and notably in the larger primates (notably the great apes and humans) than in relatively primitive forms. Control can be achieved in measure by what we earlier called biological smartness, but without doubt the strategies and tactics formulated in the pursuit of control are most efficiently designed and carried out by psychological intelligence.

Brain, Function, and Maturation

Let us consider how traditional conditioning terms might be modified and how new ones might be defined for the writing of a Rational Behaviorism intended to unify respondents, operants, and Emergents. We begin by formulating more formally assumptions about brains in their roles of enhancing survival and reproductive success for species in general.

Evolution of brains has included systems that have become highly sensitive to patterns among things and events that tend to occur either together or sequentially and to the specific temporal or predictive relations among them.

Brains have become increasingly sensitive to things and events that are of vital significance to adaptation for species in accordance with the ecological niches within which they have their histories of evolution.

Accordingly,

Brains are not neutral in their sensitivities to stimuli and experiences. Brains have become highly proficient in these operations in response to selective pressures of survival.

Brains have evolved to become increasingly sensitive to the logic structure of environments and experiences associated with them in various ecological niches. If an environment has no logic structure, it generates only noise. Brains learn nothing from noise and do not develop normally as a consequence. On the other hand, in environments where there is logic and a relation between things and events, brains become organized and mature so as to absorb a great deal of information and organize it into "best fits" among both the specifics and principles to be titrated from life experiences. This is the vector whereby the specific logic structures of early environment can result in young apes that might come literally to understand human speech.

In the extreme, the brain "learns everything," though it places differential emphasis on things according to their relative salience.

Definitions

Salience. Things and events that capture the attention may be defined as salient. Things and events might be inherently salient (for example, thunder and lightning on a clear, hot summer day) or salient due to past experience and attendant learning. Inherently weak stimuli can become highly salient because of other things or events that have reliably been associated with them, either contiguously or sequentially in time. In other words, predictive relations, once discerned, generate salience. Salience is a basic parameter of perceptual attention, learning, and performance. Salience is perhaps the most powerful parameter of learning. Naturally salient cues can be inherently powerful and used as unconditional stimuli (for example, shock, bright light, loud noise) in classical conditioning. Relatively subtle (nonsalient) cues can become salient if used as conditional stimuli in classical conditioning. If they have histories of reliable association with salient things or events, they can function as Hull's secondary reinforcer and as Skinner's conditioned reinforcer. Biological needs, as for food and water, can result in otherwise subtle cues becoming highly salient through association with events whereby those needs are met.

Stimulus. A stimulus is a unit of raw energy that impinges upon one or more receptors of the body. A stimulus may have its origin in the external environment or within the body. It may evoke a sensation depending upon its strength. (Note: a stimulus lacks definition in the perceptual field of the subject in that it lacks meaning.) To the degree that a stimulus is specific, it can acquire cue properties; to the degree that a stimulus is strong, it is salient and can induce a drive or motivation for the organism to pursue or avoid it. (This perspective is consistent with the view articulated by Miller and Dollard 1941.)

Cue. A stimulus that, due to its distinctiveness, has come to serve as a sign or marker to signify possible consequences of response is a cue. Stimuli that serve to elicit instinctive behaviors have relatively well-defined cue properties (as with sign-stimuli and releasers). As a result of experience, including those defined by conventional conditioning procedures, well-defined stimuli can acquire cue properties.

Response. A rather specific action of a muscle or gland is a response. In a conditioning experiment, a response is targeted for becoming conditioned to some conditional stimulus or discriminative stimulus. It is relatively constrained in its form and function. Examples include a reflex arc, pressing a bar, or pecking a key. A response might be reflexive or learned.

Behavior. Actions that generally entail the patterning of neural events (even as in thinking) or the coordination of muscle groups constitute behavior. Examples include running a maze, riding a bicycle, dancing, singing, climbing, talking, foraging, writing, pursuing prey, or operating a computer or phone. The term *behavior* is more generic than *response*, in that all responses are instances of behavior.

Resource. A wide array of benefits—foods, liquids, shelters, objects, money, other animates, and so on—constitute resources. Things and events can be defined as resources either because of their inherent nature or because of learning and experience.

Benefits. Benefits comprise resources harvested in and from the environment through behavior. Benefits can be inherent in certain behavioral changes and states (for example, resting or sleeping after high-energy expenditures) and can help to sustain both life and the quality of life (for example, flavorful foods instead of bland foods only for sustenance). Benefits serve to justify the execution of behaviors by their servicing biological needs and quality of life. Benefits are obtained in the field by foraging, manipulating and using objects, engaging in social interactions (grooming, play, breeding), and so on. In captive and laboratory contexts, other terms—*incentive, goal, reward*—are applied to specific kinds of benefits. Because a benefit can have the consequence of bringing sharp focus to a specific behavior and its perseveration, as in conventional instrumental conditioning procedures, it might erroneously be concluded that a specific behavior or response is all that the organism has learned. The revised framework here advanced would allow for the subject to be learning, all the while, comprehensive overarching principles about context and attendant qualities or relations for future adaptive behavior patterns. Accordingly, benefits also might be tantamount to what has been learned in situations above and beyond their pragmatics. Thus the reader should not conclude that what is here called a benefit is what traditionally has been termed a reinforcer.

Incentive. An incentive is something relatively specific to be earned or obtained, given the appropriate response or behavior in the appropriate temporal and physical contexts. Incentives can be bits of the organism's perceived or known environmental resource bank, such as food and water. An incentive also might be a controllable event or a preferred activity (such as play) as well as a tangible object (such as money or certificates of recognition).

Goal. A goal generally is more complex or comprehensive than an incentive. Nonetheless, a goal has incentive value and functions accordingly. Both incentives and goal achievement can become foci of attention, intention, and expectation.

Reward. A reward is an incentive, the access to which is under the control of another being or system, such as a vending device. A reward is properly viewed as a payment for a specific response or behavior. A reward is not to be viewed as something that has the power of directly or indirectly strengthening a connection between a stimulus and a response or between a stimulus and a stimulus; that is, it is not to be viewed as what has been called a reinforcement or reinforcer.

Costs. All responses and all behaviors entail costs of execution (fatigue, risk of injury, boredom, depletion of blood sugars, time, tissue wear, inability to execute other responses concurrently, injuries, and so on). All opportunities entail risks and costs as well as benefits.

Reinforcer and *reinforcement.* Reinforcers and reinforcement have been subsumed, viewed, or redefined as environmental resources or incentives obtained, goals attained, rewards received as benefits because of behaviors engaged in by an organism. The Rational Behavioral framework posits that the organism learns about resources, incentives, rewards, and goals, how they might be used or what they can be used for, and how they can be accessed efficiently when needed. More basic is the issue that, traditionally, it has been held that a specific response, not the organism, has been reinforced. We posit that the organism monitors its behavior and learns of its effectiveness in the continuing challenges of adaptation. Because the traditional roles of reinforcer and reinforcement as terms in traditional behaviorism are in basic conflict with the framework of Rational Behaviorism, they are not needed and hence are deleted as useful terms.

Rational Behaviorism incorporates basic learning afforded by classical and instrumental conditioning paradigms, along with learning induced by logic structures of the environment as perceived by the organism. Rational Behaviorism anticipates that what is learned by an organism is probably far more comprehensive and complex than single responses to single stimuli. Synergistic use of whatever is learned will enable the organism to be creative and clever as some positive function of the complexity of its brain (Gibson 1977, 1990; Jerison 1985), as exemplified notably in mammals, particularly primates, humans included (Bruner 1972).

Implications for Research

Psychologists and students of animal behavior need to refine research strategies and tactics to increase the probability of detecting Emergents. In turn, we need generally to be more sensitive to the possible effects that genetics, early rearing, and social contexts might have both upon what is learned and the expression of what has been learned. Generally, we should no longer be content to study only how single responses are acquired by the procedures of traditional reinforcement. To do so biases our findings to support the proclamations of Descartes and the traditional assumption that animals are stupid and that there are no rational bridges between the dynamics of their behaviors and ours.

Clearly, a more sophisticated understanding of how brains work will help research tactics for studying the products of Rational Behavioral processes. Thus the following questions are posed:

- How might the brain work to accommodate implications of this revised perspective?
- What natural mechanisms of physics and neurobiology might generate emergent behavioral options from neural systems?
- How are memories organized and stored so as to be subject to logical or systematic rather than random recall?
- How does the mechanism of a fractional stimulus event serve to redintegrate and restore the original memory system and to rationally compare it, if necessary, with new ones?
- How do motivation, intent, and strategic thinking serve to recruit memories that serve as resources to constructing new behavior options for challenges at hand?
- How do memories resonate with one another so as to initiate thinking (Hebb 1949; Lyon and Krasnegor 1996)?
- How are apparently new capabilities, such as apes' becoming able to comprehend novel sentences of request, established neurologically?
- How, in sum, do organisms become creative and insightful, equipped with new capabilities and skills for learning rather than forever subject to none but trial-and-error processes?

A Question

Behaviorally, how might relevant research be directed?

1. Problem solving generally benefits from a quiet environment; a quiet context constrains the activation of irrelevant memories, thoughts, and ideas. Background sounds should not impede thought through the activation of irrelevant memory systems. Specific contexts, across time, can support specific themes or topics of thought. How can environment be optimally defined for creative thought? Does the effectiveness of environmental support for problem-solving efforts change as a function of time and exposure?

2. Cues or hints can enhance deliberate efforts to think, to be creative. Creative thought can benefit from brainstorming ideas with others who have relevant interests and backgrounds. How can dimensions of creative thought be best defined and implemented?

3. It generally takes more time to recall memories of the distant past than those of recent experience. What kinds of assistance might be extended both to the effective encoding of learning to memory and to the facilitation of selective recall of what has been learned, both recently and in the distant past?

4. Long-term memory is served by having a period of silence and rest and a learning session. The process of consolidation is served by not having extraneous stimulation or activity following learning. Are there significant exceptions to this principle that would enhance prompt consolidation of learning so as it integrate it logically to other learning?

19

Overview and Perspective

Throughout the history of psychologists' efforts to understand animal behavior, the questions that have been front and center have been "What stimulus is the animal now responding to? What is the history of reinforcement for it to do so?" In this book we have worked to look beyond the bounds of those questions. We have worked to go beyond traditional instinctive and conditioned behavior in our exploration of animal intelligence. We posit that with evolution of the brain there have been trends not only to enlargement and complexity but toward malleability of orientations in cognition and learning. As important as been our assumption that the brain itself has been subject to the evolution of certain highly constructive, creative, and synthesizing processes. We believe that within the brain, notably of the larger primates, ourselves included, there has been a honing of inherent operations that sensitively detect predictive relations from the day-in dayout experiences of infancy and subsequent maturation. The brain stores them as memory and then, in barely understood ways, organizes and interrelates those memories.

The memory systems themselves are organized for selective recall of information to some positive degree of the relevance of that information to the here and now. For example, Lana's free recall of lists of word-lexigrams held several important surprises (Buchanan, Gill, and

Braggio 1981). First, effects of both recency and primacy were strong—the first and last lexigrams were remembered best. Second, clustering effects were noted; Lana tended to cluster her recall of word-lexigrams in relation to their categorical relations, either of background color or meaning. If she did so on the basis of color, it was at the level of a preschool child; if she did so on the basis of semantic category (food, object, color), it was in a manner that might be expected from an early elementary school–aged child. All of this effort has served to bring us to the concept of Emergents, which, with instincts, respondents, and operants, belongs to the new field we here and elsewhere have termed Rational Behaviorism.

Traditional behaviorism has been loath to give any role of agency to organisms (Mackintosh 1994): behavior is to be accounted for quite satisfactorily by stimuli, responses, and their sequalae. By contrast, Rational Behaviorism does not deny all agency of action to the organism, be it a human or other animal. Allowance is made for thinking by animals. Their learning, memory, and selective recall are all viewed as possibly relevant, if not critical, to the context within which new behavior is forged and manifest. Brains of animals differ in their style of learning and organizing memories. They also differ markedly in their capacity to orchestrate complex and constructive responses to complex and changing environments.

Hard Science, Life Science

Traditional behaviorism has patterned the development of its framework after that of the so-called hard sciences. This approach is a serious error. Although the "behavior" of atoms and molecules is a reflection of natural forces that emphasize fields of force within which there are units of matter or force that attract and repel one another, and although they organize into highly complex systems (the universe included), they don't have life in a biological sense. Although it is true that all biological systems are made of those same elements, there is a "value-added" dimension called life. That value-added dimension is not just a nicety; from an evolutionary perspective, it must have service to other systems in some manner for life even to be tolerated, let alone be selected for.

Just what that service initially was remains a topic for conjecture well beyond the scope of this book. Our point is, however, that the value-added dimension of life confers a different behavior to the systems from that of inanimate systems. Vegetable life affords some "behavior," but of a kind quite different from that of animal life. Plant behavior is limited to tropisms and mechanisms for obtaining and managing moisture and nutrition (including, in some plants, metabolizing insects). Plants have no nervous system and give us no reason to suspect that they make decisions or learn, as do animals.

By contrast, in all complex forms of animal life, the centerpiece is neural control. Animal forms that have only a few controlling ganglia surely have less capacity to learn, remember, and make choices than do animals with more complex neurological systems. Worms are biologically smart, but not psychologically intelligent. Animal forms with very complex and large brains, relative to the sizes of their bodies, count on their generative operations for survival. The brain might still afford marginal survival even when grossly damaged, but a nonfunctional brain most assuredly equals death. (Indeed, a patient who becomes brain-dead is declared legally dead—without life to the degree that necessarily justifies other patients' intensive care and rights.)

We have argued that the brain has had to prove its worth, else it would not be tolerated from the perspective of extensive metabolic demands. For it to be sustained, it simply must pay its way. It must do things! It must interpret sensory stimulations, it must coordinate all kinds of bodily processes in real time, it must learn and smartly remember things learned, it must recall what it has learned so as to enhance the probability of success in efforts to adapt, it must pilot the body to needed resources and away from fields of high risk and danger, it must govern eating and activity as it also eliminates wastes, it must govern social behaviors, and on and on. The brain must prove to be a "for profit" organization of highly costly units—or it will not be tolerated from an evolutionary perspective.

There must be more to behavior and life than response to stimuli and contingencies of the environment. That "more" includes, we assert, the honing of natural roles of agency. Organisms, humans included, do things and behave and thereby gain perspectives of themselves and their competencies both as individuals and as social agents.

Agency of the individual encourages the refinement both of motor and of behavioral and psychological competencies. Why does a young eagle ever fly? What great risk it takes with absolutely no reinforcement history of gain from having done so in sheltered conditions. Why does a young ape repeatedly climb and descend, climb and descend a single box? Why does it repeatedly climb and leap off of a cabinet? We posit that these kinds of activities are engaged in and perpetuated because they are possible, and that they are then evaluated by the doer as improving or not. Improvement is both necessary and sufficient to their operations. Play behaviors are rampant in mammals, if not in birds. Why? We posit that here again the behavior provides the player an opportunity to perceive and to score itself in terms of gains and losses. Gains encourage repetition of the behavior, and losses lead to termination or at least revisions of practice, play, and other forms of risk-taking activities.

So, here, in brief, we assert that traditional behaviorism has failed to take proper notice of the contribution of life to the behaving systems that theory seeks to understand. We posit that the brains of animal species have evolved to give the individual a running start to successful adaptation. We now know that even infants can perceive complex patterns. Instincts and reflexes are marvelous encouragements to adaptation and survival. Classical and operant or instrumental conditioning are also marvelous, affording as it does new degrees of freedom and information vital to the organism. That said, Emergents afford animals the most comprehensive and generative organizations, the most competent psychological systems for addressing the novel and complex challenges to be dealt with in the service of adaptation and reproductive success (Rumbaugh 2002).

Landmarks on the Path to Rational Behaviorism

Let's review some landmarks of our trek in somewhat greater detail.

Behaviorism

The behaviorist tradition of psychology has emphasized the search for environmental stimuli and for the reinforcement history of responses.

Behavior is a reflection of contingencies, past and present. Responses are reinforced, but not organisms. This strategy has by design left no role for the animal as an "initiating agent of what it does." Neither has it allowed any room for any form of mental operations, such as thinking, planning, weighing the probabilities of outcomes of behavioral options of choice, and so on. The causes or "instigators of behavior" were to be found in the environment. Animals responded to stimuli, but they were not capable of generating any behavior as agents of action. The results of behavior declared its survival or demise.

Animals came to be viewed as empty boxes, which certainly served to ensure objectivity. Regrettably, it also ensured that the behaviorists' account of behavior could be neither correct nor ever complete. That view ensured, most egregiously, that scientific study would wring from its behavioral bases the richness that characterizes behavior. Complex behaviors, such as choice of route in a maze or learning which of two stimuli should be selected, would be classified as responses "checked" as correct or incorrect. These data would be sufficient for the science, but not sufficient for understanding the dynamics of the behavior and what has really been learned by the organism. The relating of behavior to biological mechanisms would be of little interest to experimental psychologists of learning. Biological considerations would be left to the physiological psychologists, who were, at best, interested in the most basic forms of behaviors such as reflexes and perception. In due course, it was posited that there would be essential equivalence between the behaviorist's framework and brain science. That act of faith has not been substantiated to date.

Responses and behavior patterns were, and would remain, the grist of psychology. Cognition was dismissed as mentalistic or epiphenomenal. Although such an approach enhanced the psychologists' perceptions of themselves as hard-headed scientists, as were the physicists and chemists they emulated in their science, it also assured that their science would exclude the very attributes that signify life itself—a sense of being alive and a sense of knowing something about one's environment and what one could do.

No physical element or matter has anything akin to biological life. By contrast, probably most forms of animal life do have some level of distinguishing self from other. We now suspect that at least the more complex forms of animal life have some primitive awareness of their own existence, needs, comforts, and plights. Certainly we humans have rich perceptions of ourselves and the environments within which we cope and live. Such perceptions are there, of course, not because we are human, but because the inanimate materials that our bodies use to build cells and biological systems have evolved so as to produce emergent phenomena.

There has been avid debate regarding the extent to which animals of other species are aware of themselves and their environments (Griffin 1984). Clearly, we encourage the reader to suspect that at least the primates, notably the great apes, have senses of being that are not too different from our own.

Behavioristic schools of thought were satisfied to study so-called simple behaviors, such as maze learning and bar pressing. The assumption was that learned behavior was behavior regardless of the species and that a single set of principles and laws would account for them all. Hull (1943), for example, allowed for species effects only by some exponent in his mathematical formulations. Neither did it matter, so the early behaviorists maintained, which species generated the simple behaviors. Species were selected for study based on cost of acquisition and maintenance, on ability to reproduce in large numbers, and on relatively short lifespans. A premium was placed on "naive" subjects, be they rats or pigeons or cats. Subjects (excepting college sophomores, of course) were used once and then terminated—literally. The long-term use of subjects became acceptable in conjunction with Harlow's learning-set phenomena and studies of monkeys and apes in primate centers and the field.

The fact remains, however, that such studies of behavior have not served to elucidate the processes of complex behaviors—such as those involved in learning mathematics, composing music, writing poetry, and so on. Simple behaviors have important roles, and they might well be accounted for in terms of environmental stimuli to which organisms have been reinforced for responding. Although studies certainly can be used to get the individual to attend to complex materials, as in mathematics, composition, and the arts, they are not designed or even intended to address the processes of creativity and the generation of new ways of doing old tasks or the invention of new machines and systems. Traditional behaviorism, despite the ambitions of its leaders, generated many more principles or laws of performance and work than laws of learning or laws of creative synthesis. Although these laws of work could account for changes in simple behaviors as a function of contingencies, they do not address other significantly complex behaviors that are reflections of brain operations that entail keen and selective perception, including real-time computations of probabilities of events and consequences. Attempts to relate the here-and-now to similar events of the past are critical. A main task of the brain is to provide its carrier with a current, data-based informed assessment of the world.

An apparent unintended consequence of the empty-organism model of behavior was the propagation of indifference and abuse toward animals in laboratories and elsewhere. After all, the animals were just empty things, a view inherently compatible with the Cartesian perspective (Descartes 1637). Their behavior was uninfluenced by feelings and knowledge regarding their situation or their past or future. Though animals could and would respond, they had no "psyche." Allusions to their discomfort or pain were not to be taken literally. Indeed, Kennedy (1992, reviewed by Rumbaugh 1994) believed that it was a mistake even to consider the issue of whether animals could feel pain because it encouraged anthropomorphism. For Kennedy, no greater error could be committed. Because pain could not be assessed objectively and scientifically, he preferred that animal researchers ignore the question of pain. On the other hand, Kennedy was ready to accept the accuracy and validity of verbal reports by people about their feelings. In our view, to be consistent, Kennedy should have rejected such verbal reports—perhaps even his own. To accept prima facie the validity of introspective reports is more risky, in our assessment, than trusting well-reasoned, systematic, long-term studies of primates.

Although the stimuli of the here-and-now and the experiences of the past do influence behavior, some organisms declare their own contributions to behavior. They might not be intending literally to do so or even know that they can do so or are doing so. Their contribution might be as circumscribed as that suggested by Denny and Ratner (1970)—namely, that they generate their own discriminative stimuli in situations. The organisms most able to do so are those with relatively large brains with elaborated cortexes. But for their complex brains to operate optimally, those animals also must have had appropriately enriched early environments—ones that foster the perception of predictive relations between what is happening now and what will happen in the immediate future. The brain's capacity to control behavior is not simply a manifestation of its cytoarchitecture, it is also a function of the logic-structure of the environment within which its cognitive structures and topics of attention were established by the experiences of daily life, notably during the early formative years. By contrast, if raised in an impoverished environment for the first two years of life, apes will remain cognitively compromised (see fig. 28) and socially deficient in their abilities to acquire and interpret social communications, to copulate, and to care for their offspring (Davenport 1979; Davenport, Rogers, and Rumbaugh 1973; Menzel, Davenport, and Rogers 1970). Rhesus monkeys also suffer cognitive deficits as a consequence of early social restriction (Gluck 1979; Harlow and Harlow 1962; Harlow et al. 1971), though in our view the deficits are neither as severe nor as resistant to remediation as they are with the apes.

In striking contrast, E. Menzel (1972, 1973) reports that chimpanzees reared in a social group and a generally enriched stimulating environment will become highly communicative and cooperative. In figure 29 chimpanzees are shown working together to position and stabilize a pole so that they might get on the tree trunk safely above the coils of electric wire positioned to keep them from doing just that. The planning, social recruitment and coordination, and timely offers of assisting in a role (holding a pole being climbed by another) are very complex operations. Chimpanzees can become capable of them if the conditions of their rearing encouraged cognitive development, while chimpanzees reared in more circumscribed environs don't even see the problem to be solved, let alone how it might be solved through the coordination of efforts.

Continuity

This view of behavior and Rational Behaviorism stands in contrast to that of the past. The declaration by Descartes that animals were nothing more than beast machines is frankly wrong, but it should be evaluated as a historical statement. Descartes had no data to argue the con-

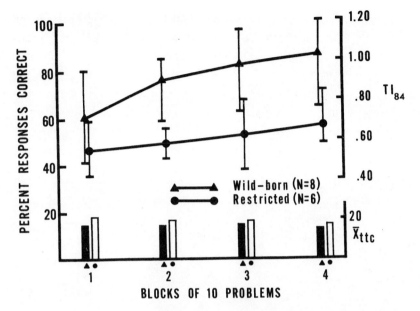

Figure 28. A comparison of chimpanzees reared in an impoverished environment for the first two years of infancy compared on transfer index (TI) testing with those reared in a social group from birth. Although simple discrimination learning was essentially the same in the two groups (lower right axis), the two groups' TI range markers overlapped only minimally when measurements were taken of their ability to transfer learning in a discrimination-reversal test situation. The chimpanzees were about fourteen-year-old young adults when tested. Even short-term impoverished rearing (here two years) can have lasting, perhaps irreversible costs to the cognitive competence of chimpanzees (Davenport, Rogers, and Rumbaugh 1973). Copyright © 1973 by the American Psychological Association. Reprinted with permission.

trary. We are confident that Descartes would reject his framework if he had the database accrued over the past fifty years. Regrettably, believing as Descartes did is likely to engender an inappropriate lack of concern about the treatment of animals and their humane care. Darwin (1859) was far more correct than Descartes. The processes of natural selection have served to provide for continuity in psychological function and "mental operations" just as they have in biology.

A basic principle to be kept in mind is that shared genetics not only foster similarities of appearance, they also foster similar psychology and even similar behaviors. Complex anatomic expressions, such

Figure 29. In contrast to the data in fig. 28, chimpanzees reared in enriched environments can come to cooperate so as to solve novel challenges. Here three chimpanzees are positioning a pole so that the electrified barrier on the trunk of the tree can be overcome by climbing. The chimpanzees came to hold the pole so as to stabilize it while it was precariously positioned on the trunk of the tree. The team effort was remarkably successful. The apes were not trained to cooperate in this manner. Photo courtesy of E. Menzel.

as the ability to see and to fly, have emerged from the integration of simpler structures and systems. Similarly, the complex psychological competencies of our species, including thought and language, have emerged from simpler, more basic competencies of our precursors. Fortunately, traces of the attributes from which our competence has been selected and honed are found in other animal forms—and notably in those most closely related to us. We are very fortunate that we are not the only species of primates. If we were, consider how distorted our view of ourselves would be. By good fortune, there still lives a rich array of nonhuman primates. Their study serves to emphasize that we are but one of many alternatives supported by the evolution of the order Primates. There is no simple ladder of expression of attributes across time. Diversity is a basic principle of changes in life forms across time, yet diversity does not deny continuity.

Research of the past decade has served to emphasize the correctness of the Darwinian perspective. All primate species are by definition unique. Although we are different from other species, we really are not "more" unique. As we have seen, there is strong new evidence for the argument that apes have substantial language skills. That they can acquire those skills best if they are reared in ways uncommon to their natural histories (that is, about as one cares for a human child; Savage-Rumbaugh et al. 1986, 1993; Savage-Rumbaugh, Brakke, and Hutchins 1992) attests to the common heritage which common genetics extends both to the apes and to us, a heritage manifested to the degree that the apes share with us a common pattern of early rearing in a language-structured environment. Given that environment, both humans and chimpanzee (notably the bonobo, *Pan paniscus*) have the requisite capacities for understanding language and for acquiring the competent use of symbols "to talk." And whereas no nonhuman primate literally "speaks," one bonobo, Kanzi, has manifested marked changes in his vocal repertoire that probably reflect his particular sensitivity to the human speech of the environment within which he was reared (Hopkins and Savage-Rumbaugh 1991. In sum, the effects of rearing on Kanzi's language skills are captured succinctly by Marler (1999): "The Kanzi project and its predecessors are stunning demonstrations of the powerful influence that the social environment can exert on behavioral development, regardless of whether or not the rubicon of true language is ever crossed."

The Computer Age and Its Impact on Comparative Research

Although computers have changed all of our lives, no change has been more important to psychology than the effect computers are having in the methods of comparative psychology. Primates are revealing not only their prowess for mastery of complex video-formatted tasks, they are manifesting extraordinary intelligence. As we have seen, not only do they learn to execute perceptual-motor skills that enable them to keep a joystick-controlled cursor within the boundaries of an erratically moving target, they are able to learn highly complex relations between events. And their psychology of learning undergoes changes. The tasks that they perform can be performed also by human adults and children. The similarities of abilities and learning are impressive. The rapidly accruing literature generated by such methods has served to redefine and to significantly upgrade our estimation of primate cognition both for monkeys and apes.

Primates do more than just respond mechanically to stimuli of the present environmental field. Rather, they predict events and calculate how responses must be altered if they are to "win" in a given task. They can express their confidence in making choices. Their behavior can be as new and as innovative as are the trials on which they test their skills. That great apes, rhesus monkeys, capuchins, and even squirrel monkeys are adroit is something of a shock. Just how did evolution provide them with such abilities? It did so inadvertently—by the same mechanisms that were used to instate our own competencies for such tasks.

It is important to note that primates' efficiency of learning and their readiness to work hard and accurately is enhanced by extending their own control of what they do—control over when they work, what incentive they work for, what task they work on, and so on. And eventually it matters little whether they are hungry and get food pellets for correct performances. Once skilled, they work on tasks because it gives them a stimulating challenge. They would much rather work on their computers than to play with objects. Thus, whereas their initial work on the computer-based tasks is surely "pellet driven," it soon becomes task driven—which is to say psychologically rather than biologically driven. The chimpanzee Panzee has been known to call up the maze-running program from the menu unintentionally left on the monitor and to work away on a series of complex mazes for half an hour at a time with her joystick—with no reward for so doing other than the intrinsic work on the task itself. Our apes are not food deprived.

The apparatus and the contexts within which behavior is studied both forms and limits the database from which conclusions are drawn

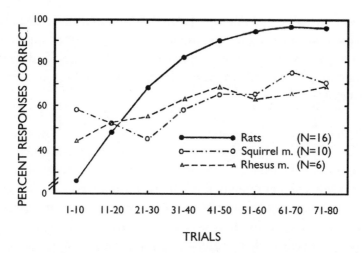

Figure 30. Rats are substantially better than either squirrel monkeys *(Saimiri sciureus)* or rhesus macaques *(Macaca mulatta)* in learning mazes (Rumbaugh 1968). Figure by John Davenport. Copyright © Academic Press.

about the effects of variables and the abilities of the primate subjects. The psychologist's perspectives of a species' learning ability are both enabled and delimited by methods of inquiry—just as the astronomer's perspective of the universe is limited by the sensitivity of his or her telescopes. If a rat is tested in a simple maze with a single right-left choice point, then both the rat's learning and the psychologist's view of the rat's learning ability are limited. Both squirrel monkeys and rhesus monkeys are much poorer at learning mazes than are rats (see fig. 30). If a monkey is tested in the standard Wisconsin General Testing Apparatus (WGTA; Harlow 1949), its learning of a variety of tasks can be explored. But because the WGTA does not provide for the dynamic interactions availed by a joystick-controlled computerized task, no perspective can be obtained regarding the monkeys' abilities on such tasks. Indeed, some psychologists don't even consider exploring many questions if they are unfamiliar with the equipment with which to do so. The conventional WGTA would not even permit the experimenter to ask whether the rhesus might be able to do such things as to shoot bullets of light at a moving target or to attend to the appearance of a specific signal in an otherwise "noisy" visual field. Such opportunities for study have been afforded to us and others because of the development of our Language Research Center's Computerized Testing System (LRC-CTS). Happily, computers enrich our research questions and programs and extend to the primates new challenges for demonstrating their smarts and for leading more stimulating lives in captive settings.

Washburn, Hopkins, and Rumbaugh (1991) reported performance of rhesus in a variant of one of their several video-formatted tasks, called SELECT. Recall in the SELECT task the rhesus can choose which task it will perform. Generally it gets only five trials on the task of its choice. Upon completion of those trials, a library of icons is re-presented and another choice must be made. In one study, one of the options was free food: the monkey received five pellets of food distributed across time at a rate comparable to that at which they would have been dispensed as reinforcers for performance on any other task. Thus the monkey was given a choice of not working but receiving food as though it had worked on a task.

Initially most subjects continued to work on real tasks. Gradually, however, the choice of the free-food option became stronger and stronger. Finally, the monkeys were "on the dole" more than on the payroll. Frankly, we were keenly disappointed. We had hoped that the tasks would prove inherently gratifying and would retain their luster over the choice of free food.

At that point, we had an intriguing idea. If one minute of free food was good, then thirty minutes of free food should be great. However, even free food comes at some cost, and in this case the cost was that the computer tasks were unavailable during the entire interval during which free food was dispensed. That is, once the monkey selected the free-food option, it would receive thirty minutes of pellets, delivered at the approximate rate that they could be obtained by working, but without the opportunity to work during that time.

Under this condition the preference for free food crashed. The work ethic was reinstated. It seems that the free-food option was attractive to the rhesus so long as it lasted but a short time. But when free food came at the expense of being able to work on other tasks for a half-hour, that option dropped from a 70 percent rate of preference to 18 percent! By contrast, when other tasks were extended thirty minutes, preference for them remained stable. The challenge of work was real.

The monkeys were greedy (they wanted the richest payout possible) but not lazy (over time, they didn't want to receive pellets for nothing). The monkeys chose not to live by pellets alone. Free food seems to be attractive only if it remains an option which can be controlled.

How does a primate become freed from the specifics of stimuli, hence able to respond to novel relations? Does a primate come to think, to plan, to reason? Do the cognitive operations of the primate change as a function of its experience? These and a host of other questions now can be addressed though use of computer-formatted tasks.

One of the several important lessons learned through the use of computers is that species do not have fixed abilities. Past research has paid little attention to the effects of rearing and maintenance conditions upon primates. Primates have been studied as though their learning and cognitive operations were somehow fixed by genetics. The idea seemingly was that if one would but keep the animals alive and healthy, one could study them without concern that the conditions of their maintenance and study would affect their abilities to learn. Any old ape or monkey would do for a study to represent the species. We now know that such is not the case.

Super-Learning and Optimization Are the Rules

Primates not only care about the task on which they work, they learn more—generally much more—than they need to learn. Sherman and Austin, two adult male chimpanzees *(Pan troglodytes)*, were given the opportunity to select between two pairs of foodwells that held their favorite chocolate candies (Rumbaugh, Savage-Rumbaugh, and Hegel 1987; Rumbaugh, Savage-Rumbaugh, and Pate 1988; Perusse and Rumbaugh 1990). The foodwells were evenly spaced, and the rule was that if the chimpanzee selected either of the two on the right, then the animal got to eat the contents of both wells on that side. Similarly, if the chimpanzee chose either of the two foodwells on the left, the contents of both wells on that side were given to the animal. The other pair of foodwells were withdrawn from reach; hence their M&M candies were not available.

Sherman and Austin were never required to choose the pair of wells that would yield the greater total number of chocolates. Rather, they always got chocolates—the ones chosen. They gradually came to choose the pair that gave them the greater total. Although they did not have to learn to select the greater total, they did so and could differentiate between even nine and ten chocolates (Perusse and Rumbaugh 1990).

It has been noted that we found that rhesus monkeys learned far more than was necessary when given the opportunity to choose between numerals 0 through 9 in a video-formatted task. The monkeys always got the quantity of pellets associated with the value of the numeral selected. Thus on a given trial with the numerals 3 and 7 paired, the monkey got three pellets if he selected 3 and seven pellets if he selected 7. Only if the rhesus chose 0 did it get nothing. In other words, the monkeys almost always got pellets, and they did not have to choose the larger numeral to obtain food.

After their training was completed and revealed a high preference for the larger of two paired numerals, seven novel trials were presented. It was on these trials that the monkeys first encountered certain possible pairings of numerals. This test was to tell us whether the monkeys had learned only which number of any specific pair was the better deal or whether they had learned something comprehensive about the relations that existed between all of the numbers—regardless of whether or not two had been paired during training.

On these novel tests, one monkey made no errors and the second one made but two. Clearly they had learned more than simply which of two numerals, of every pair previously presented to them, was the one to select for the optimum amount of food to be received. They had seemingly learned a relational matrix of the numerals that took into account their values and ordinal ranks—even though their values differed by the minimum quantity of but one pellet. And this observation, in turn, strongly suggests that the primate's brain has a natural bent or inclination for organizing information—if that information is orderly and reliably encountered across time in a context within which its most basic needs are to be met.

Thus rhesus prefer to have control over what they do, and they learn complexly and far more than they must—as do we. They learn complexly and comprehensively even in a simple task—as do we. All they had to do to get food (and they were never food deprived) was to choose a number—any number other than 0—and they would get highly nourishing banana-flavored fruit pellets. But they proceeded, quite effortlessly it appeared, to define the entire matrix of values by which the numbers were interrelated. This result tells us that the primate brain has not been designed to accept "no-brainer" conditioning of single responses. Rather, it has been designed to discern relations and to interrelate them insofar as possible.

Once the proposition is stated in this way, we recognize that a large body of evidence supports the general principle that animals and humans learn more than they must in order to handle the immediate demands of specific tasks. Why and how they do so are not trivial questions. If nothing else, the conservation of energy and the principle of least effort would seem to restrict what is learned. Learning, by that principle, should be limited to some efficient minimum.

On the other hand, this principle does not apply if we view learning in a new way—one that encourages the learner to exploit all that might be learned in a situation. Learning, of course, must be stored in memory. In highly integrated and well-organized memory, learning is available for recall and for use in the future—in new situations for which efficiency of adaptation saves the energy that would otherwise be needed. Whereas many animals hedge against the future by storing fat, the animal brain stores learning. Both fat and learning can be called upon for adaptation to challenges of the future.

Large brains, though the most expensive of all body organs, have evolved in the order Primates because they, more than small brains, afford maximum learning and organizations of new learning with past learning, and also because they afford effective memory storage systems that "pack and transport learning" to the future for possible use. It was in this manner that energy was conserved in the long run, and not by limiting the amount that might be learned in the short run. True, large brains enable the comprehension of the social dynamics of large groups, the planning of deception or cooperation, the use of symbols, and so on. But brain size was not necessarily selected for because of any of those. A host of factors probably all supported the selection of larger brains because with such brains there came a new flexibility of behaving in service of survival, adaptation, and reproductive success.

Future Orientation

Thus viewed, complex learning and the operation of the complex brain are future oriented. Recent findings regarding the ability of animals to make predictions regarding future events support this conclusion.

Savage-Rumbaugh's (1991) report on the bonobo Panbanisha yields still other data consonant with the principle that primates learn substantially more than they must. Her detailed analysis of the process by which Panbanisha came to comprehend specific spoken words and lexigrams through the course of being a participant-observer in a variety of "routines," many of which were designed to provide care necessary for her well-being and comfort. Typical routines included getting ready to go outdoors, taking a bath, looking at pictures in a book, playing games, going to specific sites in the woods, and so on. Some routines were far too abstract for the apes to comprehend at all, but others, such as having diapers changed, were sufficiently frequent and concrete that the young ape became a participant.

One of the first signs of the ape's becoming a participant was that she accepted the positioning activities imposed upon her for events such as diapering. Eventually Panbanisha came to comprehend her caregiver's speech regarding "diapers"—even to the point of helping to get a clean diaper and then lying down so as to facilitate the change.

The "blowing bubbles" routine had many components—finding the bottle of "bubble" water, opening it, finding and using the wand with which bubbles are blown, watching and chasing the bubbles, and so on. Across time, as this playful routine was engaged in over and over again, Panbanisha eventually came to behave as if she knew what had to be done next for bubbles to be produced. She even learned that she could initiate the routine by selecting the bottle of bubbles, showing it to the caregiver, putting the wand to the caregiver's mouth, and so on. Thus a transition was made from passive-receptive comprehension of blowing bubbles to active participation.

Panbanisha sometimes learned without the direction of the caregiver. She initially learned the basic elements of the task, then gradually came to comprehend and eventually to use language markers (speech heard or use of lexigrams at the keyboard) for initiating and expediting bubble blowing. And what Panbanisha couldn't formally request through her own speech or use of lexigrams, she attempted to request through actions—such as putting the bottle of bubbles in the caregiver's hands after making repeated, though unsuccessful, attempts to open the bottle on her own.

Still later the ape learned to comply with novel requests from caregivers. Such requests entailed parts of the blowing-bubble routine. They included getting the bubble bottle, putting it in the backpack, and then carrying it out into the woods, where the bottle might be asked for either by the chimpanzee or by another member of the traveling party. Comprehension of verbal markers typically occur first within established or familiar routines. Across time, however, they can be used appropriately and intelligently in variations on familiar routines, even as those routines are experienced within other routines that have not included the blowing of bubbles.

The chimpanzees and bonobos who learned language in our research program were not required to learn anything. Neither were they given specific training drills. Rather, they were observer-participants—encouraged to watch, to participate and to enjoy all of the several activities associated within the daily routines. Visiting various sites in the forest, eating various foods, and playing social games served as contexts within which elements were "predicted" by someone speaking and using the symbol-embossed keyboard.

The apes learned, and they learned a great deal more than expected. They learned because they could. They learned as their brains kept "taking the initiative" in sorting out predictive relations between events, between words the animals had heard and the events that ensued, and a variety of other experiences of life. The events were not just individually perceived and stored in memory, however. Rather, these events were integrated into logical sequences, patterns, and categories—so that in due course any of a number of words heard or lexigrams used were responded to intelligently regardless of the specifics of the context. And as we have argued earlier, that is exactly the function for which their large brains were selected. That is brain business as manifested in Emergents and emergent operations.

What was the driving force for the apes to learn the verbal markers of speech and lexigrams? Surely it was their predictive values. The verbal markers became worthy of focused attention. Once learned, they allowed the infant apes to predict parts of their world that were of particular interest—including the behavior of others and what they would have to do in order to participate or to avoid the consequences of others' behaviors.

As valuable for competence and comfort in adaptive efforts as is the induction of valid predictions, these predictions appear to be subject to integration by the brain. Thus, notably in the great ape and human children, the brain is competent to organize predictions that are valid both within contexts and between contexts. Principles are seemingly induced and general, as well as specific, dimensions of competence emerge. Thinking, reasoning, insight, organization, and prediction somehow benefit from coordinated efforts to adapt. In balance, it probably is as much the effort to adapt and the tenacity in that effort that hones the best of ape and human intelligence. The set or orientation to do so is, we believe, formed during the sensitive weeks, months, and years that begin at or even before birth. And though apes and we excel in the manifestations of intelligence, we will make a grand mistake if we begin to think, argue, or conclude that mammals of the land and sea and birds of the air lack their own very active businesses of the brain that provide for successful adaptation beyond that afforded by instinct and conditioning.

Humans are not unique in having the potential for psychological intelligence and for language. True, our potential is much greater than that of the great apes, but we have a vastly larger brain relative to the size of our body. We share with the great apes and rhesus and probably several other primate species the desire for *control* over what we do and when we do it. We all do better in our tasks if permitted to choose to perform those tasks rather than have those tasks assigned. Intelligence is serviced by large brains and elaborated cortexes. Although the amount of learning that takes place in a given situation can be far more complex and comprehensive than required, that learning is cost-efficiently acquired, then stored for transport across time for adaptive use in the future. Large brains, though metabolically very expensive, were an effective means whereby masterful control could be achieved. The achievement of control reduces the perception of helplessness. It inspires the body to try something, to try anything in desperate situations. Doing something in that mode serves to abate anxiety and apprehension. Doing something also serves to enhance the probability that a true cause-effect relation will be discovered. Such valid relations afford valid control. They also enable the development of technology and science.

Nature's grand idea of behavior and intelligence was invested exclusively in animal life. Its potential for adaptation is enormous. That potential is one that we share with all other animals, with all other primates. Neither we nor they should waste it. Neither we nor they should be wasted. Together we must work for a new and common good so that we conserve the world—the only world we have.

Epilogue

A hallmark of scientific thought is that it is receptive to new findings, new data that serve to modulate perspectives of the past and to open new vistas for the future. Even as this book nears the date of printing, Kanzi has come forth with new lessons that pertain to our understanding of language and emergent operations.

Without being trained or required to do so, Kanzi has come to modulate his vocalizations to produce different sounds that correspond to different things that he likes and as a way of expressing agreement (Taglialatela, Savage-Rumbaugh, and Baker 2003). He produces different vocalizations for at least four words—and ongoing research may reveal even more—where his meanings are unambiguously defined by concurrent lexigram selections, gestures, or other behavioral evidence. His vocal productions in contexts where prized foods are to be named or requested or just commented upon (for example, banana, grape, and juice) vary systematically and reliably on both the temporal and spectral levels. These productions are, in turn, different from his vocalization of a "yes" that conveys approval or concurrence (for example, to the question of "Kanzi, are you ready to listen?"). Spectographic analysis for these and other vocalizations reveals that the structures of the vocalizations are predictable and consistent even across wide variations in Kanzi's emotional state.

We have known for years that Kanzi's vocalizations include ones that are uncommon to bonobos generally and that are attributable to his unique, language-enriched rearing from birth (Hopkins and Savage-Rumbaugh 1991). But now Kanzi has made another major stride forward into the language domain. He is doing what generally was thought not possible for an ape: he is uttering sounds that are discernibly different in several dimensions. They are complex and produced in a variety of contexts, and the differences between these vocalizations cannot be attributed to only one or two acoustic variables. That they are complex and used reliably in a variety of contexts clearly indicates that they have meaning, both to him and to the listener. They are semantically defined. No, Kanzi does not talk in sentences, but semantic, rule-based phrases are suggested by his coordinated use of modulated vocalizations, gestures, and gaze. Although to the listener Kanzi's vocalizations are not as discernible as English, his vocalizations have every marker of meaningful words used to communicate socially what otherwise he could not.

With this brief yet very important epilogue of Kanzi's accomplishments, we should remind ourselves that future research will continue to deliver surprises that are significant to our understanding of the common ground between nonhuman and human beings.

References

Andrews, P., and L. Martin. 1987. Cladistic relationships of extant and fossil hominoids. *Journal of Human Evolution, 16,* 101–108.

Antinucci, F. (ed.). 1969. *Cognitive structure and development in nonhuman primates.* Hillsdale, N.J.: Erlbaum.

Bard, K. A., and K. H. Gardner. 1996. Influences on development in infant chimpanzees: Enculturation, temperament, and cognition. In A. E. Russon, K. A. Bard, and S. T. Parker (eds.), *Reaching into thought: The minds of the great apes* (pp. 235–256). New York: Cambridge University Press.

Bates, E. 1993. Comprehension and production in early language environment: A commentary on Savage-Rumbaugh, Murphy, Sevcik, Brakke, Williams, and Rumbaugh, "Language comprehension in ape and child." *Monographs of the Society for Research in Child Development, 58,* nos. 3–4, 222–242.

Bates, E., D. Thal, and V. Marchman. 1991. Symbols and syntax: A Darwinian approach to language development. In N. A. Krasnegor, D. M. Rumbaugh, R. L. Schiefelbusch, and M. Studdert-Kennedy (eds.), *Biological and behavioral determinants of language development* (pp. 29–65). Hillsdale, N.J.: Erlbaum.

Beck, B. B. 1980. *Animal tool behavior.* New York: Garland.

Beran, M. J. 2001. Summation and numerousness judgments of sequentially presented sets of items by chimpanzees *(Pan troglodytes). Journal of Comparative Psychology, 115,* 181–191.

Beran, M. J., K. R. Gibson, and D. M. Rumbaugh. 1999. Predicting hominid intelligence from brain size. In M. Corballis and S. Lea (eds.), *Descent of mind* (pp. 88–97). Oxford: Oxford University Press.

Beran, M. J., J. L. Pate, W. K. Richardson, and D. M. Rumbaugh. 2000. A chimpanzee's *(Pan troglodytes)* long-term retention of lexigrams. *Animal Learning and Behavior, 28,* 201–207.

Beran, M. J., and D. M. Rumbaugh. 2001. "Constructive" enumeration by chimpanzees *(Pan troglodytes)* on a computerized task. *Animal Cognition, 4,* 81–89.

Beran, M. J., D. M. Rumbaugh, and E. S. Savage-Rumbaugh. 1998. Chimpanzee *(Pan troglodytes)* counting in a computerized testing paradigm. *Psychological Record, 48,* 3–19.

Beran, M. J., E. S. Savage-Rumbaugh, K. E. Brakke, J. W. Kelley, and D. M. Rumbaugh. 1998. Symbol comprehension and learning: A "vocabulary" test of three chimpanzees *(Pan troglodytes). Evolution of Communication, 2,* 171–188.

Betz, S. K. 1981. Sentence expansion by Lana chimpanzee. Master's thesis, Georgia State University.

Birch, H. G. 1945. The relation of previous experience to insightful problem solving. *Journal of Comparative Psychology, 38,* 367–383.

Bitterman, M. E. 1975. The comparative analysis of learning: Are laws of learning the same in all animals? *Science, 188,* 699–709.

———. 1988. Vertebrate-invertebrate comparisons. In H. J. Jerison and I. Jerison (eds.), *Intelligence and evolutionary biology* (pp. 251–275). Berlin: Springer-Verlag.

———. 2000. Cognitive evolution: A psychological perspective. In Heyes and Huber 2000 (pp. 61–80).

Bitterman, M. E., and P. A. Couvillon. 1991. Failures to find adaptive specialization in the learning of honey bees. In L. J. Goodman and R. C. Fisher (eds.), *The behavior and physiology of bees* (pp. 288–305). Wallingford, U.K.: CAB International.

Blum, D. 1994. *The monkey wars.* New York: Oxford University Press.

Boesch, C., and M. Tomasello. 1998. Chimpanzee and human cultures. *Current Anthropology, 39,* 591–614.

Bolig, R., C. S. Price, P. L. O'Neil, and S. J. Suomi. 1992. Subjective assessment of reactivity level and personality traits of monkeys. *International Journal of Primatology, 13,* 287–306.

Boysen, S. T. 1993. Counting in chimpanzees: Nonhuman principles and emergent properties of number. In S. T. Boysen and E. J. Capaldi (eds.), *The development of numerical competence: Animal and human models. Comparative cognition and neuroscience* (pp. 39–59). Hillsdale, N.J.: Erlbaum.

Boysen, S. T., and G. G. Berntson. 1989. Numerical competence in a chimpanzee *(Pan troglodytes). Journal of Comparative Psychology, 103,* 23–31.

Boysen, S. T., V. A. Kuhlmeier, P. Halliday, and Y. M. Halliday. 1999. Tool use in captive gorillas. In S. T. Parker, R. W. Mitchell, and H. L. Miles (eds.), *The mentalities of gorillas and orangutans: Comparative perspectives* (pp. 179–187). New York: Cambridge University Press.

Brakke, K. B., and E. S. Savage-Rumbaugh. 1995. The development of language skills in bonobo and chimpanzees: Comprehension. *Language and Communication, 15,* 121–148.

———. 1996. The development of language skills in Pan: Production. *Language and Communication, 16,* 361–380.

Brannon, E., and H. S. Terrace. 1998. Ordering of the numerosities 1 to 9 by monkeys. *Science, 282,* 746–749.

Breland, K., and M. Breland. 1961. The misbehavior of organisms. *American Psychologist, 16,* 681–684.

———. 1966. *Animal behavior.* Toronto: Macmillan.

Bruner, J. S. 1972. Nature and uses of immaturity. *American Psychologist, 27,* 687–708.

Brunswik, E. 1943. Organismic achievement and environmental probability. *Psychological Review, 50,* 255–272.

———. 1952. The conceptual framework of psychology. *International Encyclopedia of Unified Science 1,* 1–102.

Buchanan, J. P., T. V. Gill, and J. T. Braggio. 1981. Serial position and clustering effects in a chimpanzee's "free recall." *Memory and Cognition, 9,* 651–660.

Burns, R. A., M. E. Goettl, and S. T. Burt. 1995. Numerical discriminations with arrhythmic serial presentations. *Psychological Record, 45,* 95–104.

Butler, R. A. 1965. Investigative behavior. In A. M. Schrier, H. F. Harlow, and F. Stollnitz (eds.), *Behavior of nonhuman primates: Modern research trends* (vol. 2, pp. 463–494). New York: Academic Press.

Buzsaki, G. 1989. A two state model of memory trace formation: A role for "noisy" brain states. *Neuroscience, 31,* 551–570.

Bryne, R. 1995. *The thinking ape.* Oxford: Oxford University Press.

Cantalupo, C., and W. D. Hopkins. 2001. Asymmetric Broca's area in great apes: A region of the ape brain is uncannily similar to one linked with speech in humans. *Nature, 414,* 505.

Capaldi, E. J., and D. J. Miller. 1988. Counting in rats: Its functional significance and the independent cognitive processes that constitute it. *Journal of Experimental Psychology: Animal Behavior Processes, 14,* 3–17.

Capretta, P. J., and L. H. Rawls. 1974. Establishment of a flavor preference in rats: Importance of nursing and weaning experience. *Journal of Comparative and Physiological Psychology, 86,* no. 4, 670–673.

Chiszar, D., C. Andren, G. Nilson, B. O'Connell, J. S. Mestas, Jr., H. M. Smith, and C. W. Radcliffe. 1982. Strike-induced chemosensory searching in Old World vipers and New World pit vipers. *Animal Learning and Behavior, 10,* no. 2, 121–125.

Clayton, N. S., D. P. Griffith, and A. Dickinson. 2000. Declarative and episodic-like memory in animals: Personal musings of a scrub jay. In Heyes and Huber 2000 (pp. 273–288).

Cowles, J. T. 1937. Food-tokens as incentives for learning by chimpanzees. *Comparative Psychology Monographs, 14.*

Crespi, L. P. 1942. Quantitative variation of incentive and performance in the white rat. *American Journal of Psychology, 55,* 467–517.

Darwin, C. 1859. *The origin of species.* London: Murray.

———. 1871. *The descent of man, and selection in relation to sex.* 2 vols. New York: Appleton.

Davenport, R. K. 1979. Some behavioral disturbances of great apes in captivity. In D. Hamburg and E. R. McCown (eds.), *The great apes* (pp. 341–356). Menlo Park, Calif.: Benjamin/Cummings.

Davenport, R. K., and C. W. Rogers. 1970. Intermodal equivalence of stimuli in apes. *Science, 168,* 279–280.

Davenport, R. K., C. W. Rogers, and D. M. Rumbaugh. 1973. Long-term cognitive deficits in chimpanzees associated with early impoverished rearing. *Developmental Psychology, 9,* 343–347.

Davey, G. C., and G. G. Cleland. 1982. Topography of signal-centered behavior in the rat: Effects of deprivation state and reinforcer type. *Journal of the Experimental Analysis of Behavior, 38,* no. 3, 291–304.

Deacon, T. W. 1997. *The symbolic species: The co-evolution of language and the brain.* New York: Norton.

Denny, M. R., and S. C. Ratner. 1970. *Comparative psychology: Research in animal behavior* (rev. ed). Homewood, Ill.: Dorsey.

Descartes, R. 1637, rpt. 1956. *Discourse on method.* New York: Liberal Arts Press.

de Waal, F. 2001a. *The ape and the sushi master: Cultural reflections of a primatologist.* New York: Basic.

———(ed.). 2001b. *Tree of origin: What primate behavior can tell us about human social evolution.* Cambridge: Harvard University Press.

de Waal, J. 1982. *Chimpanzee politics.* New York: Harper and Row.

———. 1989. *Peacemaking among primates.* Cambridge: Harvard University Press.

Domjan, M. 1993. *The essentials of conditioning and learning* (3d ed.). Pacific Grove, Calif.: Brooks/Cole.

———. 1998. *The principles of learning and behavior* (4th ed.). Pacific Grove, Calif.: Brooks/Cole.

———. 2003. *The principles of learning and behavior* (5th ed.). Belmont, Calif.: Wadsworth/Thomson Learning.

Dooley, G. B., and Gill, T. 1977. Acquisition and use of mathematical skills by a linguistic chimpanzee. In Rumbaugh 1977 (pp. 247–260).

Dunbar, R. I. M. 1992. Neocortex size as a constraint on group size in primates. *Journal of Human Evolution, 20,* 469–493.

Ehrlich, A. 1970. Response to novel objects in three lower primates: Greater galago, slow loris, and owl monkey. *Behavior, 37,* 55–63.

Ellen, P., B. J. Soteres, and C. Wages. 1984. Problem solving in the rat: Piecemeal acquisition of cognitive maps. *Learning and Motivation, 12,* no. 2, 232–237.

Essock, S. M. 1977. Color perception and color classification. In Rumbaugh 1977 (pp. 207–223).

Essock, S. M., T. V. Gill, and D. M. Rumbaugh. 1977. Language relevant object- and color-naming tasks. In Rumbaugh 1977 (pp. 193–206).

Essock-Vitale, S. M. 1978. Comparison of ape and monkey modes of problem solution. *Journal of Comparative Physiological Psychology, 92,* 942–957.

Fernandez-Carriba, S., A. Loeches, A. Morcillo, W. D. Hopkins. 2002. Functional asymmetry of emotions in primates: New findings in chimpanzees. *Brain Research Bulletin, 57,* nos. 3–4, 561–564.

Filion, C. M., D. A. Washburn, and J. P. Gulledge. 1996. Can monkeys *(Macaca mulatta)* represent invisible displacement? *Journal of Comparative Psychology, 110,* 386–395.

Fobes, J. L., and J. E. King. 1982. Measuring primate learning abilities. In J. L. Fobes and J. E. King (eds.), *Communication and behavior* (pp. 289–326). New York: Academic Press.

Fouts, R. S. 1973. Acquisition and testing of gestural signs in four young chimpanzees. *Science,* 180, 978–980.

———. 1976. Transfer of signed responses in American Sign Language from vocal English stimuli to physical object stimuli by a chimpanzee *(Pan). Learning and Motivation,* 7, 458–475.

———. 1997. *Next of kin: What chimpanzees have taught me about who we are.* New York: Morrow.

Fouts, R. S., and D. H. Fouts. 1989. Loulis in conversation with cross-fostered chimpanzees. In Gardner, Gardner, and van Cantfort 1989 (pp. 293–307).

Fouts, R. S., D. H. Fouts, and T. E. van Cantfort. 1989. The infant Loulis learns signs from cross-fostered chimpanzees. In Gardner, Gardner, and van Cantfort 1989 (pp. 280–292).

Furness, W. 1916. Observations on the mentality of chimpanzees and orangutans. *Proceedings of the American Philosophical Society,* 45, 281–290.

Gallistel, C. R. 1992. *Animal cognition.* Cambridge: MIT Press.

Gallup, G., M. K. McClure, S. D. Hill, and R. A. Bundy. 1971. Capacity for self-recognition in differentially reared chimpanzees. *Psychological Record,* 21, 69–74.

Garber, J., and M. E. P. Seligman (eds.). 1980. *Human helplessness: Theory and applications.* New York: Academic Press.

Garcia, J., F. R. Ervin, and R. A. Koelling. 1966. Learning with prolonged delay of reinforcement. *Psychonomic Science,* 5, 121–122.

Garcia, J., and W. G. Hankins. 1977. On the origin of food aversion paradigms. In L. M. Barker, M. R. Best, and M. Domjan (eds.), *Learning mechanisms in food selection* (pp. 460–467). Waco, Texas: Baylor University Press.

Garcia, J., D. J. Kimeldorf, and E. L. Koelling. 1955. Conditioned aversion to saccharin resulting from exposure to gamma radiation. *Science, 122,* 157–158.

Garcia, J., and R. Koelling. 1966. Relation of cue to consequence in avoidance learning. *Psychonomic Science, 4,* 123–124.

———. 1967. A comparison of aversions induced by x-rays, toxins, and drugs in the rat. *Radiation Research Supplement,* 7, 439–450.

Garcia, J., B. K. McGowan, F. R. Ervin, and R. Koelling. 1968. Cues: Their relative effectiveness as a function of the reinforcer. *Science, 160,* 794–795.

Gardner, B. T., and R. A. Gardner. 1971. Two-way communication with an infant chimpanzee. In A. M. Schrier and F. Sollnitz (eds.), *Behavior of Nonhuman Primates* (vol. 4, pp. 117–185) New York: Academic Press.

Gardner, R. A., and B. T. Gardner. 1969. Teaching sign language to a chimpanzee. *Science, 165,* 664–672.

———. 1989. A cross-fostering laboratory. In Gardner, Gardner, and van Cantfort 1989 (pp. 1–28).

——— (eds.). 1998. *The structure of learning: From sign stimuli to sign language.*
Mahwah, N.J.: Erlbaum.

Gardner, R. A., B. T. Gardner, and T. E. van Cantfort (eds.). 1989. *Teaching sign
language to chimpanzees.* Albany: State University of New York Press.

Garner, W. R., H. W. Hake, and C. W. Erikson. 1956. Operationism and the
concept of perception. *Psychological Review, 63,* 149–159.

Gibson, K. R. 1977. Brain structure and intelligence in macaques and human infants from a Piagetian perspective. In S. Chevalier-Skolnikoff and F. Poirier
(eds.), *Primate biosocial development* (pp. 113–158). New York: Garland.

———. 1990. New perspectives on instincts and intelligence: Brain size and the
emergence of hierarchical mental constructional skills. In Parker and
Gibson 1990 (pp. 248–255).

Gill, T. V. 1977. Conversations with Lana. In Rumbaugh 1977 (pp. 225–246).

Glickman, S. E., and R. W. Sroges. 1966. Curiosity in zoo animals. *Behavior, 26,*
151–188.

Gluck, J. P. 1979. The intellectual consequences of early social restriction in rhesus monkeys *(Macaca mulatta).* In G. C. Ruppenthal (ed.), *Nursery care
of nonhuman primates* (pp. 541–543). New York: Plenum.

Gordon, W. C., C. F. Flaherty, and E. P. Riley. 1973. Negative contrast as a function of the interval between preshift and postshift training. *Bulletin of the
Psychonomic Society, 1,* no. 1a, 25–27.

Gottlieb, G. 1984. Development of species identification in ducklings: XII. Ineffectiveness of auditory self-stimulation in wood ducklings *(Aix sponsa).*
Journal of Comparative Psychology, 98, no. 2, 137–141.

Gould, J. L. 1982. *Ethology: The mechanisms and evolution of behavior.* New York:
Norton.

Greenberg, G., and M. M. Haraway. 2002. *Principles of comparative psychology.*
Boston: Allyn and Bacon.

Greenfield, P., and E. S. Savage-Rumbaugh. 1993. Comparing communicative
competence in child and chimp: The pragmatics of repetition. *Journal of
Child Language, 20,* 1–26.

Greenough, W. T. (1987). Experience effects on the developing and the mature
brain: Dendrite branching and synaptogenesis. In N. A. Krasnegor, E. M.
Blass, M. A. Hofer, and W. P. Smotherman (eds.), *Perinatal development:
A psychobiological perspective* (pp. 195-221). Orlando, Fla.: Academic Press.

Greenough, W. T., J. E. Black, and C. S. Wallace. 1987. Experience and brain development. *Child Development, 58,* 539–559.

Griffin, D. R. 1958. *Listening in the dark.* New Haven: Yale University Press.

———. 1984. *Animal thinking.* Cambridge: Harvard University Press.

Gulledge, J. 1999. *Judgments of Arabic numerals and arrays of dots by monkeys: Evidence for concept of number.* Master's thesis, Georgia State University.

Guthrie, E. R. 1935. *The psychology of learning*. New York: Harper and Row.
———. 1952. *The psychology of learning* (rev. ed.). New York: Harper and Row.
———. 1959. Association by contiguity. In S. Koch (ed.), *Psychology: A study of a science* (vol. 2, pp. 158–195). New York: McGraw-Hill.
Guthrie, E. R., and G. P. Horton. 1946. *Cats in a puzzle box*. New York: Rinehart.
Hall, K. R. L. 1963. Tool using performances as indicators of behavioral adaptability. *Current Anthropology, 4*, 479–494.
Hammond, K. R. 2000. *Judgments under stress*. New York: Oxford University Press.
Harlow, H. F. 1949. The formation of learning sets. *Psychological Review, 56*, 51–65.
Harlow, H. F., and M. K. Harlow. 1949. Learning how to think. *Scientific American, 180*, 36–39.
———. 1962. The effects of rearing conditions on behavior. *Bulletin of the Menninger Clinic, 26*, 213–224.
Harlow, H. F., M. K. Harlow, K. A. Schlitz, and D. J. Mohr. 1971. The effects of early adverse and enriched environments on the learning ability of rhesus monkeys. In L. E. Jarrard (ed.), *Cognitive processes of nonhuman primates* (pp. 67–74). New York: Academic Press.
Harris, K. D., D. A. Henze, H. Hirase, X. Leinekugel, G. Dragoi, A. Czurko, and G. Buzsaki. 2002. Spike train dynamics predicts theta-related phase precession in hippocampal pyramidal cells. *Nature, 417*, 738–741.
Hayes, C. 1951. *The ape in our house*. New York: Harper.
Hayes, K. J., and C. Hayes. 1951. The intellectual development of a home-raised chimpanzee. *Proceedings of the American Philosophical Society, 95*, 105–109.
———. 1952. Imitation in a home raised chimpanzee. *Journal of Comparative and Physiological Psychology, 45*, 450–459.
Hayes, K. J., and C. Nissen. 1971. Higher mental functions of a home-raised chimpanzee. In A. M. Schrier and F. Stollnitz (eds.), *Behavior of nonhuman primates: Modern research trends* (vol. 4, pp. 59–115). New York: Academic Press.
Hebb, D. O. 1949. *The organization of behavior: A neuropsychological theory*. New York: Wiley.
———. 1953. On human thought. *Canadian Journal of Psychology, 7*, 99–110.
Herberg, L. H. 1963. Seminal ejaculation following positively reinforcing electrical stimulation of the rat hypothalamus. *Journal of Comparative and Physiological Psychology, 56*, 679–685.
Herman, L. M., S. A. Kuczaj, M. Holder. 1993. Responses to anomalous gestural sequences by a language trained dolphin: Evidence for processing of semantic relations and syntactic information. *Journal of Experimental Psychology: General, 122*, 184–194.
Hewes, G. W. 1977. Language origin theories. In Rumbaugh 1977 (pp. 3–54).

Heyes, C., and L. Huber. 2000. *The evolution of cognition.* Cambridge: MIT University Press.

Hillix, W. A., and D. M. Rumbaugh. 2003. *Animal bodies, human minds: Ape, dolphin, and parrot language skills.* New York: Plenum.

Honig, W. K., and J. G. Fetterman. 1992. *Cognitive aspects of stimulus control.* Hillsdale, N.J.: Erlbaum.

Hopkins, W. D. 1999. Heritability of hand preference in chimpanzees *(Pan troglodytes):* Evidence from a partial interspecies cross-fostering study. *Journal of Comparative Psychology, 113,* no. 3, 307–313.

Hopkins, W. D., and S. Fernandez-Carriba. 2000. The effect of situational factors on hand preferences for feeding in 177 captive chimpanzees *(Pan troglodytes). Neuropsychologia, 38,* no. 4, 403–409.

Hopkins, W. D., and L. A. Fowler. 1998. Lateralized changes in tympanic membrane temperature in relation to different cognitive tasks in chimpanzees *(Pan troglodytes). Behavioral Neuroscience, 112,* no. 1, 83–88.

Hopkins, W. D., L. Marino, J. K. Rilling, and L. A. MacGregor. 1998. Planum temporale asymmetries in great apes as revealed by magnetic resonance imaging (MRI). *NeuroReport, 9,* 2913–2918.

Hopkins, W. D., and K. Pearson. 2000. Chimpanzee *(Pan troglodytes)* handedness: Variability across multiple measures of hand use. *Journal of Comparative Psychology, 114,* no. 2, 126–135.

Hopkins, W. D., and D. L. Pilcher. 2001. Neuroanatomical localization of the motor hand area using magnetic resonance imaging: The left hemisphere is larger in great apes. *Behavioral Neuroscience, 115,* 1159–1164.

Hopkins, W. D., and E. S. Savage-Rumbaugh. 1991. Vocal communication as a function of differential rearing experiences in *Pan paniscus:* A preliminary report. *International Journal of Primatology, 12,* 559–583.

Hopkins, W. D., D. A. Washburn, L. Berke, and M. Williams. 1992. Behavioral asymmetries of psychomotor performance in rhesus monkeys *(Macaca mulatta):* A dissociation between hand preference and skill. *Journal of Comparative Psychology, 106,* no. 4, 392–397.

Hull, C. L. 1943. *Principles of behavior.* New York: Appleton-Century-Crofts.

Hume, D. A. (1748, rpt. 1902). An enquiry concerning human understanding. L. A. Selby-Bigge (ed.), 2d ed. Oxford: Clarendon.

Humphrey, N. 2002. *The mind made flesh: Frontiers of psychology and evolution.* Oxford University Press.

Jenkins, H. M., and B. R. Moore. 1973. The form of the autoshaped response with food or water reinforcers. *Journal of the Experimental Analysis of Behavior, 20,* 163–181.

Jerison, H. J. 1985. On the evolution of mind. In D. A. Oakley (ed.), *Brain and mind* (pp. 1–31). London: Methuen.

Jolly, A. 1964. Prosimian's manipulation of simple object problems. *Animal Behavior, 12,* 560–570.

Kamin, L. J. 1969. Predictability, surprise, attention, and conditioning. In B. A.

Campbell and R. M. Church (eds.), *Punishment and adversive behavior* (pp. 415–437). New York: Appleton-Century-Crofts.

Kellogg, W. N. 1980. Communication and language in the home-raised chimpanzee. In T. A. Sebeok and J. Umiker-Sebeok, (eds.), *Speaking of apes: A critical anthology of two-way communication with man* (pp. 61–70). New York: Plenum.

Kellogg, W. N., and L. A. Kellogg. 1933. *The ape and the child.* New York: McGraw-Hill.

Kennedy, J. S. 1992. *The new anthropomorphism.* New York: Cambridge University Press.

Köhler, W. 1925. *The mentality of apes.* London: Routledge and Kegan Paul.

Krechevsky, I. 1938. A study of the continuity of the problem solving process. *Psychological Review, 45,* 107–133.

Kuhlmeier, V. A. and S. T. Boysen. 2002. Chimpanzees *(Pan troglodytes)* recognize spatial and object correspondences between a scale model and its referent. *Psychological Science, 13,* 60–63.

Kummer, H. 1968. *Social organization of Hamadryas baboons.* Chicago: University of Chicago Press.

Kuo, Z. Y. 1967. *The dynamics of behavior development.* New York: Random House.

Le Gros Clark, W. E. 1959. *The antecedents of man.* Edinburgh: Edinburgh University Press.

Levin, P. S., and D. A. Levin. 2002. The real biodiversity crisis. *American Scientist, 90,* 6–8.

Lorenz, K. 1950. The comparative methods in studying innate behavior patterns. In *Physiological mechanisms in animal behavior* (pp. 221–268). New York: Academic Press.

———. 1965. *Evolution and modification of behavior.* Chicago: University of Chicago Press.

Lyn, H., and E. S. Savage-Rumbaugh. 2000. Observational word learning in two bonobos *(Pan paniscus):* Ostensive and non-ostensive contexts. *Language and Communication, 20,* 255–273.

Lyon, G. R., and N. A. Krasnegor (eds.). 1996. *Attention, memory, and executive function.* Baltimore: Paul H. Brookes.

Mackintosh, N. J. (ed.). 1994. *Animal learning and cognition.* New York: Academic Press.

Marler, P. 1972. Song learning and preparedness. In M. E. P. Seligman and J. L. Hager (eds.), *Biological boundaries of learning* (pp. 336–376). New York: Appleton-Century-Crofts.

———. 1999. How much does a human environment humanize a chimp? *American Anthropologist, 101,* no. 2, 432–436.

Marx, M. H., and W. A. Hillix. 1979. *Systems and theories in psychology.* New York: McGraw-Hill.

Mason, W. A. 1958. *Primary role of primates in comparative psychology.* Paper presented at the American Psychological Association Annual Convention, Washington, D.C.

———. 2002. The natural history of primate development: An organismic perspective. In D. J. Lewkowicz and R. Lickliter (eds.), *Conceptions of development: Lessons from the laboratory* (pp. 105–134). New York: Psychology Press.

Matsuzawa, T. 1985a. Color naming and classification in a chimpanzee *(Pan troglodytes)*. *Journal of Human Evolution, 14,* 283–291.

———. 1985b. Use of numbers by a chimpanzee. *Nature, 315,* 57–59.

———. 1990. The perceptual world of a chimpanzee. Project no. 63510057 Inuyama, Aichi, 484 Japan.

———. 1994. Field experiments on use of stone tools by chimpanzees in the wild. In R. W. Wrangham, W. C. McGrew, F. B. M. deWaal, and P. G. Heltne (eds.), *Chimpanzee cultures* (pp. 351–370). Cambridge: Harvard University Press.

McGrew, W. C. 1992. *Chimpanzee material culture.* Cambridge: Cambridge University Press.

Meador, D. M. 1984. Effects of color on visual discrimination of geometric symbols by severely and profoundly mentally retarded individuals. *American Journal of Mental Deficiency, 89,* no. 3, 275–286.

Meador, D. M., D. M. Rumbaugh, M. Tribble, and S. Thompson. 1984. Facilitating visual discrimination learning of moderately and severely retarded children through illumination of stimuli. *American Journal of Mental Deficiency, 89,* no. 3, 313–316.

Menzel, C. R. 1999. Unprompted recall and reporting of hidden objects by a chimpanzee *(Pan troglodytes)* after extended delays. *Journal of Comparative Psychology. 113,* 426–434.

Menzel, E. W., Jr. 1972. Spontaneous invention of ladders in a group of young chimpanzees. *Folia Primatologica, 17,* 87–106.

———. 1973. Further observations on the use of ladders in a group of young chimpanzees. *Folia Primatologica, 19,* 450–457.

Menzel, E. W., Jr., R. K. Davenport, and C. M. Rogers. 1970. The development of tool using in wild born and restriction reared chimpanzees. *Folia Primatologica, 12,* 273–283.

Menzel, E. W., Jr., E. S. Savage-Rumbaugh, and J. Lawson. 1985. Chimpanzee *(Pan troglodytes)* spatial problem solving with the use of mirrors and televised equivalents of mirrors. *Journal of Comparative Psychology, 99,* 211–217.

Mettrie, J. O. de la. 1748, rpt. 1912. *Man a machine.* Chicago: Opencourt.

Meyer, D. R., F. R. Treichler, and P. M. Meyer. 1965. Discrete-trial training techniques and stimulus variables. In A. M. Schrier, H. F. Harlow, and F. Stollnitz (eds.), *Behavior of nonhuman primates: Modern research trends* (vol. 1, pp. 303–321). New York: Academic Press.

Mill, J. S. 1843, rpt. 1956. *A system of logic.* London: Longmans.

Miller, G. A. 1983. Informavores. In F. Machlup and U. Mansfield (eds.), *The study of information: Interdisciplinary messages* (pp. 111–113). New York: Wiley.

Miller, N. E., and J. Dollard. 1941. *Social learning and imitation.* New Haven: Yale University Press.

Mitchell, R. W. 1999. Deception and concealment as strategic script violation in great apes and humans. In S. T. Parker, R. W. Mitchell, and H. L. Miles (eds.), *The mentalities of gorillas and orangutans: Comparative perspectives* (pp. 295–315). New York: Cambridge University Press.

Mitchell, R. W., P. Yao, P. Sherman, and M. O'Regan. 1985. Discriminative responding of a dolphin *(Tursiops truncatus)* to differentially rewarded stimuli. *Journal of Comparative Psychology, 99,* 218–225.

Morgan, C. L. 1894. *An introduction to comparative psychology.* London: Scott.

Morris, R. D., W. D. Hopkins, and L. Bolser-Gilmore. 1993. Assessment of hand preference in two language-trained chimpanzees *(Pan troglodytes):* A multimethod analysis. *Journal of Clinical and Experimental Neuropsychology, 15,* 487–502.

Muenzinger, K. F. 1938. Vicarious trial and error at a point of choice: I. A general survey of its relation to learning efficiency. *Journal of Genetic Psychology, 53,* 75–86.

Napier, J. R., and P. H. Napier. 1994. *The natural history of primates.* Cambridge: MIT Press.

Nissen, H. W. 1951. Phylogenetic comparison. In S. S. Stevens (ed.), *Handbook of experimental psychology* (pp. 347–386). New York: Wiley.

Nottebohm, F. 1981. A brain for all seasons: Cyclical anatomical changes in song control nuclei of the canary brain. *Science, 214,* 1368–1370.

Novikoff, A. B. 1945. The concept of integrative levels and biology. *Science, 101,* 209–215.

Papini, M. R. 2002. *Comparative psychology: Evolution and development of behavior.* Upper Saddle River, N.J.: Pearson Education.

Parker, C. E. 1969. Responsiveness, manipulation, and implementation behavior in chimpanzees, gorillas, and orangutans. In C. R. Carpenter (ed.), *Proceedings of Second International Congress on Primatology, 1,* 160–166.

———. 1974a. The antecedents of man the manipulator. *Journal of Human Evolution, 3,* 493–500.

———. 1974b. Behavioral diversity in ten species of nonhuman primates. *Journal of Comparative and Physiological Psychology, 37,* 930–937.

Parker, S. T., and K. R. Gibson. 1990. *"Language" and intelligence in monkeys and apes: Comparative developmental perspectives.* New York: Cambridge University Press.

Parker, S. T., M. Kerr, H. Markowitz, and J. Gould. 1999. A survey of tool use in zoo gorillas. In S. T. Parker, R. W. Mitchell, and H. L. Miles (eds.), *The*

mentalities of gorillas and orangutans: Comparative perspectives (pp. 188–
193). New York: Cambridge University Press.

Parr, L. A., J. T. Winslow, W. D. Hopkins, and F. B. M. de Waal. 2000. Recognizing facial cues: Individual discrimination by chimpanzees *(Pan troglodytes)* and rhesus monkeys *(Macaca mulatta). Journal of Comparative Psychology, 114(1),* 47–60.

Pate, J. L., D. M. Rumbaugh. 1983. The language-like behavior of Lana chimpanzee: Is it merely discrimination and paired-associate learning? *Animal Learning and Behavior,* 11, 134–138.

Patterson, F. G. 1977. The gestures of a gorilla: Language acquisition in another pongid species. In D. Hamburg, J. Goodall, and R. E. McCown (eds.), *Perspectives on human evolution* (pp. 26–29). Menlo Park, Calif.: Benjamin.

———. 1978. The gestures of a gorilla: Sign language acquisition in another pongid species. *Brain and Language, 5,* 72–97.

Pavlov, I. P. 1927. *Conditioned reflexes.* London: Oxford University Press.

———. 1955. *Selected works.* Moscow: Foreign Languages Publishing.

Perkins, C. C., Jr. 1968. An analysis of the concept of reinforcement. *Psychological Review, 75,* 155–172.

Perusse, R., and D. M. Rumbaugh. 1990. Summation in chimpanzees *(Pan troglodytes):* Effects of amounts, number of wells, and finer ratios. *International Journal of Primatology, 11(5),* 425–437.

Piaget, J. 1930. *The child's conception of physical causality.* London: Routledge and Kegan Paul.

———. 1974. *Understanding causality.* New York: Norton.

Povinelli, D. J., K. E. Nelson, and S. T. Boysen. 1990. Inferences about guessing and knowing by chimpanzees *(Pan troglodytes). Journal of Comparative Psychology, 104,* 203–210.

Premack, A. 1976. *Why chimps can read.* New York: Harper and Row.

Premack, D. 1963. Prediction of the comparative reinforcement values of running and drinking. *Science, 139,* 1062–1063.

———. 1965. Reinforcement theory. In D. Levine (ed.), *Nebraska symposium on motivation* (vol. 13, pp. 335–337). Lincoln: University of Nebraska Press.

———. 1970. A functional analysis of language. *Journal of the Experimental Analysis of Behavior, 14,* 107–125.

———. 1971. On the assessment of language competence in the chimpanzee. In A. M. Schrier and F. Sollnitz (eds.), *Behavior of Nonhuman Primates* (vol. 4, pp. 808–822). New York: Academic Press.

———. 1976. *Intelligence in ape and man.* Hillsdale, N.J.: Erlbaum.

Premack, D., and A. J. Premack. 1983. *The mind of an ape.* New York: Norton.

Premack, D., and G. Woodruff. 1978. Does the chimpanzee have a theory of mind? *Behavioral and Brain Sciences, 4,* 515–526.

Purdy, J. E., M. R. Markham, B. L. Schwartz, and W. C. Gordon (eds.), 2001. *Learning and memory.* Wadsworth.

Rescorla, R. A. 1988a. Behavioral studies of Pavlovian conditioning. *Annual Review of Neuroscience, 11,* 329–352.

———. 1988b. Pavlovian conditioning: It's not what you think it is. *American Psychologist 43,* 151–160.

Rescorla, R. A., and A. R. Wagner. 1972. A theory of Pavlovian conditioning: Variations in the effectiveness of reinforcement and non-reinforcement. In A. H. Black and W. F. Prokasy (eds.). *Classical conditioning II* (pp. 372–381). Englewood Cliffs, N.J.: Prentice-Hall.

Revusky, S., and E. W. Bedarf. 1967. Association of illness with prior ingestion of novel foods. *Science, 155,* 219–220.

Riesen, A. H. 1982. Effects of environments on development in sensory systems. In W. D. Neff (ed.), *Contributions to sensory physiology* (pp. 45–77). New York: Academic Press.

Rilling, J. K., and T. R. Insel. 1999. Differential expansions of neural projection systems in primate brain evolution. *NeuroReport, 10,* 1453–1459.

Roitblat, H. L. 1982. The meaning of representation in animal memory. *The Behavioral and Brain Sciences, 5,* 353–406.

———. 1985. *Introduction to comparative psychology.* New York: Freeman.

———. 1988. A cognitive action theory of learning. In J. Delacour and J. C. S. Levy (eds.), *Systems with learning and memory abilities* (pp. 353–406). Amsterdam: Elsevier.

Roitblat, H. L., T. Bever, and H. Terrace. 1984. *Animal cognition.* Hillsdale, N.J.: Erlbaum.

Romanes, G. J. 1882. *Animal intelligence.* New York: Appleton.

Rumbaugh, D. M. 1965. Maternal care in relation to infant behavior in the squirrel monkey. *Psychological Reports, 16,* 171–176.

———. 1968. The learning and sensory capacities of the squirrel monkey in phylogenetic perspective. In L. A. Rosenblum and R. C. Cooper (eds.), *The Squirrel Monkey* (pp. 255–317). New York: Academic Press.

———. 1970. Learning skills of anthropoids. In L. Rosenblum (ed.), *Primate behavior: Developments in field and laboratory research* (pp. 1–70). New York: Academic Press.

——— (ed.) 1977. *Language learning by a chimpanzee: The Lana Project.* New York: Academic Press.

———. 1985. Comparative psychology: Patterns in adaptation. In A. M. Rogers and C. J. Schrier (eds.), *The G. Stanley Hall Lecture Series,* vol. 5 (pp. 7–53). Washington, D.C.: American Psychological Association.

———. 1990. Comparative psychology and the great apes: Their competence in learning, language, and number. *Psychological Record, 40,* 15–39.

———. 1994. Anthropomorphism revisited [review of *The new anthropomorphism*]. *Quarterly Review of Biology, 69,* 248–251.

———. 1995. Emergence of relations and the essence of learning: A review of Sidman's *Equivalence Relations and Behavior: A Research Story. Behavior Analyst, 38(3),* 367–375.

————. 1997. The psychology of Harry F. Harlow: A bridge from radical to rational behaviorism. *Philosophical Psychology, 10*, no. 2, 197–210.

————. 2002. Emergents and rational behaviorism. *Eye on Psi Chi, 6,* 8–14.

Rumbaugh, D. M., and R. C. Arnold. 1971. Learning: A comparative study of Lemur and Cercopithecus. *Folia Primatologica, 14,* 154–160.

Rumbaugh, D. M., and T. V. Gill. 1976. The mastery of language-type skills by the chimpanzee *(Pan). Annals of the New York Academy of Sciences, 280,* 562–578.

Rumbaugh, D. M., T. V. Gill, and E. C. von Glasersfeld. 1973. Reading and sentence completion by a chimpanzee *(Pan). Science, 182,* 731–733.

Rumbaugh, D. M., W. D. Hopkins, D. A. Washburn, and E. S. Savage-Rumbaugh. 1989. Lana chimpanzee learns to count by "Numath": A summary of a videotaped experimental report. *Psychological Record, 39,* 459–470.

————. 1993. Chimpanzee competence for counting in a video-formatted task situation. In H. L. Roitblat, L. M. Herman, and P. E. Nachtigall (eds.), *Language and communication: Comparative perspectives* (pp. 329–346). Hillsdale, N.J.: Erlbaum.

Rumbaugh, D. M., and D. McCormack. 1967. The learning skills of primates: A comparative study of apes and monkeys. In D. Stark, R. Schneider, and H. J. Kuhn (eds.), *Progress in primatology* (pp. 289–306). Stuttgart: Gustav Fischer.

Rumbaugh, D. M., and J. A. McQueeney. 1963. Learning set formation and discrimination reversal: Learning problems to criterion in the squirrel monkey. *Journal of Comparative Physiological Psychology, 56,* 435–439.

Rumbaugh, D. M., and J. L. Pate. 1984. The evolution of cognition in primates: A comparative perspective. In Roitblat, Bever, and Terrace 1984 (pp. 569–587).

Rumbaugh, D. M., and M. B. Pournelle. 1966. Discrimination-reversal skills of primates: The reversal/acquisition ratio as a function of phyletic standing. *Psychonomic Science, 4,* 45–46.

Rumbaugh, D. M., W. K. Richardson, D. A. Washburn, E. S. Savage-Rumbaugh, and W. D. Hopkins. 1989. Rhesus monkeys *(Macaca mulatta),* video tasks, and implications for stimulus response spatial contiguity. *Journal of Comparative Psychology 103,* 32–38.

Rumbaugh, D. M., A. H. Riesen, and R. E. Lee. 1970. *Survey of the primates.* Film. Atlanta: Georgia State University.

Rumbaugh, D. M., A. H. Riesen, and S. C. Wright. 1972. Creative responsiveness to objects: A report of a pilot study with young apes. *Folia Primatology, 17,* 397–403.

Rumbaugh, D. M., M. E. Sammons, M. M. Prim, and S. Phillips. 1965. Learning set in squirrel monkeys as affected by pretraining with differentially rewarded single objects. *Perceptual Motor Skills, 21,* 63–70.

Rumbaugh, D. M., and E. S. Savage-Rumbaugh. 1994. Language in comparative perspective. In Mackintosh 1994 (pp. 307–333).

Rumbaugh, D. M., E. S. Savage-Rumbaugh, and M. Hegel. 1987. Summation in the chimpanzee *(Pan troglodytes)*. *Journal of Experimental Psychology: Animal Behavior Processes, 13,* (2), 105–113.

Rumbaugh, D. M., E. S. Savage-Rumbaugh, and J. L. Pate. 1988. Addendum to "Summation in the chimpanzee *(Pan troglodytes)*." *Journal of Experimental Psychology: Animal Behavior Processes, 14,* 118–120.

Rumbaugh, D. M., E. S. Savage-Rumbaugh, and D. A. Washburn. 1996. Toward a new outlook on primate learning and behavior: Complex learning and emergent processes in comparative perspective. *Japanese Psychological Research, 38,* no. 3, 113–125.

Rumbaugh, D. M., and G. T. Steinmetz. 1971. Discrimination-reversal skills of the lowland gorilla *(Gorilla g. gorilla)*. *Folia Primatologica, 16,* 144–152.

Rumbaugh, D. M., and G. M. Sterritt. 1986. Intelligence: From Genes to Genius in the Quest for Control. In W. Bechtel (ed.), *Science and philosophy: Integrating the disciplines* (pp. 309–322). Boston: Martinus Nijhoff.

Rumbaugh, D. M., and D. A. Washburn. 1993. Counting by chimpanzees and ordinality judgements by macaques in video-formatted tasks. In S. T. Boysen and E. J. Capaldi (eds.), *The development of numerical competence: Animal and human models* (pp. 87–106). Hillsdale, N.J.: Erlbaum.

Rumbaugh, D. M., D. A. Washburn, and W. A. Hillix. 1996. Respondents, operants, and emergents: Toward an integrated perspective on behavior. In K. Pribram and J. King (eds.), *Learning as a self-organizing process* (pp. 57–73). Hillsdale, N.J.: Erlbaum.

Rumbaugh, J. R. 1973. Long-term and short-term retention in a talapoin monkey. *Perceptual and Motor Skills, 36,* no. 3, 800.

Savage-Rumbaugh, E. S. 1986. *Ape language: From conditioned response to symbol.* New York: Columbia University Press.

———. 1991. Language learning in the bonobo: How and why they learn. In N. A. Krasnegor, D. M. Rumbaugh, R. L Schiefelbusch, and M. Studdert-Kennedy (eds.), *Biological and behavioral determinants of language development* (pp. 209–233). Hillsdale, N.J.: Erlbaum.

Savage-Rumbaugh, E. S., K. Brakke, and S. Hutchins. 1992. Linguistic development: Contrasts between co-reared *Pan troglodytes* and *Pan paniscus.* In T. Nishida (ed.), *Proceedings of the 13th International Congress of Primatology* (pp. 293–304). Tokyo: University of Tokyo Press.

Savage-Rumbaugh, E. S., and R. Lewin. 1994. *Kanzi: At the brink of the human mind.* New York: Wiley.

Savage-Rumbaugh, E. S., K. McDonald, R. A. Sevcik, W. D. Hopkins, and E. Rubert. 1986. Spontaneous symbol acquisition and communicative use by pygmy chimpanzees *(Pan paniscus)*. *Journal of Experimental Psychology: General, 115,* 211–235.

Savage-Rumbaugh, E. S, J. Murphy, R. A. Sevcik, K. E. Brakke, S. Williams, and D. M. Rumbaugh. 1993. Language comprehension in ape and child.

Monographs of the Society for Research in Child Development, serial no. 233, vol. 58, nos. 3–4, pp. 1–242.

Savage-Rumbaugh, E. S., J. L. Pate, J. Lawson, S. T. Smith, and S. Rosenbaum. 1983. Can a chimpanzee make a statement? *Journal of Experimental Psychology: General, 112,* 457–492.

Savage-Rumbaugh, E. S., D. M. Rumbaugh, and S. Boysen. 1978. Symbolic communication between two chimpanzees *(Pan troglodytes). Science, 201,* 641–644.

Savage-Rumbaugh, E. S., D. M. Rumbaugh, S. T. Smith, and J. Lawson, J. 1980. Reference: The linguistic essential. *Science, 210,* 922–924.

Savage-Rumbaugh, E. S., S. G. Shanker, and T. J. Taylor. 1998. *Apes, language, and the human mind.* New York: Oxford University Press.

Savage-Rumbaugh, E. S., R. A. Sevcik, and W. Hopkins. 1991. Symbolic cross-modal transfer in two species of chimpanzees *(Pan paniscus* and *Pan troglodytes). Child Development, 59,* 617–625.

Savage-Rumbaugh, E. S., S. L. Williams, T. Furuichi, and T. Kano. 1996. Language perceived: *Paniscus* branches out. In B. McGrew, L. Marchant, and T. Nishida (eds.), *Great apes societies* (pp. 173–184). London: Cambridge University Press.

Schiller, P. A. 1952. Innate constituents of complex responses in primates. *Psychological Review, 59,* 177–191.

———. 1957. Innate motor action as a basis of learning. In C. H. Schiller (ed.), *Instinctive behavior* (pp. 14–24). New York: International Universities Press.

Schurcliff, A., D. Brown, and F. Stollnitz. 1971. Specificity of training required for solution of a stick problem by rhesus monkeys *(Macaca mulatta). Learning and Motiviation, 2,* 255–270.

Schusterman, R. J. 1981. Behavioral capabilities of seals and sea lions: A review of their hearing, visual, learning, and diving skills. *Psychological Record, 31,* 125–143.

Seligman, M. E. P. 1975. *Helplessness: On depression, development, and death.* San Francisco: Freeman.

Sheffield, F. D., and T. B. Roby. 1950. Reward value of a non-nutritive sweet taste. *Journal of Comparative Physiological Psychology, 43,* 471–481.

Sibley, C. G., and J. E. Ahlquist. 1987. DNA hybridization evidence of hominoid phylogeny: Results from an expanded data set. *Journal of Molecular Evolution, 26,* 99–121.

Sidman, M. 1994. *Equivalence relations and behavior: A research story.* Boston: Authors Cooperative.

Skinner, B. F. 1938. *The behavior of organisms: An experimental analysis.* New York: Appleton-Century-Crofts.

———. 1950. Are theories of learning necessary? *Psychological Review, 57,* 193–216.

———. 1953. *Science and human behavior.* New York: Macmillan.

———. 1957. *Verbal behavior.* New York: Appleton-Century-Crofts.

Smith, J. D., W. E. Shields, and D. A. Washburn. (in press). The comparative psychology of uncertainty monitoring and metacognition. *Behavioral and Brain Sciences.*

Spence, K. W. 1956. *Behavior theory and conditioning.* New Haven: Yale University Press.

———. 1960. *Behavior theory and learning: Selected papers.* Englewood Cliffs, N.J.: Prentice-Hall.

Stanford, C. B. 1995. Chimpanzee hunting behavior. *American Scientist, 83,* no. 3, 256–261.

Stebbins, W. C. 1976. Comparative hearing function in the vertebrates. In R. B. Masterson, M. E. Bitterman, C. B. G. Campbell, and N. Hotton (eds.), *Evolution of brain and behavior in vertebrates* (pp. 107–113). Hillsdale, N.J.: Erlbaum.

Sternberg, R. J. (ed.). 1994. *Encyclopedia of Human Intelligence,* vol. 1. New York: Macmillan.

Sternberg, R. J., and E. L. Grigorenko. 2001. Unified psychology. *American Psychologist, 56,* 1069–1079.

Sterritt, G. M., and M. P. Smith. 1965. Reinforcement effect of specific components of feeding in young leghorn chicks. *Journal of Comparative and Physiological Psychology, 59,* 171–175.

Suddendorf, T., and A. Whiten. 2001. Mental evolution and development: Evidence for secondary representation in children, great apes, and other animals. *Psychological Bulletin, 127,* no. 3, 629–650.

Suomi, S. J. 2002. How gene-environment interactions can shape the development of socioemotional regulation in rhesus monkeys. In B. S. Zukerman and A. F. Lieberman (eds.), *Socioemotional regulation: Dimensions, developmental trends, and influences* (pp. 265–279). Skillman, N.J: Johnson and Johnson.

Taglialatela, J. P., S. Savage-Rumbaugh, and L. A. Baker. 2003. Vocal production by a language-competent bonobo, *Pan paniscus. International Journal of Primatology, 24,* no. 1, 1–17.

Terrace, H. S. 1979. *Nim.* New York: Knopf.

Terrace, H. S., L. A. Petitto, R. J. Sanders, and T. G. Bever. 1979. Can an ape create a sentence? *Science, 206,* 891–900.

Thomas, R. K., D. Fowlkes, and J. D. Vickery. 1980. Conceptual numerousness judgments by squirrel monkeys. *American Journal of Psychology, 93,* 247–257.

Thorndike, E. L. 1898. Animal intelligence: An experimental study of the associative processes in animals. *Psychological Review Monograph Supplements 2,* no. 8, 1–109.

———. 1911. *Animal intelligence: Experimental studies.* New York: Macmillan.

———. 1932. Reward and punishment in animal learning. *Comparative Psychology Monographs, 8.*

Thorpe, W. H. 1956. *Learning and instinct in animals.* London: Methuen.

———. 1972. Vocal communication in birds. In R. A. Hinde (ed.), *Nonverbal communication* (pp. 153–176). Cambridge: Cambridge University Press.

Tinbergen, N. 1951. *The study of instinct.* Oxford: Oxford University Press.

Tolman, E. C. 1932. *Purposive behavior in animals and men.* New York: Century.

———. 1948. Cognitive maps in rats and men. *Psychological Review, 55,* 189–208.

Tomasello, M. 1999. *The cultural origins of human cognition.* Cambridge: Harvard University Press.

Tomasello, M., E. S. Savage-Rumbaugh, and A. C. Kruger. 1993. Imitative learning of actions on objects by children, chimpanzees, and enculterated chimpanzees. *Child Development, 64,* 1688–1705.

Torigoe, T. 1985. Comparison of object manipulation among 74 species of non-human primates. *Primates, 26,* no. 2, 182–194.

Toth, N., K. D. Schick, E. S. Savage-Rumbaugh, R. A. Sevcik, and D. M. Rumbaugh. 1993. *Pan* the tool-maker: Investigations into the stone tool-making and tool-using capabilities of a bonobo *(Pan paniscus). Journal of Archaeological Science, 20,* 81–91.

Tulving, E., and H. J. Markowitsch. 1998. Episodic and declarative memory: Role of the hippocampus. *Hippocampus, 8,* 198–204.

Tuttle, R. H. 1986. *Apes of the world: Their social behavior, communication, mentality, and ecology.* Park Ridge, N.J.: Noyes.

Visalberghi, E., and D. M. Fragaszy. 1990. Do monkeys ape? In Parker and Gibson 1990 (pp. 829–836).

von Glasersfeld, E. 1977. The Yerkish language and its automatic parser. In Rumbaugh 1977 (pp. 91–130).

Wagner, A. R. 1961. Effects of amount and percentage of reinforcement and number of acquisition trials on conditioning and extinction. *Journal of Experimental Psychology, 61,* 234–242.

———. 1969. Frustrative non-reward: A variety of punishment? In B. A. Campbell and R. M. Church (eds.), *Punishment* (pp. 554–569). New York: Appleton-Century-Crofts.

Wagner, A. R., and W. S. Terry. 1975. Backward condition to a CS following an expected vs. a surprising UCS. *Animal Learning and Behavior, 3,* 370–374.

Washburn, D. A., W. D. Hopkins, and D. M. Rumbaugh. 1989. Automation of learning-set testing: The video-task paradigm. *Behavior Research Methods, Instruments, and Computers, 21,* 281–284.

———. 1991. Perceived control in rhesus monkeys *(Macaca mulatta):* Enhanced video-task performance. *Journal of Experimental Psychology, 17,* 123–129.

Washburn, D. A., and D. M. Rumbaugh. 1991a. Rhesus monkey *(Macaca mulatta)* complex learning skills reassessed. *International Journal of Primatology 12,* no. 4, 377–388.

————. 1991b. Ordinal judgments of numerical symbols by macaques *(Macaca mulatta). Psychological Science, 2,* no. 3, 190–193.

————. 1992a. Comparative assessment of psychomotor performance: Target prediction by humans and macaques *(Macaca mulatta). Journal of Experimental Psychology: General, 121,* no. 3, 305–312.

————. 1992b. Testing primates with joystick-based automated apparatus: Lessons from the Language Research Center's Computerized Test System. *Behavior Research Methods, Instruments, and Computers, 24,* 157–164.

Watson, J. B. 1913. Psychology as the behaviorist views it. *Psychological Review, 20,* 158–177.

Wechsler, D. 1935, rpt. 1969. *The range of human capacities.* New York: Hafner.

————. 1944. *The measurement of adult intelligence.* 3d ed. Baltimore: Williams and Wilkins.

————. 1974. *Selected papers of David Wechsler.* New York: Academic Press.

Whiten, A., J. Goodall, W. C. McGrew, T. Nishida, V. Reynolds, Y. Sugiyama, C. E. G. Tutin, R. W. Wrangham, and C. Boesch. 1999. Cultures in chimpanzees. *Nature, 399,* 682–685.

Wilson, E. O. 2002. *The future of life.* New York: Knopf.

Wolkin, J. R., and R. H. Myers. 1980. Characteristics of a gibbon-siamang hybrid ape. *International Journal of Primatology, 1,* no. 3, 203.

Yerkes, R. M. 1916. *The mental life of monkeys and apes: A study of ideational behavior.* Behavior Monographs 3, 1–145.

————. 1943. *Chimpanzees: A laboratory colony.* New Haven: Yale University Press.

Yerkes, R. M., and B. Learned. 1925. *Chimpanzee intelligence and its vocal expressions.* Baltimore: Williams and Wilkins.

Yerkes, R. M., and A. Yerkes. 1929. *The great apes.* New Haven: Yale University Press.

Recommended Reading

Bandura, A. 1971. *Social learning theory.* New York: General Learning.

Benchley, B. J. 1942. *My friends, the apes.* Boston: Little, Brown.

Benson, J., P. Fries, W. Greaves, K. Iwamoto, E. S. Savage-Rumbaugh, and J. Taglialatela. 2002. Confrontation and support in bonobo-human discourse. *Functions of Language, 9,* 1–38.

Bickerton, D. 1995. *Language and human behavior.* Seattle: University of Washington Press.

Blum, D. 1994. *The monkey wars.* New York: Oxford University Press.

Bruner, J. S. 1983. *Child's talk: Learning to use language.* New York: Norton.

Buirski, P., R. Plutchik, and H. Kellerman. 1978. Sex differences, dominance, and personality in the chimpanzee. *Animal Behavior, 26,* 123–129.

Byrne, R. 1995. *The thinking ape.* Oxford: Oxford University Press.

———. 1996. The misunderstood ape: Cognitive skills of the gorilla. In A. E. Russon, K. A. Bard, and S. T. Parker (eds.), *Reaching into thought: The minds of the great apes* (pp. 111–130). New York: Cambridge University Press.

Call, J., and M. Tomasello. 1996. The effects of humans on the cognitive development of apes. In A. E. Russon, K. A. Bard, and S. T. Parker (eds.), *Reaching into thought: The minds of the great apes* (pp. 371–403). New York: Cambridge University Press.

Calvin, W. H. 1994. The emergence of intelligence. *Scientific American, 271,* 100–107.

———. Unpublished. Searching for intelligence: Evolution in the brain.

Candland, D. K. 1993. *Feral children and clever animals.* New York: Oxford University Press.

Chomsky, N. 1965. *Aspects of a theory of syntax.* Cambridge: MIT Press.

———. 1980. Human language and other semiotic systems. In T. A. Sebeok and J. Umiker-Sebeok (eds.), *Speaking of apes: A critical anthology of two-way communication with man* (pp. 429–440). New York: Plenum.

———. 1988. *Language and problems of knowledge: The Managua.* Cambridge: MIT Press.

Corballis, M. C., and S. E. G. Lea (eds.). 1999. *The descent of mind: Psychological perspectives on hominid evolution.* London: Oxford University Press.

Cory, A. T. 1840. *The hieroglyphics of Horapollo Nilous.* London: William Pickering.

Dewsbury, D. A. 1984. *Comparative psychology in the twentieth century.* New York: Hutchinson Ross.

Epstein, R. 1987. Reflections on thinking in animals. In G. Greenberg and E. Tobach (eds.), *Cognition, language, and consciousness: Integrative levels.* Hillsdale, N.J.: Erlbaum.

Fernandez-Carriba, S., and W. D. Hopkins. 2002. Asymmetry in facial expressions of emotions by chimpanzees. *Neuropsychologia, 40,* 1523–1533.

Ferster, C. B., and B. F. Skinner. 1957. *Schedules of reinforcement.* New York: Appleton-Century-Crofts.

Flynn, J. R. 1999. Searching for justice: The discovery of IQ gains over time. *American Psychologist, 54,* 5–20.

Gannon, P. J., R. L. Holloway, D. C. Broadfield, and A. R. Braun. 1998. Asymmetry of the chimpanzee planum temporale: Humanlike pattern of Wernicke's brain language area homolog. *Science, 279,* 220–222.

Garner, R. L. 1892. *The speech of monkeys.* London: Heinemann.

———. 1896. *Gorillas and chimpanzees.* London: Osgood, McIlvane.

Goodall, J. 1986. *The chimpanzees of Gombe.* Cambridge: Harvard University Press.

Gossette, R. L. 1967. Successive discrimination reversal (SDR) performances of four avian species on a brightness discrimination task. *Psychonomic Science, 6,* 17–18.

Hauser, M. D. 2000. *Wild minds.* New York: Holt.

Herman, L. M. 1987. Receptive competencies of language-trained animals. In J. S. Rosenblatt, C. Beer, M. C. Busnel, and P. J. B. Slater (eds.), *Advances in the Study of Behavior,* vol. 17 (pp. 1–60). Orlando, Fla.: Academic Press.

———. 1988. The language of animal language research: Reply to Schusterman and Gisiner. *Psychological Record, 38,* 349–362.

Herman, L. M., P. Morrel-Samuels, and A. A. Pack. 1990. Bottlenosed dolphin and human recognition of veridical and degraded video displays of an artificial gestural language. *Journal of Experimental Psychology: General, 119,* 215–230.

Herman, L. H., A. A. Pack, and P. Morrel-Samuels. 1993. Representational and conceptual skills of dolphins. In H. L. Roitblat, L. M. Herman, and P. E. Nachtigall (eds.), *Language and communication: Comparative perspectives* (pp. 404–442). Hillsdale, N.J.: Erlbaum.

Herman, L. H., D. G. Richards, and J. P. Wolz. 1984. Comprehension of sentences by bottlenosed dolphins. *Cognition, 16,* 129–219.

Hobson, P. 2002. *The cradle of thought.* Macmillan.

Hockett, Charles F. 1982, rpt. of 1960 article in *Scientific American.* The origin of speech. In *Human Communication.* San Francisco: Freeman.

Hoyt, A. Maria. 1941. *Toto and I: A gorilla in the family.* Philadelphia: Lippincott.

Jensen, A. R. 1998. *The g factor: The science of mental ability.* Westport, Conn.: Praeger.

Jensvold, M. L. A., and R. A. Gardner. 2000. Interactive use of sign language by cross-fostered chimpanzees *(Pan troglodytes). Journal of Comparative Psychology, 114,* 335–346.

Kappelman, J. 1996. The evolution of body mass and relative brain size in fossil hominids. *Journal of Human Evolution, 30,* 243–276.

Keleman, G. 1948. The anatomical basis of phonation in the chimpanzee. *Journal of Morphology, 82,* 229–256.

———. 1949. Structure and performance in animal language. *Archives of Otolaryngology, 50,* 740–744.

Kimble, G. A. 1981. Biological and cognitive constraints on learning. In L. T. Benjamin, Jr. (ed.), *The G. Stanley Hall Lecture Series* (vol. 1, pp. 205–225). Washington, D.C.: American Psychological Association.

King, J. E. 1999. Personality and the happiness of the chimpanzee. In F. Dolin (ed.), *Animal perspectives* (pp. 101–113). Cambridge: Cambridge University Press.

Kohts, N. 1935. *Infant ape and human child.* Scientific Memoirs of the Museum Darwinianum in Moscow. 2 vols.

Konner, M. 1982. *The tangled wing: Biological constraints in the human spirit.* New York: Harper and Row.

Kortlandt, A. 1965. How do chimpanzees use weapons when fighting leopards? *Yearbook of American Philosophical Society,* 327–332.

Krasnegor, N. A., O. R. Lyon, and P. S. Goldman-Rakic. 1997. *Development of the prefrontal cortex: Evolution, neurobiology, and behavior.* Baltimore: Paul H. Brookes.

Krasnegor, N. A., D. M. Rumbaugh, R. L. Schiefelbusch, M. Studdert-Kennedy. 1991. *Biological and behavioral determinants of language development.* Hillsdale, N.J.: Erlbaum.

Lieberman, P. 1968. Primate vocalizations and human linguistic ability. *Journal of the Acoustical Society of America, 44,* 1157–1164.

Lieberman, P. 1984. *The biology and evolution of language.* Cambridge: Harvard University Press.

Limber, J. 1977. Language in child and chimp? *American Psychologist, 32,* 280–293.

Locke, J. 1690, rpt. 1894. *An essay concerning human understanding.* Vol. 1. Ed. A. C. Fraser. Oxford: Oxford University Press.

Marchant, L., and T. Nishida (eds.). 1996. *Great apes societies.* London: Cambridge University Press.

Marino, L. 2002. Convergence of complex cognitive abilities in cetaceans and primates. *Brain, Behavior and Evolution, 59,* 21–32.

Martin, R. D. 1990. *Primate origins and evolution: A phylogenetic reconstruction.* London: Chapman and Hall.

Maryanski, A., and J. H. Turner. 1992. *The social cage.* Stanford, Calif.: Stanford University Press.

Matsuzawa, T. 1989. Spontaneous pattern construction in a chimpanzee. In P. Heltne and L. A. Marquardt (eds.), *Understanding chimpanzees.* Cambridge: Harvard University Press.

McGuire, M. T., M. J. Raleigh, and D. B. Pollack. 1994. Personality features in vervet monkeys: The effects of sex, age, social status, and group composition. *American Journal of Primatology, 33,* 1–13.

McHenry, H. M. 1992. Body size and proportions in early hominids. *American Journal of Physical Anthropology, 87,* 407–431.

————. 1994. Behavioral ecological implications of early hominid body size. *Journal of Human Evolution, 27,* 77–87.

Menzel, E. W., Jr. 1969. Chimpanzees utilization of space and responsiveness to objects. Age differences and comparison with macaques. In C. R. Carpenter (ed.), *Proceedings of Second International Congress on Primatology, 1,* 72–80.

Michotte, A. 1963. *The perception of causality.* Trans. T. R. Miles. New York: Basic.

Miles, H. L. 1990. The cognitive foundations for reference in a signing orangutan. In S. T. Parker and K. R. Gibson (eds.), *"Language" and intelligence in monkeys and apes: Comparative developmental perspectives* (pp. 451–468). New York: Cambridge University Press.

Parker, S. T., and K. R. Gibson. 1979. A model of the evolution of language and intelligence in early hominids. *Behavioral and Brain Sciences, 2,* 367–407.

Parker, S. T., R. W. Mitchell, and M. Boccia (eds.). 1994. *Self-awareness in animals and humans: Developmental perspectives.* New York: Cambridge University Press.

Patterson, F. L. 1990. Language acquisition in a lowland gorilla: Koko's first ten years of vocabulary development. *Word, 41,* no. 2, 97–143.

Patterson, F. L., and E. Linden. 1981. *The education of Koko.* New York: Holt, Rinehart, and Winston.

Pepperberg, I. M. 1985. Social modeling theory: A possible framework for understanding avian vocal learning. *Auk, 102,* 854–864.

————. 1999. *The Alex studies: Cognitive and communicative abilities of Grey parrots.* Cambridge: Harvard University Press.

Povinelli, D. J., and J. M. Bering. 2002. The mentality of apes revisited. *Current Directions in Psychological Science, 11,* 115–119.

Pribram, K. H. 1963. Reinforcement revisited: A structural view. *Nebraska Symposium on Motivation,* 113–159.

————. 1991. *Brain and perception: Holonomy and structure in figural processing.* Hillsdale, N.J.: Erlbaum.

Rapoport, S. I. 1999. How did the human brain evolve? A proposal based on new evidence from in vivo brain imaging during attention and ideation. *Brain Res. Bull. 50,* 149–165.

Rapoport, S. I. 2003. How did longevity promote brain expansion during primate evolution? In C. E. Finch, J.-M. Robine, and Y. Christen (eds.), *Brain and Longevity,* pp. 99–110. Berlin: Springer-Verlag.

Riley, D. A., and H. L. Roitblat. 1978. Selective attention and related cognitive processes in pigeons. In S. H. Hulse, H. Fowler, and W. K. Honig (eds.),

Cognitive processes in animal behavior (pp. 107–114). Hillsdale, N.J.: Erlbaum.

Rilling, J., C. Kilts, S. Williams, M. Beran, M. Giroux, J. M. Hoffman, S. Rapoport, S. Savage-Rumbaugh, and D. Rumbaugh. 2000. A comparative PET study of linguistic processing in humans and language-competent chimpanzees. *American Journal of Physical Anthropology, 111* (S), 263. [Abstract].

Rilling, J., C. Kilts, S. L. Williams, J. W. Kelley, M. J. Beran, M. Giroux, J. M. Hoffman, E. S. Savage-Rumbaugh, and D. M. Rumbaugh. 1999. Functional neuroimaging of linguistic processing in chimpanzees. *Society for Neuroscience Abstracts, 25,* 2170. [Abstract].

Ristau, C. A., and D. Robbins. 1982. Language in the great apes: A critical review. In R. J. Schusterman, J. A. Thomas, and F. G. Wood (eds.), *Dolphin cognition and behavior: A comparative approach.* Hillsdale, N.J.: Erlbaum, 1986.

Roitblat, H. L., and J. A. Meyer. 1995. *Comparative approaches to cognitive science.* MIT Press.

Romski, M. A., and R. A. Sevcik. 1991. Patterns of language learning by instruction: Evidence from nonspeaking persons with mental retardation. In Krasnegor at al. 1991 (pp. 429–446).

Rumbaugh, D. M. 1995. Primate language and cognition: Common ground. *Social Research, 62,* 711–730.

———. 1997. Competence, cortex, and animal models: A comparative primate perspective. In Krasnegor, Lyon, and Goldman-Rakic 1997 (pp. 117–139).

Rumbaugh, D. M., and E. S. Savage-Rumbaugh. 1996. Biobehavioral roots of language: Words, apes, and a child. In B. M. Velichkovsky and D. M. Rumbaugh (eds.), *Communicating meaning: The evolution and development of language* (pp. 257–274). Mahwah, N.J.: Erlbaum.

Rumbaugh, D. M., E. S. Savage-Rumbaugh, and R. A. Sevcik. 1994. Biobehavioral roots of language: A comparative perspective of chimpanzee, child, and culture. In R. W. Wrangham, W. C. McGrew, F. B. M. de Waal, and P. G. Heltne (eds.), *Chimpanzee cultures* (pp. 319–334). Cambridge: Harvard University Press.

Rumbaugh, D. M., E. C. von Glasersfeld, H. Warner, P. Pisani, T. V. Gill, J. V. Brown, and C. L. Bell. 1973a. Exploring the language skills of Lana chimpanzee. *International Journal of Symbology, 4,* 1–9.

———. 1973b. A computer-controlled language training system for investigating the language skills of young apes. *Behavior Research Methods and Instrumentation, 5,* 385–392.

Rumbaugh, D. M., and Washburn, D. A. 1994. Animal intelligence: Primate. In R. J. Sternberg (ed.), *Encyclopedia of Human Intelligence* (vol. 1, pp. 96–102). New York: Macmillan.

Sarich, V. 1983. Retrospective on hominid macromolecular systematics. In R. L.

Ciochon and R. S. Corruccini (eds.), *New interpretations of ape and human ancestry* (pp. 137–150). New York: Plenum.

Savage, E. S., and B. J. Wilkerson. 1978. Socio-sexual behavior in *Pan paniscus* and *Pan troglodytes:* A comparative study. *Journal of Human Evolution, 7,* 327–344.

Savage, E. S., B. J. Wilkerson, and R. Bakeman. 1977. Spontaneous gestural communication among conspecifics in the pygmy chimpanzee *(Pan paniscus).* In G. H. Bourne (ed.), *Progress in ape research* (pp. 99–116). New York: Academic Press.

Savage-Rumbaugh, E. S. 1984. Acquisition of functional symbol usage in apes and children. In H. L. Roitblat, T. G. Bever, and H. S. Terrace (eds.), *Animal cognition* (pp. 291–310). Hillsdale, N.J.: Erlbaum.

———. 1990. Language as a cause-effect communication system. *Philosophical Psychology 3,* 55–76.

———. 1993. Language learnability in man, ape, and dolphin. In H. L. Roitblat, L. M. Herman, and P. E. Nachtigall (eds.), *Language and communication: Comparative perspectives, comparative cognition, and neuroscience* (pp. 457–484). Hillsdale, N.J.: Erlbaum.

Savage-Rumbaugh, E. S., M. A. Romski, W. D. Hopkins, and R. A. Sevcik. 1989. Symbol acquisition and use by *Pan troglodytes, Pan paniscus,* and *Homo sapiens.* In L. A. Marquardt and P. G. Heltne (eds.), *Understanding chimpanzees* (pp. 266–295). Cambridge: Harvard University Press.

Savage-Rumbaugh, E. S., and D. M. Rumbaugh. 1993. The emergence of language. In K. R. Gibson and T. Ingold (eds.), *Tools, language, and cognition in human evolution* (pp. 86–108). Cambridge: Cambridge University Press.

Savage-Rumbaugh, E. S., D. M. Rumbaugh, and S. Boysen. 1978. Linguistically-mediated tool use and exchange by chimpanzees *(Pan troglodytes).* *Behavioral and Brain Sciences, 4,* 539–554.

Savage-Rumbaugh, E. S., R. A. Sevcik, K. E. Brakke, D. M. Rumbaugh, and P. Greenfield. 1990. Symbols: Their communicative use, comprehension, and combination by bonobos *(Pan paniscus).* In C. Rovee-Collier and L. P. Lipsitt (eds.), *Advances in infancy research,* vol. 6 (pp. 221–271). Norwood, N.J.: Ablex.

Savage-Rumbaugh, E. S., S. Shanker, and T. J. Taylor. 1998. *Apes, language, and the human mind.* New York: Oxford University Press.

Schrier, A. M., H. F. Harlow, and F. Stollnitz. 1965. *Behavior of nonhuman primates,* vols. 1 and 2. New York: Academic Press.

Seidenberg, M. S., and L. A. Pettito. 1979. Signing behavior in apes: A critical review. *Cognition, 7,* 177–215.

Terman, L. M. 1916. *The measurements of intelligence.* Boston: Houghton Mifflin.

———. 1921. Mental growth and the IQ. *Journal of Educational Psychology, 12,* 325–341, 401–407.

Thomas, E. M. 1993. *The hidden life of dogs.* Boston: Houghton Mifflin.

Thomas, R. K. 1996. Investigating cognitive abilities in animals: Unrealized potential. *Cognitive Brain Research 3*, 157–166.

Thorpe, W. H. 1972. Comparison of vocal communication in animals and man. In R. A. Hinde (ed.), *Nonverbal communication* (pp. 27–47). Cambridge: Cambridge University Press.

Tomasello, M. 1996. The cultural roots of language. In B. M. Velichkovsky and D. M. Rumbaugh (eds.), *Communicating meaning: The evolution and development of language* (pp. 275–308). Mahwah, N.J.: Erlbaum.

Tomasello, M., and J. Call. 1997. *Primate cognition*. New York: Oxford University Press.

Trinkhaus, E., and P. Shipman. 1993. *The Neanderthals*. London: Cape.

Tuttle, R. H. 1986. *Apes of the world: Their social behavior, communication, mentality, and ecology*. Park Ridge, N.J.: Noyes.

Umiker-Sebeok, J., and T. A. Sebeok. 1980. Introduction: Questioning apes. In T. A. Sebeok and J. Umiker-Sebeok (eds.), *Speaking of apes: A critical anthology of two-way communication with man* (pp. 1–59). New York: Plenum.

Wallman, J. 1992. *Aping language*. New York: Cambridge University Press.

Warden, C. J., and L. H. Warner. 1928. The sensory capacities and intelligence of dogs with a report on the ability of the noted dog "Fellow" to respond to verbal stimuli. *Quarterly Review of Biology, 3*, 1–28.

Wasserman, E. A. 1995. The conceptual abilities of pigeons. *American Scientist, 83*, no. 3, 246–255.

White, P. A. 1995. *The understanding of causation and the production of action: From infancy to adulthood*. East Sussex, England: Erlbaum.

Whiten, A. 2000. Chimpanzee cognition and the question of mental re-representation. In D. Sperber (ed.), *Metarepresentation: A multidisciplinary perspective* (pp. 139–167). Vancouver Studies in Cognitive Science, vol. 10. Oxford: Oxford University Press.

Wilson, E. O. 1980. Comparative social theory. *Tanner Lectures on Human Values, 49–73*.

Wood, B. 1992. Origin and evolution of the genus Homo. *Nature, 355.* 783–790.

Index

Abel, 168
adaptive behaviors: animal intelligence, 30–32; biological smartness, 24–27; brain function, 32–35, 270; brain size, 283, 286; comparative psychology, 16–20; ecological niches, 20, 24; emergent behavior, 235, 270; psychological intelligence, 24; species, 17–23; stimulation-response behaviors, 26–27
Akili, 129
Albert, 60, 79–82
Alia, 136–142
Alvila, 82
Ameslan, 91
analogues, 205
anecdotes, use of, 7–8
animal behavior: activity refinement, 270; cause-effect reasoning, 197–202, 259–260; empty-organism model, 7, 271–273; instinctive behaviors, 197; misbehavior of organisms, 168–174; pain, 273; rational behaviorism, 250–253; rationality, 8, 51; self-awareness, 271–272; shared anatomical structures, 53. *See also* respondent conditioning
animal intelligence: adaptive behaviors, 30–32; apes, 14, 30, 132–133, 252, 274; counting, 122–123, 178–179, 185–190; creative behaviors, 31–36, 259–260; learning process, 35–36, 249–250; learning-set process, 10; numerical cognition, 178–184, 185–190; primates, 14; reinforcement stimuli, 6–8, 26–27; thought processes, 8, 247–248, 268; understanding of, 3, 11–12. *See also* cognitive processes
apes: active participation, 281–285; animal intelligence, 14, 30, 132–133, 252; ape-monkey differences, 174–175; characteristics, 51–52; comprehension, 112–113, 115–119, 128–129, 131–142; discrimination learning, 76; discrimination reversal experiments, 69–72; genetic mutations, 22; imitation, 175–

176; language, 88–94, 131–143, 277; learning process, 19, 246–247, 249–250; problem-solving skills, 205–207, 252; responsivity, 15–16; social interaction, 274–276; theory of mind, 176; tool use, 175–176; transfer skills, 67–72. *See also* chimpanzees; primates
arboreal primates, 64–66, 83
associative drift, 169, 174
associative learning: brain size, 74–76; conditional stimuli (CS), 39–40, 233–234; emergent behavior, 238; learning process, 241; macaque monkeys, 174; meaningful failures, 171–174; primates, 17, 74–76, 154; reinforcers, 221; rhesus monkeys, 171–174; testing apparatus, 148–149
attention, 160–162, 210–212, 214, 216, 218–219, 224, 226–227
auditory feedback, 28, 29
Austin: brain complexity, 76, 207–208; categorization, 125–127, 254–255; cognitive processes, 167–168; concept formation, 114–127; cross-modal perception, 110; imitation, 167–168; novel behaviors, 117–121, 124–125; numerical cognition, 184, 188, 281–282; sharing, 121–123
autonoetic consciousness, 206–207
autonomic nervous system, 205
auto-shaping, 220
avoidance conditioning, 44, 225–226

background cues, 64–66
backward conditioning, 44, 195, 218
bar pressing, 197, 203, 218–219, 222, 231
Bata, 60
bats, 20, 29–30
behavior: adaptive behaviors, 17, 20–35, 270, 283, 286; animals, 14–15, 250–253, 271–274; benefits, 263; brain complexity, 60, 273–274; comparative psychology, 17–18; continuity, 274–277; costs,